TAX INCENTIVES FOR PRIVATE INVESTMENT IN DEVELOPING COUNTRIES

INTERNATIONAL BAR ASSOCIATION
Tax Committee, Section on Business Law

TAX INCENTIVES FOR PRIVATE INVESTMENT IN DEVELOPING COUNTRIES

Reporter:

Robert Anthoine
Partner of Winthrop, Stimson, Putnam & Roberts
Adjunct Professor of Law,
Columbia University

1979
Springer-Science+Business Media, B.V.

Cover design: Pieter J. van der Sman

Library of Congress Cataloging in Publication Data

Main entry under title:

Tax incentives for private investment in developing countries.

At head of title: International Bar Association.
1. Underdeveloped areas - Taxation - Addresses, essays, lectures. 2. Underdeveloped areas - Investments, Foreign - Law and legislation - Addresses, essays, lectures. I. Anthoine, Robert. II. International Bar Association.

K4528.Z9T39 343.04'09172'4 79-18798

ISBN 978-94-017-4471-3 ISBN 978-94-017-4469-0 (eBook)
DOI 10.1007/978-94-017-4469-0

Originally published by Kluwer, Deventer, The Netherlands 1979
Softcover reprint of the hardcover 1st edition 1979

Table of Contents

About the IBA Section on Business Law

The Section on Business Law was formed in 1970 to promote an interchange of information among Members as to laws, practices and procedures affecting business, financial and commercial activities throughout the world. It works through the following 20 Committees:

(A) Maritime and transport law
(B) Aeronautical law
(C) Antitrust law and monopolies
(D) Procedures for settling disputes
(E) Commercial banking
(F) Environmental law
(G) Business organizations
(H) Insurance
(I) Investment companies funds and trusts
(J) Creditors' rights, insolvency, liquidations and reorganizations
(K) Public utilities
(L) Patents, trademarks, copyrights
(M) Sales of goods
(N) Taxes
(O) Energy and natural resources
(P) Labour law
(Q) Issues and trading in securities
(S) Consumer affairs, advertising, unfair competition and products liability
(T) International construction contracts
(U) Savings and building societies

The Section publishes the *International Business Lawyer* and arranges Conferences and Seminars. Membership enables lawyers to make contact with others practising in the same fields and to contribute to law reforms of direct interest to the practising lawyer.

Further details of the Section and how to join may be obtained from the IBA, Byron House, 7-9 St James's Street, London SW1A 1EE, England.

Chairman's page

'Tax Incentives for Private Investment in Developing Countries' are an important aspect of the so-called North-South Dialogue and the transfer of technology from industrial countries to developing countries. The Section on Business Law of the International Bar Association is greatly indebted to the Editor, Robert Anthoine, the Chairman of the Committee on Taxes, Jean-Claude Goldsmith, its Vice-Chairmen, John H. Young and Raoul Lenz, and the members of the Committee, who have contributed, for their joint efforts in preparing this first book of the Committee on Taxes.

It has been written by practising lawyers with the knowledge and experience of their own daily work but also with the knowledge of what a practitioner is looking for.

I am confident that this book will prove of real assistance to practising lawyers world-wide, as did previous publications of other Committees of the Section on Business Law. I wish it full succes.

I hope that you may wish to join the Section on Business Law and thereby make contact and work with lawyers with similar interests in commercial law.

Dr. Walter Oppenhoff

Chairman of the Section on Business Law

Preface by the Chairman of the Tax Committee

Dear friends and colleagues,

Our Committee is now in its ninth year of existence since it was formed, concurrently with the Business Section as a whole, at the IBA Congress in Tokyo in 1970.

A number of topics have since been selected for their highly practical implications, and considered and discussed at the Committee meetings. A good number of them were covered by reports in writing which were published in The International Business Lawyer or in Tax Management. Others were presented and surveyed in the form of a panel-floor exchange of views on the seminar model.

Until now, none have resulted in the publication of a full book. The main reason is that it is not very easy to achieve the harmonization and editing of national reports in a single language, even on the basis of a specific and detailed questionnaire.

This gap is now filled up by the issue of two books published by Kluwer Law and Taxation Publishers, one on 'Tax Incentives for Private Investment in Developing Countries' and the other on 'Tax Status of Regional Headquarters of Multinational Companies'.

It is my personal pleasure and pride to introduce the book on tax incentives, indeed a most important subject in international business. I hope it may prove to be a useful companion in your practice.

I look forward to our next meeting in Zurich.

With my best regards,

Yours sincerely

J. C. Goldsmith
Chairman-Committee 'N' : 'Taxes'
Section on Business Law

Editor's Preface

The purpose of this book is to provide within a single volume a comparative analysis of the tax laws of developed countries bearing upon direct private investment in developing countries, and a representative sample of developing country laws bearing upon the receipt of such investment. This study was initiated by the Tax Committee of the Business Section of the International Bar Association under the leadership of Jean-Claude Goldsmith of the Paris Bar. I undertook to act as the reporter, to browbeat colleagues in other countries to write national reports, and to provide the reporter's overview statement.

This report includes studies of fourteen developed countries prepared by national reporters and summaries of five other developed country laws. Noteworthy are the detailed examinations of the laws of the Federal Republic of Germany and of Japan, the two developed countries that have provided the most comprehensive system of incentives for private investment in developing countries. Also contained herein are reports from eight developing countries, including a thorough examination of the laws of Brazil.

Attention is paid in the developed country reports not only to those tax provisions that act as in inducement to foreign investment but also to those that favor domestic investment and hence act as a disincentive to foreign investment. Relevant double taxation agreements are discussed, and other aspects such as exchange control and government grants are also mentioned.

I am grateful to the national reporters who took the time from their busy practices to prepare reports which en masse provide an excellent view of the current state of tax incentives for private investment in developing countries.

New York, New York
May, 1979

Robert Anthoine

Statement of Reporter

Robert Anthoine

INTRODUCTION

The Tax Committee of the Business Section of the International Bar Association under the leadership of Jean-Claude Goldsmith of the Paris bar has initiated a project to study tax incentives for private investment in developing countries.[1] The Association sought to fill a need for systematic study of tax incentives in law and in practice. No other body is engaged in such work, including the United Nations, which over the years has played the most significant role in identifying and supporting the interests of the developing countries.[2]

Your Reporter submitted a preliminary Report at the Business Section meeting in Atlanta in November, 1977 and a substantially complete report at the biannual meeting in Sydney in September, 1978. This is his final report.

SCOPE OF STUDY

This Report is addressed primarily to the tax laws of the developed countries but reports from a number of developing countries are included. A complete study limited even to the tax factor should include not only the provisions of developed country laws that induce foreign investments but also those that favor domestic investment and hence act as a disincentive to foreign investment. Likewise the tax laws of developing countries should be examined not

1. For recent publications on this subject see Anthoine, Tax Systems of Major Capital Exporting Countries: An Examination of Incentives for Private Investment at Home and in Developing Countries, 32 Tax Law Rev. 323 (1977); Bryan, Developed Nation Tax Law and Investment in LDC's, Columbia Journal of Transnational Law, July, 1978.

2. Tax Treaties Between Developed and Developing Countries (UN Sales No. E.69.XVI.2); Tax Treaties Between Developed and Developing Countries, Second Report (UN Sales No. E.71.XVI.2); Tax Treaties Between Developed and Developing Countries, Third Report (UN Sales No. E.72.XVI.4); Tax Treaties Between Developed and Developing Countries, Fourth Report (UN Sales No. E.73.XVI.4); Tax Treaties Between Developed and Developing Countries, Fifth Report (UN Sales No. E.75.XVI.1); Tax Treaties Between Developed and Developing Countries, Sixth Report (UN Sales No. E.76.XVI.3); Tax Treaties Between Developed and Developing Countries, Seventh Report (UN Sales No. E.78.XVI.1); Guidelines for Tax Treaties Between Developed and Developing Countries (UN Sales No. E.74.XVI.5). See also Muten, 'Appropriate Tax Systems for Developing Countries', in Associated Business Programmes Ltd., International Tax Conference, Nairobi (1976); Shoup, 'Report on Tax Incentives in Developing Countries' (December, 1975), an unpublished report prepared for the United Nations Centre for Development Planning, Projections and Policies; United Nations: Economic and Social Council: 'The Impact of Multinational Corporations on the Development Process and on International Relations', E/5500/Add 1/Rev. 1-St/ESA/6 (1974).

only for provisions encouraging inward investment but also for those favoring capital outflows. An attempt is made in this report to deal with both aspects of developed country laws.

The tax incentives with which we are concerned here are those that induce the movement of capital and technology, not labor. (The developing countries are largely exporters of labor, apart from the technicians from the developed world who come for limited periods of service.) And we should be focusing upon those incentives that induce investment that would not have been made but for the incentive. Unfortunately, it is extremely difficult to identify such incentives and to distinguish them from those which merely improve the well-being of those who receive them. The subject of 'Tax Incentives as an Instrument for Achievement of Governmental Goals' was one of the two topics discussed at the Thirtieth Congress of the International Fiscal Association held in 1976 and in the accompanying volume there are national reports from 19 countries (Volume LXIa Cahiers de Droit Fiscal International). These studies are useful as are the tax expenditure budgets prepared by the United States and Germany, and to a considerable extent by Japan, in which systematic consideration is given to tax expenditures by budget category in an effort to estimate the cost in revenue loss of those provisions that are identified as departing from a presupposed norm. However, although tax expenditure budgets provide highly useful information – often the only available information concerning the extent to which particular provisions are actually being used – they cannot tell us what expenditures would not have been made but for the incentive.

THE SETTING

The setting for the dialogue between the developed and developing countries has changed radically in recent years. The external debts of the oil importing developing countries amount to over $ 100 billion [3] – loans incurred both to meet balance of payments deficits and to fund projects developed under previous expenditure patterns that were not or could not be wound down quickly enough. The rapid increase in population of the developing countries places a great burden on their economies to maintain a tenable standard of

3. The developing countries, other than the oil exporters, owed at the end of 1976 in the neighborhood of 180 billion to foreign governments, commercial banks and international lending institutions. Of that total about 48 billion was owed to governments, primarily those of the US and Western European countries and it is those debts that the developing countries have urged be written off to help them increase economic development. On October 12, 1977, the government of Sweden announced that it planned to cancel more than 200 million in debts owed by the governments of 8 poor countries, following by a month a similar announcement by the Prime Minister of Canada that his nation was in the process of cancelling 254 million in debts from developing countries. Both countries followed a similar criterion in that the nations whose debts they chose to cancel were drawn from a list of the poorest countries in the world compiled five years ago by the United Nations Conference on Trade and Development. The Netherlands and Switzerland thereafter took similar action and others have promised to follow. See the Economist, July 29, 1978, p. 68.

living. And, as if they did not have trouble enough, when the developing countries succeed in forging new exports capable of penetrating the markets of industrialized countries, often they are faced with the threat of new tariff restrictions.

In view of the nature and urgency of the problems of the developing countries, it is understandable that they should ask primarily for debt relief, liquidity support and commodity price stabilization.[4] The 1979 renegotiation of the Lomé Convention, involving over 50 nations from the Third World and the EEC, and the GATT discussions in Geneva have provided a current discussion of financial and commercial issues. Indeed, the developing countries boycotted the April, 1979 signing ceremonies in Geneva for the new agreement to liberalize world trade on the ground that the new agreement does little for the world's poorer countries and fails to provide the special advantages they were promised when the trade talks opened in Tokyo more than five years ago.

From the private sector of the developed world the developing countries want primarily technology and technical cooperation but they remain interested in foreign private capital and particularly in country credit loans. They do not wish to give up equity in their natural resources or essential industries, and do not want to favor foreign controlled or even 49 percent foreign owned ventures over local businesses. In this new setting what is the importance of the tax factor? Attitudes and conditions differ so much that they require a country-by-country analysis. In any event, the relevance of tax incentives is limited to countries that welcome private capital inflow from abroad. Such private capital will generally move into a developing country only in search of profits, through the exploitation of local or regional markets or the acquisition of raw materials. Tax systems are undoubtedly important but it must be recognized that our study deals with only one important factor in making the investment decision. Consideration must also be given to the guarantee and credit facilities and exchange control laws of the potential investor's country, to the credit facilities of international and regional financial institutions, and in the host country to investment laws, exchange control, political stability, financing facilities, infrastructure, labor, local markets and raw materials.

1. Comparison of Incentive Provisions in Developed Countries

A comparison of the incentive provisions in the laws of developed countries reveals that the Federal Republic of Germany and Japan are in the lead: In addition to effectively exempting dividend income from foreign subsidiaries and income from foreign permanent establishments, they offer a significant direct tax incentive to investment in developing countries through the creation of reserves for such investments that reduce current income from other sources. France is similarly generous, although within a narrower range of activity.

All of the developed countries surveyed other than the United States and

4. See Jahangir Amuzegar, Requiem for the North-South Conference, 56 Foreign Affairs 136 (1977).

Italy apply, through internal law or tax treaty or a combination thereof, one of two methods to avoid negating a developing country's efforts to stimulate the inflow of foreign private capital through tax concessions: The exemption method or the tax sparing method and often a combination of the two where the exemption method applies only to dividend income and tax sparing is applied to other categories of foreign source income. Hence, they achieve effective local tax exemption of income remitted by way of dividend from a foreign subsidiary or income earned or remitted by a foreign permanent establishment.[5] Italy is the least generous to foreign investment of the developed countries, principally because its foreign tax credit is limited to direct taxes, and even then to a maximum of two-thirds of the Italian tax payable with respect to the item, but Italy has not been in any position to invest overseas and its tax policy thus appears to be in tune with its national policies. On the other hand, the United States is a major capital exporting nation and of all such countries, only the United States makes no tax concession to private investment in developing countries.

2. Taxation of Undistributed Foreign Subsidiary (Tax Haven) Income

All of the developed countries surveyed respect the separate entity of a bona fide foreign subsidiary engaged in production or manufacturing or trading with unaffiliated persons and do not tax the foreign corporate earnings until they are actually or constructively remitted to the domestic parent. Accordingly, as long as the profits of such companies are reinvested, there will be no tax interference from the capital exporting country. The U.S. is the only country that has seriously considered changing this principle. As recently as 1978, the legislative branch of the government defeated the proposal of the executive branch that would have taxed the US 10 % or greater shareholder of a foreign corporation in which over 50 % of the voting power was held by such US persons upon its pro rata share of the undistributed foreign corporate earnings. Moreover, no exception was provided for subsidiaries in developing countries.

The United States, Canada, the Federal Republic of Germany and Japan have adopted special provisions taxing certain of their citizens or residents

5. The Australian tax system will become much less congenial to foreign investment if the proposals of the Asprey Committee are implemented. See pp. 21-23, *infra*. Switzerland does impose a tax under certain circumstances, usually at a low effective rate, on dividends received from foreign sources by Swiss companies that are not pure holding companies. Several countries require as a condition precedent to tax exemption a minimum local equity ownership in the foreign corporation, often 25 percent. The Netherlands requires that the recipient of the dividends own 5 percent or more of the paid in capital of the subsidiary as an active participation rather than as a porfolio investment and that the foreign income be subject to a foreign national profits tax of some amount, but income exempt because a tax holiday can still qualify for exemption. A number of countries such as The Netherlands apply the 'exemption with progression' method, under which foreign income is first included in the tax base and is then deducted after it has served the sole purpose of determining the tax rate to be applied to the other taxable income. Where the corporate tax is a proportional tax, the progression only applies to noncorporate taxpayers.

upon their pro rata shares of the undistributed income of controlled foreign corporations where the corporate income is largely of a 'tax haven' nature, such as dividends, interest, rents and royalities. The Japanese report notes the interesting variation on that theme adopted in 1978. The approach of singling out the particular tax haven countries and the exception for local business and management may set a pattern for tax haven legislation by other developed countries.[6]

3. Incentives Provided by Developing Countries

Many developing countries have adopted five to ten year income tax holiday provisions. Others do not permit such exemption but do undertake not to increase existing rates over a succeeding period of years and often provide tax reduction for reinvested profits or for investments in depressed areas or for export profits. Relief from customs duties and other charges appears universal.

These favorable provisions are undoubtedly important but difficult to evaluate. Standing alone the tax incentive has a questionable impact upon investment but it may prove effective when combined with other favorable investment law provisions such as interest subsidization of loans to finance almost all local expenditure (an incentive easy to direct selectively without balance of payments effects), the right to bring in duty-free equipment to be set up on the books in dollars and ultimately to be repatriated in dollars, the freedom to remit currently a reasonable amount of dividends (or royalties) without having to earn the foreign exchange through exporting a whacking percentage of the firm's output to export markets that do not exist rather than selling in good local markets, and effective decision-making implementation of investment laws that free the foreign investor from bureaucratic harassment and are well integrated into the country's legal system. The political stability of the country and the region may be determinative. In this connection, it will be interesting to observe the effect of the Middle East accord upon foreign investment in Egypt which has heretofore been at a disappointingly low level.[7]

It is occasionally suggested that the developing countries should concentrate

6. See Brockman, Japan: Taxes of Undistributed Proceeds of 'designated Tax Haven Subsidiaries', TM Int'l J. March 1979.

7. Egypt's law 43 adopted in 1974 provided considerable encouragement in the form of a 5 to 8 year complete income tax holiday and freedom from customs duties and numerous other charges. However, under law 43 investment capital had to be introduced into Egypt at the official rate of exchange which was $2.50 per Egyptian pound whereas the free market rate was about $1.30. Although the problem could have been overcome in many cases by the foreign investor through bringing into Egypt only assets in kind, such as machinery and materials, and by borrowing locally to meet all working capital requirements, the exchange control rules must have provided some deterrent. Also, the law was heavily export oriented: in order to be able to remit profits currently, the investor would have had to export about 60% of its production to earn the necessary foreign exchange. These unfavorable aspects were eliminated by Law 32 adopted in June 1977. Now investment capital and earnings can be transferred to and from Egypt at the highest prevailing exchange rate. Moreover, current earnings can be remitted by a company whose activities are oriented towards import substitution rather than exports. In addition, the privileges extended to foreigners are now also granted to Egyptian investors. See Chown and Stathopoulos, Investing in the Eastern Mediterranean (1977).

the tax holiday or reduced rate in the first few years of the investor's venture on the ground that the private investor will discount future revenue at a much higher rate than the government and will be much more moved to invest by strong relief in the early period. However, the premise does not seem valid in the case of high technology ventures when the first few years of tax relief may not provide much, if any, benefit and a holiday period of less than ten years might not be regarded as meaningful.

4. Effect of Developed Country Tax Incentives Upon Investment in Developing Countries

The impact of the tax incentives is difficult to measure. Looking at the statistics, one would conclude that the tax provisions have certainly not been dominant because United States private enterprise owns over 50 % of the stock of direct private investment made by all OECD-DAC members in developing countries. The US position was accumulated during a period when the tax provisions favorable to overseas investment were insubstantial (and nonexistent after 1976). The reporter from the Federal Republic of Germany notes that the impact of the German tax incentives on LDC investment' is probably not too important', and the reporter on Japan holds a similar view. However, the tax regime of the host country may be very important, interfacing with the developed country approach of not taxing earnings of foreign subsidiaries until distributed. The US reporter notes the agreeable interrelation provided by the US system of allocating dividends to the most recently accumulated earnings and profits, thereby preserving the benefits of the developing country's tax holiday to the extent that profits are reinvested during the holiday period. The change in US law proposed by the executive branch in 1978 would have changed all that and would have put US private investment at a marked disadvantage in comparison with all other developed country investment.

5. Incentives for Domestic Investment in Developed Countries

The impact of incentives for overseas investment must be judged by reference to disincentives to such investment, notably tax and other incentives to invest at home. The national reports reveal that the developed countries provide powerful incentives to local investment. A tax expenditure type budget would demonstrate the much greater value of domestic as compared with foreign investment incentives. Moreover, these domestic incentives are on the increase. In April 1979 the French government adopted a FFr 5.8 billion package of measures to stimulate investment and the Prime Minister stated that the government would not hesitate to provide an added stimulus to the building and public works sectors if the economic situation justified it. In the same month the Canadian government announced the introduction of fiscal measures to encourage high technology. In the US, there are proposals to provide more rapid depreciation for capital equipment.

Moreover, developed countries have competed fiercely in offering both tax and nontax incentives to induce multinational corporations to construct major plants within the jurisdiction. In 1979 Ireland defeated Scotland in the competition to secure an American controlled $ 80 million microchip plant that will provide about 1100 jobs within three years. Ireland won because the Irish Industrial Development Agency was able to offer a more attractive financial package consisting of development grants up to 50 % of the capital cost and to guarantee that profits on exports would be exempted from all taxes until 1990. The membership of Ireland in the Common Market makes the freedom from tax on exports very meaningful. As this is being written, France and Austria among others, are competing for a new Ford Motor $ 1 billion European car plant. It is understood that the French government, hopeful of inducing the company to locate in Lorraine where there is high unemployment, is offering a financial package worth about $ 400 million. Austria is said to be offering Ford about $ 300 million in grants and a free site near Vienna. In the United States, states and even communities within the same state compete with one another for the introduction of new industry.

6. Joint Ventures in the Developing Countries

Private industry in the developed world will have to adapt to the requirement of joint ventures in the developing world with a maximum equity participation of 50%. Developing countries are increasingly expressing their national policies of retaining domestic control over local enterprises by adopting investment laws that limit foreign equity participation to 50 % or less. Another approach has been the 'buy back' arrangement under which initial foreign ownership will gradually be replaced, in whole or significant part, by local ownership. It is understandable that a country whether developing or developed should want its residents to have control over major local enterprises. Witness the Foreign Investment Review Law of Canada which reflects Canada's fear that it may be squashed by the friendly elephant to the south. In certain sensitive industries the inability to hold 100 % or even operating control of the local subsidiary may compel withdrawal by the company from the country. This has happened in the cases of IBM in India and Nigearia and Coca Cola in India.

A number of developing countries with different political and social systems which provide the joint venture approach, including Egypt, Hungary and Yugoslavia, have recently liberalized their investment laws in an effort to attract more foreign investment. But these moves come at a time when the developed countries are suffering from depressed industries, serious unemployment and understandable labor union militancy. It is now realized that in some areas such as textiles, shoes and electronics, some of the developing countries do indeed provide stiff competition. Politically the developed countries will find it difficult to take any action that would favor overseas investment. They will do well to allow a larger amount of free trade for imports from developing countries.

7. Regulation of Multinational Enterprises

The United Nations, the OECD, and the United States have all been actively investigating the investments and the conduct of multinational enterprises and the economic and social impact that these powerful venturers are having upon international development. Of major importance has been the attempt to frame international codes of conduct for multinational enterprises. In June, 1976 the OECD Council of Ministers issued a set of voluntary guidelines which includes tax provisions. The United Nations Centre for Transnational Corporations has been evaluating the impact of the multinationals upon international development and has been working on a code of conduct. The Centre issued a major report in March 1978 which is required reading (Transnational Corporations in World Development: A Reexamination; E78.IIA 5). The US Reporter notes the legislation adopted in 1976 and 1977 to regulate the conduct of US multinationals in which the tax law is used, in part, as a powerful sanction. These studies and measures may prove highly significant in relation to future investment in the developing countries.

8. Tax Treaties Between Developed and Developing Countries

The general subject of tax treaties is beyond the scope of this study but mention should be made of the confrontation between the developing countries and the capital exporting countries with respect to the allocation of taxing jurisdiction. The developing countries are not satisfied with the OECD model. Through the United Nations they have been making progress in the development of a model more to their liking.[8] It is understood that the US Treasury is also engaged in producing a draft of a model treaty, such a model for treaties between developed countries having been published by the Treasury in 1976.

As previously noted, all of the major capital exporting countries other than the United States provide in their treaties with developing countries for the significant tax incentive of tax sparing with respect to some categories of income. This is very agreeable to the developing countries but beyond the range of tax sparing, they seek a greater allocation to them – the country of source – of the right to tax business income, royalty and services income, capital gains, shipping income, and dividends and interest. It seems likely that progress will be made in negotiations between the developed and the developing countries in arriving at treaty rules that will promote trade with, investment in, and technology flows to the developing countries.

Countries such as the United States that provide an investment credit as an incentive for local investment should consider extending the domestic invest-

8. See Guidelines, *supra* note 2; Surrey, United Nations group of experts and the Guidelines for tax treaties between developed and developing countries, 19 Harv. Int'l Law J. p. 1 (Winter 1978) and appendix thereto which contains a model treaty prepared by students associated with the Journal.

ment credit by treaty to investors that make qualified direct investments in developing coutries. The US Report notes that such a credit appeared in three US tax treaties but the provisions never became effective. In some respects, the application of the investment credit of the capital exporting country would be more advantageous than tax sparing. It would achieve greater neutrality of the investor's income tax law; the benefits of the credit – just as in the case of the reserves allowed by France, Germany and Japan – would be received by the private investor at the time of the investment rather than on the subsequent receipt of dividends; the retention of earnings in the developing country would be encouraged because, under the old US proposal, additional investment credits would be allowed for reinvested profits; competition among developing countries for the inward investment through eliminating or reducing their taxes would be unnecessary with respect to investment from the foreign tax credit countries because the investment credit would reduce the investor's local income tax and the investor would later obtain the credit for the host country's income tax upon the distribution of dividends.

The US Report also notes a provision in one treaty which never became effective that deserves support among the developed countries: The deferral of any income tax on the transfer of industrial property rights, technical information and know-how in exchange for stock of the foreign corporation in the developing country.

OBSERVATIONS

a. The explanation for the infrequent appearance in tax treaties of a credit for taxes spared on the underlying corporate profits out of which a dividend distribution has been made is that for countries using the exemption method for dividends from developing country corporations, there is no need to provide such a credit in order to eliminate the developed country's income tax. The direct credit for taxes spared on other types of income produces an equivalent result to exemption. Both Japan and the United Kingdom, which apply the foreign tax credit rather than the exemption method of avoiding double taxation, do permit in their treaties with specific developing nations that a credit shall be given for the spared foreign income taxes on the underlying corporate profits out of which the dividends have been paid. The net result is the same as total exemption. However, under both the exemption and the tax credit approaches, upon distribution of their tax free profits to the shareholders by corporations in 'imputation' tax regimes, a corporate tax equivalent to the amount allowed as a credit to the shareholder is extracted. France permits a credit against the precompte in certain cases. Canada and Japan grant the shareholder a credit without actual corporate tax.

b. Tax and credit incentives for overseas activities of the private sector are often provided by governments to support exports or to facilitate the gathering of needed natural resources. Japan is a good example of a country that has welded its tax policies to its national purposes.

c. The Brazilian and United Kingdom reports demonstrate the importance of exchange control in regulating overseas remittances and investment.

d. Brazil and Spain both present the interesting picture of a country that is both developing and developed. Greece must concentrate on internal development and has adopted a comprehensive regime to encourage investment and the establishment of regional headquarters.

e. An important development in the last decade has been the movement toward regional agreements and common markets and the growing force in economic development of regional development banks (African, Asian, European, Inter-American). The EEC, the leading common market, has made progress towards tax harmonization. The Central American Common Market is mentioned in the report from Guatemala. The Andean Common Market (ANCOM) was established in 1969 and presently consists of Bolivia, Colombia, Ecuador, Peru and Venezuela. It is a subregional entity within the Latin American Free Trade Association (LAFTA). Also active are the Caribbean Free Trade Association (CARIFTA) and Common Market (CARICOM), the Central African Customs and Economic Union (CACEU), and the Arab Economic Community. These regional groups may eventually succeed in harmonizing tax systems and tax incentives. In another connection, location within a common market may vastly increase the value of local tax incentives, as in the cases of Ireland and Italy.

f. It is axiomatic that taxes are paid for governmental services rendered. In the case of many developing countries, it is only fair that the tax imposed on the foreign investor be on the low side because often the investor has to provide a considerable amount of the services that would be provided by the government in a developed country. The United States which is unique in taxing its nonresident citizens on worldwide income has not adequately taken into account the absence of US government services (and the provision of those services by others) in reducing the US income tax burden on those who are bona fide resident abroad.

g. One area that the developing countries have neglected in their enactment of investment laws and tax incentives is an improvement in the tax regime applicable to the foreign managers and technicians who will come there to live for several years. Often the individual tax system is very burdensome, requiring various devices to reduce the effective tax rate to tolerable levels. A favorable tax system for the visiting family would help attract the talent needed.

h. As noted, many of the developing countries have enacted tax holidays. These and other tax incentive measures in both developed and developing countries attract the ire of tax 'purists' who sing the praises of direct cash subsidies that can be seen and understood as against indirect, unsupervised tax subsidies. However, a tax holiday does have the advantage of being simple to enact and to administer and unlike the cash subsidy it does not cost the country anything unless profits are realized. Moreover, as distinguished from investment credits and fast depreciation, it does not favor capital intensive enterprises.

i. It has been suggested that the developing countries should do more to help themselves by subjecting residents to tax on worldwide income rather than applying the territorial principle. At the end of 1975 there were at least

18 countries that would be classified as 'developing' which do not subject their residents to tax on income from foreign sources. Such a tax system does encourage capital outflow. However, many of the developing countries do not have tax administrations that are capable of enforcing worldwide taxation. Many of these countries have been independent nations for a very short period. In 1949 there were 59 members of the United Nations; today there are 151. Perhaps in due time, after negotiating extensive exchange of information provisions in treaties with developed countries it will be possible for them to apply and enforce worldwide income taxation.

j. The developed countries should reach some regional understanding to reduce the battle of tax incentives to induce industry location.

k. In view of the effective tax exemption of income from the developing world that the developed countries other than Italy and the United States have granted, it is understandable that the developing countries should not be enthusiastic about alternative suggestions for fiscal assistance to them which have been made through the Committee of Experts of the United Nations. However, these proposals deserve circulation.[9]

9. Suggestions have been made through the United Nations for devices other than tax exemption and tax sparing as a means of assisting the developing countries – with a particular focus on the United States, which appears firmly set against uch devices. Two proposals on which no action has yet been taken by any country may be summarized: (1). *A Proposed Investment Assistance Allowance.* An investment assistance allowance would be made by the developed countries to assist investments by their residents in particular developing countries. This allowance would be certified and administered by a government agency in the developed country which would be given full details of the nature of the investment, the amount invested, the amount of reinvested profits and so forth. The amount paid would constitute a direct government grant and would be an amount consisting of a proportion of capital investment or perhaps reinvested earnings. No fiscal sacrifice by the developing country would be required.
(2). *Purchase and Leaseback.* The developing country would purchase newly constructed plant and equipment from the foreign owned and financed enterprise and would then lease these assets to the same enterprise at a low rental. The host country would not grant any tax preference to the enterprise; accordingly no problem would arise with respect to a credit for spared tax. The host country would borrow the purchase money from and pay interest to the parent of the local enterprise or some intergovernmental organization whose capital might come from subscriptions made by firms or agencies in the capital exporting countries. The investor's profits would be enhanced by the low rental which would be provided by a lease for about ten years, with an option to renew for another longer period but at a market rental. The interest payments by the host country would be financed out of the taxes collected from the profits of the enterprise.
The leaseback plan has potential advantages, but the developing countries, generally, have thought it too complex. A distinct advantage to the leaseback arangement is that it requires no governmental action on the part of the developed country: No internal legislation is needed and no tax treaty need be executed. However, the financial sacrifice in the form of a direct subsidy required of the developing country under the leaseback arrangement – although comparable to that attending the loss of revenue under tax incentive measures – is somewhat greater in the leaseback situation. It would shift ownership of industrial plant from the investor to the developing country, which would assume the risk of ownership and of the debt service, and the repayment of the loan, even if the enterprise were not profitable. The investor would not be concerned with expropriation, probably a more serious risk than failure of the country to observe the lease and loan terms. See *Tax Treaties Between Developed and Developing Countries, Fifth Report, supra,* note 2.

Direct investment flows from Development Assistance Committee member countries[1] to developing countries[2] 1965-1976

(Millions of dollars)

Country	*Annual average*			*1974*	*1975*	*1976*
	1965-1967	*1970-1972*	*1973*			
United States	1.147.0	1.909.3	2.887.0	3.788.0	7.241.0	3.119.0
Japan	80.2	229.3	1.301.1	705.4	222.7	1.084.2
Germany, Federal Republic of	146.6	425.6	786.6	701.3	815.9	765.4
United Kingdom	204.0	321.5	698.8	718.7	796.5	722.6
Canada	33.7	105.4	125.0	193.0	300.0	430.0
France	339.1	212.0	287.1	239.4	274.2	245.5
Netherlands	89.6	211.6	88.5	241.7	228.5	244.7
Belgium	46.8	44.0	48.3	49.5	68.8	235.8
Switzerland	46.3	64.7	80.5	128.0	208.2	226.1
Italy	58.6	205.7	245.6	99.9	150.1	212.9
Sweden	27.2	39.5	21.9	49.0	82.2	125.0
Australia	22.5	85.3	104.0	117.1	48.3	74.7
Other countries [3]	3.9	36.3	36.2	53.1	57.4	106.7
Grand total	2.245.4	3.882.7	6.710.6	7.084.1	10.493.8	7.592.6

Source: United Nations Centre on Transnational Corporations, based on Organisation for Economic Co-operation and Development, *Development Co-operation* (Paris, issues for 1974 to 1977).

1. Countries are listed in descending order of percentage share in total flow in 1976.
2. Including flows to the following European countries which are not classified as developing countries according to the United Nations definition: Cyprus, Gibraltar, Greece, Malta, Portugal, Spain, Turkey and Yugoslavia.
3. Austria, Denmark, New Zealand, Norway, Finland; figures prior to 1972 exclude Finland and New Zealand whose combined flow in 1973 amounted to $1 million.

Stock of Direct Private Investment in Developing Countries by Countries of Origin

End 1975

DAC Member	*$ million*	*Percentage of total*
Australia	724	0.95
Austria	36	0.04
Belgium	1,019	1.34
Canada	2,529	3.33
Denmark	142	0.19
Finland	6	0.01
France	5,009	6.60
Germany	5,205	6.86
Italy	2,233	2.94
Japan	3,883	5.12
Netherlands	3,258	4.29
New Zealand	5	0.01
Norway	110	0.15
Sweden	540	0.71
Switzerland	1,431	1.89
United Kingdom	8,600 [1]	11.33
United States	41,170	54.24
Total DAC Members	75,900	100.00

1. Excluding oil investments (roughly estimated at $2 billion).

STATEMENTS OF DEVELOPED COUNTRIES

Australia

Kevin J. Edwards *

A. AUSTRALIAN TAX STRUCTURE AND TAXATION INCENTIVES

1. Taxation Structure

In general terms the liability to income tax in Australia depends on two tests:
(a) the residence of the tax payer, and
(b) the source of the income.

Under (a) the tax payer is taxed on the whole of his or its income where ever it may be earned. Under (b) if the tax payer is not a resident of Australia he or it will be liable to tax in Australia on the income which he or it has earned there.

A resident for income tax purposes is:
(i) an individual who resides in Australia or has been in Australia during more than one half of a tax year
(ii) a company which is incorporated in Australia, or
(iii) a company incorporated outside Australia but which carries on business in Australia and has either a central management in control in Australia or its voting power controlled by shareholders who are residents of Australia

The other important matter to be decided is the source of the income. This is determined by examining all aspects of a particular case to determine whether the income concerned has been earned in Australia.

Bearing in mind the above a potential investor will have to consider the basis on which he or it will conduct operations in Australia. On the assumption the investor decides to carry on operations in Australia through a corporate structure, the following are the alternatives:

(a) the establishment of a branch in Australia of a foreign company. Income tax will be payable by the foreign company on the profits or income which it earns in Australia at a flat rate of 46 %. In addition the Government has just recently announced a proposal to levy and additional tax on profits earned by an Australian Branch of a non-resident company. The tax to be assessed will be 5 % of the income earned in Australia or derived from Australia by a non-resident company. The income on which the tax is assessed

* Stone James & Co., Perth.

is the taxable income namely assessable income less allowable deductions of the non-resident company, but excluding the following types of income:

(i) dividends which are included in the assessable income
(ii) amounts included in the taxable income of a non-resident from operating ships in Australia, and
(iii) certain other amounts applicable to non-resident insurers and life assurance companies.

(b) the incorporation of an Australian Company. On this basis income tax will be payable on the profits or income of the subsidiary company earned anywhere, not only those earned in Australia by that company; again the tax liability is at the flat rate of 46 %. If however, the income earned by that company outside Australia is taxed in the country where it is earned a credit is given against the Australian tax for the tax paid in the other country. This constitutes a major departure from the practice previously adopted, namely that if the income earned by a company outside Australia was taxed in the country where it was earned the income would not also be taxed by Australia. The change takes place as from 1st July, 1978 if enacted into law.

The other important feature of this amendment is that foreign source dividends received by an Australian Company will now be subject to Australian tax and no rebate will be given. However the credit to be allowed will include:

(i) direct tax paid on the dividends in the other country
(ii) foreign dividend withholding tax and
(iii) part of any direct tax payable by the foreign company which provided the dividends if the Australian company has a shareholding of 10 % as made in the foreign company.

Dividends paid by an Australian subsidiary to its foreign parent will also attract tax. Such dividends are liable to withholding tax at the flat rate of 30 % in cases where the dividend is paid to a company situated in a country with which Australia has no tax treaty. In the case of a treaty country the withholding tax is reduced to a flat rate of 15 % on the gross amount of the dividends. Australian resident companies are obliged to deduct the tax from the dividend before it is paid.

(c) The establishment of a joint venture with an Australian resident. This would be an alternative to carrying on a business by means of a jointly owned Australian incorporated company. The basis of a joint venture is that each joint venturer receives a share of the product produced or manufactured by the joint venturers and can claim as a tax deduction his contribution to the costs of the joint venture. In this case, income tax is payable by each joint venturer on the net income realised by the disposal of its share of the product less any deductions allowable to it. The rate of tax payable will be 46 %.

In addition to the above there are further considerations which must be taken into account.

Firstly the Income Tax Assessment Act lays down certain tests to determine whether a company is a public or private company for income tax purposes. Normally a company whether a resident or non-resident will be classed as a public company for income tax purposes if its ordinary shares are quoted on a stock exchange anywhere in the world *and* at no time during a tax year 20 or less persons held more than 75 % of the ordinary shares of the company.

The significance of this test relates to what is commonly called undistributed profits tax. If a private company does not distribute a certain portion of its income to its shareholders within a prescribed period it suffers an additional tax of 50 % on the amount not distributed. This is in addition to the income tax payable by the company as mentioned above. The amount required to be so distributed to avoid the undistributed profits tax is 40 % of its net trading profit and 90 % of its net property income. This provision applies to a non-resident private company which carries on business in Australia through a branch and no relief from payment of this tax is given by a tax treaty.

Secondly, where interest is paid or credited by an Australian subsidiary company to its parent on moneys which may be borrowed from the parent a withholding tax at the rate of 10 % on the gross amount is payable. The Australian subsidiary is obliged by the Act to deduct the Australian withholding tax.

Under the new branch profits tax interest which is derived or deemed to be derived from Australian sources by a non-resident company will be subject to the 5 % tax unless it is liable to interest withholding tax. However, the liability for interest withholding tax does not arise if the interest is derived by a non-resident carrying on business in Australia at or through a permanent establishment.

Thirdly, dividends paid by an Australian subsidiary to its foreign parent are not subject to the new branch profits tax because they are expressly excluded from the concept.

Fourthly, royalties paid by an Australian resident to a non-resident are deemed to have an Australian source and the Act obliges the person or company paying the royalty to a non-resident to deduct the tax from the royalty payment. The rate is 10 % in the case of a royalty payable to a Country with which Australia has a tax treaty unless the company receiving the payment has a permanent establishment in Australia in which event it will be subject to tax at the normal rate. If the royalty is payable to a company resident in a Country with which Australia has no tax treaty then the royalty will be assessed to Australian tax as ordinary income.

The term royalty is given a very wide meaning under the Act. It includes payments made for:

(i) the right to use a copyright, patent, design, trade-mark, formula or other similar property
(ii) the right to use industrial, commercial or any scientific equipment
(iii) the supply of scientific, technical, industrial or commercial knowlegde or information
(iv) the supply of assistance in connection with the above matters

Royalties of this type will be subject to the branch profits tax unless there is a specific treaty exemption. It must be noted however, that the tax treaty will not give any exemption if the royalty is derived by non-residents in carrying on business through a permanent establishment in Australia.

2. Tax Incentives for Petroleum and Gas Exploration and Development

The Act has for many conferred incentives by way of deduction from taxable income of various types of expenditure over a broad field. For example, primary producers have been allowed substantial deductions for expenditure items of a capital nature which would not ordinarily be deductable under the general provisions of the Act. In more recent years we have seen the Government setting out to encourage investment in Australia in mining projects and lately particularly in the exploration and development of gas and oil fields on the mainland or adjacent to the Australian coast. The types of deduction available in this type of investment are as follows:

(i) expenditure incurred on exploration or prospecting in Australia for the purpose of discovering petroleum and natural gas. This type of expenditure is now deductable against the tax payers income from any source not necessarily income from petroleum.

(ii) expenditure incurred in carrying on prescribed petroleum operations in Australia which again includes natural gas. This expenditure is also deductable against income from any source. The type of expenditure covered includes certain storage facilities, drilling plant, equipment and other improvements and also expenditure incurred on plant for the purpose of liquifying natural gas.

(iii) certain items of expenduture deductable under the heading of investment allowance. This allowance permits a deduction of 20 % of the expenditure incurred on certain new plant acquired or constructed by the tax payer for its exclusive use in Australia in the production of assessable income. The conditions for the deduction are:

(a) the item must be acquired or constructed before the 1st July 1985

(b) the item must be first used or installed ready for use prior to the 1st July 1986

(c) the deduction is allowed in the first year in which the property is used or installed ready for use by the tax payer. It does not apply to structural improvement accept in limited cases. Most complete new items of plant are covered but the allowance does not apply to reconditioned or rebuilt items. The important feature about this type of deduction is that it is an addition to any allowance for depreciation.

(iv) Expenditure on certain facilities used primarily for the transport of petroleum produced in Australia. It is felt that these deductions are available for the cost of the pipeline from off shore fields to the refinery on shore together with port facilities to the extent that they have not been allowed under another provision of the Act. The deductions can be taken over a period of 10 or 20 years at the election of the taxpayer. The government has indicated that the deductions allowed under this heading will include harbour surveys, initial dredging of the harbour, channel construction, break waters, access roads and storage facilities for products awaiting shipment. The deduction will be available to a tax payer who contributes towards the cost of the facility, he need not own it nor need he have actually produced the petroleum.

(v) In addition to the above there are also deductions available for depreciation of plant and articles owned by the taxpayer and used by it to produce its assessable income. The rates vary from item to item and are prescribed by the Commissioner as being rates which are reasonable for the particular item of plant and the operation in which it is being used.

It does appear that most of the facilities which do not qualify are items (ii) and (iv) above and will be depreciable at the rate of 20 % on the diminishing value. As this type of business is relatively new to Australia problems will no doubt arise in determining which item of expenditure will fall under which headings and in some cases the rates of depreciation will have to be agreed with the Commissioner.

Although special mention has been made of the deductions available for expenditure on petroleum and gas projects it must be borne in mind that the provisions relating to deductions for Investment Allowance and Depreciation are available to other types of plant used for the production of assessable income.

B. INCENTIVES AND DISINCENTIVES FOR AUSTRALIANS TO INVEST OVERSEAS

The Australian Tax Legislation, particularly in the light of proposed amendments, gives little encouragement for Australians to invest overseas. When recently introducing changes to the system of taxation of overseas income the Treasurer said:

'More significantly the present rules lend themselves to tax avoidance through the diversion of income to low tax or no tax countries. The Asprey committee has recommended that Australia introduces a credit system of taxing foreign source income of Australian residents and this lines up with the practice of most major developed countries.'

The Asprey committee referred to in the Treasure's statement was a Governmental Committee of enquiry headed by the Hon. Mr. Justice K. W. Asprey. The Committee after a 3 year enquiry in 1975 produced a voluminous report on the Australian taxation system and suggestions for its amendment. A number of the Asprey Committee suggestions have been followed by the Government in proposed amendments to the Income Tax Assessment Act and this report is useful reading for those seeking a background both to the existing system and to proposed amendments.

1. Existing System

Under Section 23 (q) of the Act Australian residents are exempt from Australian Income Tax on foreign source income that is subject to tax in the country of source. This exemption does not apply to dividends, nor to royalties or interest received by an Australian resident when the rate of tax imposed by the foreign country is reduced by a double tax agreement with Australia. In all other cases however, the exemption applies no matter how low the foreign tax is so long as some tax is payable.

Section 23 (q) does not apply to Papua New Guinea but an Australian tax payer is given credit for any tax paid in Papua New Guinea. Section 46 of the Act gives to Australian companies an advantage over individuals receiving foreign source dividends. A company receiving dividends can obtain a rebate equal to the Australian rate of tax which effectively exempts foreign source dividends received by a company whether or not the profits from which the dividends were paid or the dividends themselves have been subject to foreign tax. For individuals, on the other hand, Section 45 allows a credit to an Australian resident who receives a foreign source dividend in respect of foreign source income tax imposed on that dividend by the source country. Therefore, the Australian company will receive a foreign dividend tax free whereas the Australian resident will only receive a credit based upon the tax paid in the country of source.

This system constituted a considerable incentive for manufacturing or trading companies to set up manufacturing or buying subsidiaries in foreign countries particularly where low rates of tax prevailed.

Occasional problems were encountered in importing the goods manufactured by the foreign subsidiary through the tariff barrier which exists in Australia for most manufactured goods. The extent to which highly inflated import or highly reduced export prices can be used to avoid Australian Tax is limited by Division 2 Sub-Division C of the Act (Sectons 38-42), as well as possibly the recently introduced Section 31 C in relation to transfers of trading stock at excessive prices between parties not dealing with each other at arms length, and also Section 36 (9) where the Commissioner can write back the value of shares and other choses in action to prevent 'tax avoidance schemes' utilising the trading stock provisions of Section 36.

2. Proposed New System

The Federal Treasurer (as mentioned in Part A of the paper) has announced a proposed new system of taxing foreign source income as at 1.7.78 (no Bill to effectuate this has yet been introduced into the Parliament). The Treasurer said in his announcement:

'The basic rule will be that all foreign source income of Australian resident people and companies will be taxable in Australia, however the Australian tax on that income will be reduced by credit for foreign tax.

It is proposed that foreign source salary and wages which are taxed in the country of source will continue to be exempted upto a maximum of $ 10,000 per annum. Amounts in excess of this will be subject to Australian tax with a credit being payable for the foreign tax paid on the excess. The exempted amount will be taken into account for the purpose of determining the rate of tax applicable to the taxpayers assessable income...

A credit will be allowed for a tax imposed at one or another Government level in the country in which the income is derived if the tax is one comparable with the Australian income tax. The foreign tax must have been paid and must ordinarily be a tax which the tax payer was personally liable.'

The credit for foreign tax will be limited to thc amount of the Australian foreign tax on the foreign source income of the year. The rebate for inter company dividends will be removed in respect of foreign source dividends but a credit will be allowed for any foreign dividend withholding or other tax paid.

'In addition a credit for the underlying company tax on the profits out of which the dividends are paid will on what is known as a 'gross up' basis be allowed to Australian companies that have something more than portfolio investment in a foreign company. This credit will provide a direct recognition of the payment of any foreign company tax on those profits and will at base be allowed where the Australian company hase a direct 10 % or greater shareholding in a foreign company. The credit for underlying tax will be extended beyond the underlying tax paid by the foreign company in which the Australian company has a direct 10 % or greater interest to include such tax paid by a foreign company one further stage removed. If the Australian company has through the first tier of the company at least a 10 % shareholding interest in the further company.'

Under the new system Australian taxpayers will presumably be allowed a deduction for expenditure incurred in Australia in gaining overseas income, although the deduction may only be allowed to the extent that it is not taken into account in calculating the Foreign Tax. Previously such expenditure would not have been deductible because the income was exempt from Australian tax.

The new rules also give a concession against the double taxation of both company profits and shareholder dividend, which still applies to Australian companies.

The effect of the proposed changes will be to reduce significantly the incentive for Australian companies to invest in overseas subsidiaries or branches.

3. Trusts

Under the law previously applicable to foreign domiciled trusts (as decided by the High Court of Australia in the *Union Fidelity Case* 69ATC 4084) the net income of a trust estate for the purposes of the Australian tax act comprises only Australian source income. Accordingly, trust incomes could be accumulated overseas and capital paid to Australian residents so as to avoid Australian taxation. The effect of the new scheme is to tax the worldwide income of 'Australian resident trusts' being trusts of which at least one trustee is a resident which is managed and controlled in Australia. If the income is accumulated it will be taxed in the hands of the trustees or in the hands of the beneficiaries if they are presently entitled. Credits will be given under the new foreign tax credit system for foreign tax paid on foreign source income which is taxed in Australia to a trustee or beneficiary.

4. Tax Treaties

Australia has a limited number of tax treaties only one of which, namely the Singapore agreement, is with a country which could be classed as a developing country. Only in the Singapore agreement is there any provision for passing on to the Australian residents tax incentives available in the treaty country. Under Article 18.3 of the Singapore agreement Australia is required to give credit for Singapore tax foregone on certain interests and royalties under the Singapore Economic Expansion Incentives Act.

5. Non Tax Incentives

(1) Cash Grants

For some time the Government has been operating a system of cash grants to reimburse exporters for export development expenditure under the Export Market Development Grant Scheme. This scheme provides a maximum of $ 100,000 (or 10 % of export earnings, whichever is the lower) taxable grant calculated at the rate of 70 % of expenditure by a corporation on export development.

A new Export Incentive Grant Scheme was announced on 13th April 1978 to come into operation from 1st July 1977. This program will operate in conjunction with the Export Market Development Grant Scheme and will give a taxable grant based on the increase in exports over the base period, being the average annual exports in the 3 years immediately preceding the grant year. Rates of grant are to be calculated on the basis of the amount of the increase on the following scale:

Increase in Exports over base period	*Grant Rate Cents / Dollar*
Upto 500,000	15
500,000 to 5,000,000	10
5,000,000 to 10,000,000	5
over 10,000,000	2.5

Some exports are excluded from consideration including minerals, petroleum and by-products, precious stones, all wheat and sugar, and livestock and meat exported to the USA and Canada under quota.

(2) Non-Cash Assistance

The Export Finance and Insurance Corporation is a Government body whose endeavour is to encourage trade and commerce with overseas countries. It does this in 3 ways:

1. by providing various types of insurance to Australian exporters of goods and services and to Australian investors and overseas enterprises.
2. by giving guarantees to banks and other financial institutions
3. by making loans in support of particular classes of capital goods transactions.

Although the loans are expressed to be at a concessional rate of interest this rate does not compare with concessional export lenders set up in the United States and Japan.

(3) Australian Overseas Project Corporation

This is a proposed Federal statutory body promoted to give Australian companies and individuals sufficient standing by Association in foreign countries (particularly the Middle East) to give them a chance of competitive tendering. Its resources and proposed areas of activity are not yet known.

6. Conclusion

The present tax system applicable to foreign income earnt by Australian residents creates a favourable environment for Australian residents to invest abroad, particularly in developing countries where tax incentives can be anticipated. This situation is entirely changed by the proposed amendments described above. There are no other significant incentives (tax-based or otherwise) for investment in developing countries.

C. INCENTIVES AND DISINCENTIVES FOR FOREIGN INVESTMENT IN AUSTRALIA

1. Authority to Invest

Investment can only be made in Australia by investors if all pre-requisite authorities are obtained. These are as follows:

(A) Federal Authorities

Foreign Investment in Australia is monitored in three ways:

(a) by the Treasurer, in the assistance of the Foreign Investment Review Board (FIRB) under the Foreign Takeovers Act
(b) by the application of the Banking (Foreign Exchange) Regulations made under the Banking Act. These regulations are imposed by the Reserve

Bank of Australia, but policy matters are referred to FIRB for consideration

(c) by a system of voluntary restraints and guidelines promulgated from time to time by the Government and administered by the FIRB. There is no legislative support for these guidelines, apart from any coincidental requirements for approvals under the Foreign Takeovers Act or Banking Foreign Exchange Regulations, in which case approvals are not given until FIRB has made a determination under the 'voluntary guidelines'.

(1) Foreign Investment Review Board - Voluntary Restraints

It is the Government policy to prevent foreign investment in banking, radio, television, newspapers and certain forms of aviation. The Government has also determined that a foreign investor cannot hold more than a 25 % interest in the production of uranium, and in addition, the uranium venture must be controlled by Australian residents.

Apart from these restrictions, a foreign investor who is proposing to acquire Australian assets or to make investments in Australia, must submit his proposals to the Review Board.

The Foreign Takeovers Act lays down guidelines for determining what is a foreign investor for the purposes of the Act. A foreign investor is:

(a) A natural person who does not normally reside in Australia.

(b) An Australian business or corporation which is controlled by a foreign resident.

(c) An Australian business or corporation in which a foreign investor ownes 15 % or more, or a number of foreign investors together own 40 % or more of the business or corporation irrespective of who actually controls it.

There is a deemed control by the foreign interest in cases where:

(i) a natural person who does not ordinarily reside in Australia, or a corporation incorporated outside Australia, holds an interest of 15 % or more in the ownership or voting power of the Australian corporation; or

(ii) two or more natural persons not ordinarily resident in Australia or corporations incorporated outside Australia, have aggregate interests of 40 % or more in the ownership or voting power of the corporation.

It is, however, open to the foreign investor to prove to the Board that he or they do not, in fact, control the corporation.

The next step is to determine whether the particular proposal is one which is required to be submitted to the Board for its review. The following are the proposals which must be submitted to the Board under the guidelines:

(a) The acquisition of an interest in an Australian business or company where the acquisition would give the foreign investor or investors more than the percentage of shareholding referred to under (c) above.

(b) The acquisition of the assets of an Australian business.

(c) An increase in the representation of a foreign investor on the Board of Directors of an Australian corporation.

(d) An arrangement conferring on a foreign investor the right to use the assets of an Australian business or to participate in the mangement or profits of an Australian business.
(e) The establishment of a new non-banking financial institution or an insurance company.
(f) The establishment of other new business, including mining, involving an investment of $ 5 million or more.
(g) An increase in the ownership of a foreign investor in an existing business where that interest is already substantial.
(h) Certain real estate transactions, including those involving an expenditure of more than $ 250,000.

Any proposed investments which are not listed in the above categories do not require the approval of the Foreign Investments Review Board.

In determining whether approval will be given to the foreign investment, the Board has regard as to whether the proposal is generally in the Australian interest. The guidelines laid down by the Government to enable the Review Board to arrive at its determination in many cases overlap some of those mentioned above. However in particular, the Board must consider the following matters:

(i) Is the investment controlled by Australian residents at the Board level and what is the percentage of Australian equity participation? In the latter respect it is the desire of the Government to aim for not less than a 50 % Australian equity. The Government recently modified the interpretation of this requirement, so that in applying the 50 % Australian ownership objective for new investment projects in the area of natural resources, (other than uranium) a new concept of 'naturalisation' of foreign companies was introduced. Under the new policy a company will be regarded as having achieved the status of at least 50 % Australian share ownership and 50 % Australian voting strength at a board of directors meeting if it has:
(a) minimum 25 % Australian equity;
(b) Articles of Association which provides for a majority of the Board of Directors to be Australian citizens; and
(c) made a public commitment to increase Australian equity to 51 % subject to understandings between the Company, major shareholder interests and the Government; and to have regular discussions with the Foreign Review Board on progress to achieve 51 % Australian ownership.

The Government's aim is to assist development of new projects by foreign companies which are already substantially Australian owned and which do not have, but are prepared to introduce, majority Australian ownership. There are no time limits and the Government has not said how it proposes to enforce undertakings made by companies. However, the Government has said that it expects the 'naturalisation' process to take place permanently by way of new share issues to Australians to find new projects and expansions rather than by takeovers which remain subject to examination under the Foreign Takeovers Act. Other relevant points are:

(a) Naturalisation will not be relevant in situations where the Foreign Takeovers Act comes into operation. Naturalised status will be relevant in relation to new projects which are subject to the minimum 50 % Australian ownership and control guidelines. So, a naturalising company will be able to proceed with a new project in its own right even though at the commencement of a project it does not have, as a question of fact 50 % Australian share ownership and not less than 50 % Australian voting strength on the board of directors.
(b) A naturalising company may not enter into a joint venture with a wholly foreign owned company as the requirement of 50 % Australian ownership of a new project as such would not be satisfied.
(c) Mineral exploration is not subject to the Federal Government's 50 % rule and such activities may be undertaken by wholly foreign owned companies.

(ii) Is the proposed business for the economic benefit of Australia with respect to the following matters?
- The competition and efficiency which will be afforded by new business.
- The introduction of new technology and skills to Australia.
- The access to new export and local markets.
- The utilisation of Australian materials and labour.
- The involvement of Australians in the management and on the Board of Directors of the Business.

It is very difficult to determine whether any particular proposal will be approved by the Board. The only satisfactory way is to submit the proposal for its review. However, in general terms, the Government has announced that the Board will make every endeavour to adivse constructively on proposed new investment and to make recommendations as to ways and means by which the proposal will satisfy the guidelines.

For example, there have been cases where for one reason or another a proposal has not satisfied the guideline as to 50 % Australian equity. If the business is one which the Government is anxious to obtain in Australia, it has approved the proposal with a recommendation that as soon as circumstances are appropriate the Australian equity should be raised to the requisite percentage.

(2) Foreign Takeovers Act

Any foreign investor seeking to take up an interest in an Australian Company must comply with this Act. The Government will not normally seek to intervene if the Assets of the company being taken over are less than $2 million, unless there are special circumstances or the business is in the financial sector.

The Act *requires* notification of certain activities, and provides penalties for non-compliance.

The Act requires persons to whom clause 26 of the Act applies – (who are basically the same persons or companies who fall within the definition of foreign interest in the guideliness) – to give forty days notice of any proposal to acquire or to increase an interest of 15 % or more of the ownership or voting power of an Australian corporation.

Notification is compulsory, but the Act also provides for voluntary notification to the Treasurer for a number of other proposals affecting Australian business. Examples of such proposals are:

(a) A proposed acquisition by a foreign person of any interest in the assets of an Australian business, whether or not thc business is carried on by a corporation;

(b) A proposed agreement which would enable increased representation on the Board of an Australian corporation, which directly or through a subsidiary carries on an Australian business, by a foreign person who has an interest of 15 % or more in the ownership or voting power of the Australian corporation concerned;

(c) A proposed arrangement under which a foreign person would lease or be granted other rights to use the assets of an Australian business (whether or not carried on by a corporation or would be entitled to participate in the management or profits of such a business).

The definition 'Australian business' is very wide and includes activities carried on in Australia by foreigners as well as Australians, whether through a local or subsidiary or a branch office.

As stated, proposals of the nature outlined above are not subject to compulsory notifications. However, notification (whether compulsory or voluntary) has the effect of setting in train time limits upon the Treasure's capacity to make prohibition and other orders in respect of the matter notified. The effect of notification is to ensure that examinable proposals which could result in a change of control of a business are submitted for Government consideration before they are concluded.

Where notification is given of a proposal, examination of the proposals then normally carried out in two stages:

(A) Preliminary examination must be completed within 30 days of receipt of notification.

Preliminary examination may result in a quick clearance of the proposal or if it is not so cleared then an interim order will be made prohibiting implementation of the proposal for a period of up to ninety days. Such an order must be made by the Treasurer within 30 days of the date of receipt of notification and it must be published in the Government Gazette within 10 days of the date on which it is made.

(B) Detailed investigation will follow an Interim Order and must be completed within 90 days.

Detailed investigation will conclude either with a clearance of the proposal or with its prohibition by order made under various sections of the Act. Such an order must be made by the Treasurer within 90 days of the date of publication of the interim order (or within 30 days of the date of notification) and it must be published in the Government Gazette within 10 days of the date on which it is made.

Where an examinable acquisition or arrangement is completed:

(i) without notification having been given to the Treasurer;

(ii) after notification has been given but within 40 days of the date on which the Treasurer received the notification; or

(iii) in defiance of an Interim Order or a Prohibition Order made by the Treasurer and published in the Gazette within due time and where the Treasurer is satisfied that:
   (a) the acquisition or arrangement resulted in a change in control of the business concerned;
   (b) the result and control is foreign; and
   (c) the foreign control concerned is against the national interest;
   the Treasurer may then make an order:
   (a) requiring the foreign person to sell within such period of time as is specified in the order the shares or assets so require; or
   (b) requiring in effect the un-winding within such period of time as is specified in the order of the arrangement so entered into.

In addition the Act provides that an examinable proposal may be prohibited by the Treasurer if the Treasurer is satisfied that the proposal would result in a change of control of the business concerned, the result and control would be foreign and the foreign control concerned would be against the national interest.

Although there are extensive definition clauses in the Act, it does not define a change in control, and so the question of whether a proposed acquisition or arrangement would result in a foreign person or persons being in a position to determine the policy of a business often cannot be determined absolutely.

As stated earlier proposals notifiable under the Act are addressed to the Foreign Investment Review Board.

(3) The Trade Practices Act 1974

The Trade Practices Act is another piece of complex legislation that will have to be allowed for by any potential foreign investor.

The basic approach of the Act is to prohibit restrictive trade practices. Within the meaning of the Act they are:
(a) Restraint of trade;
(b) Monopolisation;
(c) Re-sale price maintenance;
(d) Exclusive dealings;
(e) Discriminatory dealings; and
(f) Anti-competitive mergers.

The Act also prohibits unfair practices operating against consumers.

For foreign investors even if they have obtained a clearance under the Foreign Takeovers Act of any investment proposal it will then become necessary to consider whether or not the proposal is in breach of any of the provisions of the Trade Practices Act.

The Act provides that authorisation can be sought on public benefit grounds for individual cases of restraint of trade and exclusive dealing and for mergers.

As with the Foreign Takeovers Act, and the foreign investment guidelines this Act also provides that the Trade Practices Commission, which is the body having the general responsibility of enforcing the Act, is to make a case by case study of each application to it.

(4) Reserve Bank

The Bank has the authority under the Exchange Control Regulations made by the Federal Government (under the Bankruptcy Act) to control not only the movement of currency both to and from Australia, but also to control a number of arrangements entered into by Australian residents with non-residents.

In these Regulations the test is one of residence, which in the case of an individual means a person who is ordinarily resident in Australia and in the case of a company, one which is incorporated in Australia but also one which is incorporated outside Australia if it has a place of business there.

All contracts, agreements or arrangments of whatever nature (except contracts for the purchase of goods) entered into by a resident with a non-resident must have the prior approval of the Reserve Bank.

In addition, any agreement relating to an Australian asset made between two non-residents requires the approval of the Bank. For the purposes of these regulations and the Foreign Investment Review Board, such a transaction is treated as a new dealing.

All borrowing by Australian residents from non-residents and the allotment or transfer of securities, including shares, to non-residents, also requires the Bank's approval.

In recent years, the Government has on a number of occasions introduced a regulation requiring a resident who is borrowing from overseas to deposit with the Bank a portion of those borrowings free of interest.

Currently, there is no such requirement. If the borrowing does not exceed $ 200,000 no approval is required.

If it is intended to open a branch office in Australia or incorporate a subsidiary company in Australia the approval of the Reserve Bank will be required. However, it must be borne in mind that when the time comes to remit any profits or capital moneys to a non-resident, the Bank's approval will be requisite.

Currently the Bank does not purport to restrict the movement of such moneys out of Australia, but it will not give an advance ruling of the policy which may be applicable at a future date.

In addition to its normal functions mentioned above the Bank is required to obtain a clearance from the Commissioner of Taxation with respect to transactions with certain specified countries, commonly known as tax havens, and the Commissioner of Taxation will need to be satisfied that the transaction will not result in the avoidance of Australian tax.

A certificate will also be required to remit funds from Australia. The Foreign Exchange Regulations also require a license for the export of certain goods from Australia. Normally these are granted by the Bank.

(B) State Governments

Apart from the general necessity to comply with the laws of the State in which the foreign investor is conducting his business, it may be necessary to negotiate a special agreement with the government of that State.

A common example occurs in cases where companies are mining, transporting and exporting minerals such as iron ore and coal from Australia.

Normally transport and other facilities such as railways and harbours, are controlled and dealt with by instrumentalities of the State. The purpose of the agreement which is ratified by a special Act of Parliament of the State is to permit the company concerned to conduct the full range of its operations.

For example in most States there are a number of special agreements permitting companies to mine, transport by rail and export on ships, iron ore. This type of agreement normally permits the company to construct roads, construct and operate railways, construct and operate a port, construct towns, and other facilities. Without the special agreement, the company would not be able to conduct the full scale of its operations.

It should also be noted that in relation to mining projects in the State of New South Wales, that State's Government policy requires a minimum Australian equity participation of 51 % in respect of mining leases for new and additional projects and the policy goes even further in promoting a high level of Australian participation as is practicable.

2. Relevant Taxation Provisions

Income tax is imposed upon

(a) Australian residents on their world wide income irrespective of source, subject to double taxation relief (explained below);

(b) non-residents on income having an Australian source as stated in Part A of this paper, at the several rates there explained in detail.

It can be said that the Australian Taxation laws deal in a complex way with the taxation of persons and corporations investing in Australia and the balance of this section of the paper gives only a general resume of the relevant provisions.

The treatment of dividends interest and royalties for tax purposes by companies trading in Australia has already been dealt with in general terms under Part A of the paper.

While some unilateral relief is provided to residents in respect of ex Australian income that that has borne foreign taxes, no relief is provided to non-residents in respect of double taxation of income received from Australia. Any unilateral relief must be sought in the non-residents own country.

There are simply no special tax concessions provided under Australian law as incentives to attract foreign investment.

As mentioned earlier in the papier Australia has concluded general tax treaties with nine countries to give relief from double taxation. Those countries are France, Germany, Japan, Netherlands, New Zealand, Singapore, United Kingdom, Belgium, USA and Canada. The first seven are based on the 1963 OECD Draft Convention.

In general terms of the treaties, particularly those based on the OECD Draft, reduce the tax rate in the country of source to 15 % in respect of dividend income to 10 % in respect of interest income and to 10 or 15 % in respect of royalty income.

The treaties generally provide that the country of residence will grant a credit for the taxes paid in the country of source in respect of dividend, interest and royalty income.

Where an Australian resident corporation pays dividends to a non-resident corporation, then:

(i) where the non-resident company is a resident of a treaty country, the normal withholding tax rate on dividends is reduced from 30 % to 15 %,

(ii) the dividends paid to a non-resident which has a permanent establishment in Australia are normally subject to tax at the company rate of 46 %.

The treaties don't have any real effect on interest, as the Australian withholding tax rate on interest of 10 % is the same as the general treaty rare of 10 %.

In general terms the treaties (other than the US and Canadian treaties) impose a rate limitation of 10 or 15 % on the gross amount of royalties paid by a resident company to a non-resident company. Royalties paid to US and Canadian recipients and residents of non-treaty countries, are taxed on an assessment basis as indicated earlier in this paper.

3. Economic Data

There are a number of reports put out by the Australian Government Statistician and the Foreign Investment Review Board detailing the extent of foreign investment in Australia.

Some samples from the first source are attached to the end of this paper and indicate the level of foreign investment activity in Australia.

4. Conclusion - Incentives and Disincentives for foreign investment

Having read under sub-clauses 1 and 2 of this part of this paper of the various authorities before whom an investor must get approval and also the various complex taxation provisions that might apply, a would be investor might be forgiven for thinking that there are no incentives for foreign investment in Australia.

However, all is certainly not gloom for the foreign investor.

In general terms, it may be said that foreign investment is sought by both the Federal and State Governments, as it is in many cases the only means of getting some of the bigger projects off the ground. For example, the proposed off-shore gas development in the north west of Western Australia.

In recent years, a more nationalistic approach has been adopted to that permitted in earlier years when foreign investment had more or less unrestricted right of entry to Australia. This is particularly so with some of the large mineral developments.

In more recent times, the Federal Government has adopted a policy of requiring the maximum possible investment for Australians, and in this respect, an Australian interest of at least 50 % is regarded as desirable as detailed earlier. In many industries foreign investment is permitted if it can be demonstrated that it is in the Australian interest that a particular industry or project should be developed.

The Trade Union movement now seems to adopt the view that development of natural resources particularly should be restricted to Australian interests. The environmentalists too have opposed the development of certain industries and are particularly vocal on the proposal of the Federal Government to develop the uranium industry. The Union view too is fairly hard on this particular industry, and some unions have voiced considerable opposition to its development.

The effect of the double-tax treaties is not to discourage foreign investment in Australia and at the same time to limit the taxation on foreign investors at source to a reasonable level and allow a further tax to be levied in the country of residence. This is in line with the present Government's policy of permitting some investments in the appropriate areas while not offering unusual incentives to attract investment.

Certainly non-residents are not under any disadvantage tax-wise as against residents, as they are both treated equally under the tax laws, although it might be argued that the tax treaties favour a non-resident as against a resident investor. The new branch profits tax will not be of any substantive effect, and apart from this tax it can be concluded that the Australian tax laws do not discriminate against non-residents; on the other side and as stated earlier, there are no tax incentives for foreign investors greater than those available to residents. The position is virtually one of equality, once the investor gets through the various authorities.

The brief figures detailed below evidence a conclusion that foreign investors seem to believe that the Australian tax laws are fair and reasonable and do not constitute a disincentive to investment by non-residents in Australia.

OUTFLOW OF AUSTRALIAN INVESTMENT IN FOREIGN ENTERPRISES BY COUNTRY AND BROAD TYPE OF INVESTMENT (SA MILLION)

	EEC				*Papua*			
Year	*UK*	*Other*	*New Zealand*	*USA and Canada*	*New Guinea*	*ASEAN*	*Other countries*	*Total*
				UNDISTRIBUTED INCOME				
1967-68	..	(b)	8	..	5	(b)	(c)6	20
1968-69	—2	(b)	9	1	—3	(b)	(c)6	12
1969-70	3	.	6	1	1	3	4	17
1970-71	3	..	9	2	—2	2	5	19

1971-72	2	. .	7	2	7	2	10	30
1972-73	9	.	9	2	(b)	—1	(d)54	73
1973-74	13	.	19	2	(b)	3	(d)62	99
1974-75	5	—7	15	2	—7	5	14	28
1975-76	11	2	18	5	22	—2	9	65
1976-77	18	—3	37	5	16	4	14	90

OTHER DIRECT INVESTMENT

1967-68	6	(b)	—1	2	14	(b)	(c)6	27
1968-69	14	(b)	5	. .	28	(b)	(c)1	48
1969-70	27	. .	4	8	70	—2	3	110
1970-71	. .	1	11	4	27	3	8	53
1971-72	—7	2	20	11	45	7	14	91
1972-73	2	21	13	6	—5	8	—22	23
1973-74	26	28	8	32	6	21	15	135
1974-75	—6	5	33	8	—4	33	11	79
1975-76	24	5	—8	19	19	12	19	90
1976-77	12	10	18	24	14	11	31	121

PORTFOLIO INVESTMENT AND INSTITUTIONAL LOANS

1967-68	. .	(b)	. .	—1	2	(b)	(c)—1	1
1968-69	5	(b)	. .	. .	. .	(b)	(c)—2	3
1969-70	7	. .	. .	—4	. .	. .	2	6
1970-71	—2	. .	1	—1	. .	. .	—1	—4
1971-72	—5	. .	. .	—2	. .	. .	—3	—10
1972-73	—13	. .	2	12	. .	. .	17	17
1973-74	2	1	2	6	. .	. .	8	18
1974-75	3	. .	3	—1	4	. .	—3	5
1975-76	—5	1	1	19	5	. .	—1	20
1976-77	1	1	. .	11	—3	. .	—7	2

TOTAL

1967-68	6	(b)	8	2	21	(b)	(c)10	48
1968-69	17	(b)	14	1	25	(b)	(c)5	63
1969-70	37	. .	10	5	72	1	9	133
1970-71	1	. .	21	5	25	4	12	68
1971-72	—10	2	26	11	53	9	22	112
1972-73	—2	21	24	20	(b)	7	(d)44	114
1973-74	41	29	28	39	(b)	24	(d)91	252
1974-75	2	—1	51	9	—7	38	21	112
1975-76	30	8	11	43	46	10	27	175
1976-77	31	8	55	40	26	15	38	213

(a) From January 1976, includes portfolio investment in Papua New Guinea. Prior to April 1975 excludes such investment; between April and December 1975, includes transactions with Papua New Guinea only where amounts involved were denominated in kina.
(b) Not available; included in 'Other countries'.
(c) Includes Other EEC and ASEAN.
(d) Includes Papua New Guinea.

INFLOW OF FOREIGN INVESTMENT IN ENTERPRISES IN AUSTRALIA, BY BROAD TYPE OF INVESTMENT, INDUSTRY GROUP AND COUNTRY (SA MILLION)

Country	*1974-75*			
	Direct investment		*Portfolio investment and institutional loans*	*T*
	Undistributed income	*Other direct investment*		
EEC — United Kingdom	24	1	—10	
— Other	—18	7	25	
US	46	—23	35	
Canada	—4	(a)	(a)	
Japan	7	6	7	
Other countries	14	5	13	
Total	*68*	*—4*	*71*	
EEC — United Kingdom	33	52	31	
— Other	..	22	75	
USA	99	45	34	
Canada	—1	1	7	
Japan	—3	5	—1	
Other countries	2	28	41	
Total	*130*	*153*	*186*	
EEC — United Kingdom	32	25	—78	-
— Other	—17	53	10	
USA	49	31	34	
Canada	7	(a)	(a)	
Japan	—1	40	5	
Other countries	—27	105	8	
Total	*43*	*254*	*—20*	
EEC — United Kingdom	89	77	—57	
— Other	—34	82	110	
USA	194	53	103	
Canada	2	2	11	
Japan	2	51	12	
Other countries	—12	138	58	
Total	*241*	*403*	*237*	

(a) Not available for publication; Included in 'Other countries'.
(b) See footnote (a), Table 5.

1975-76				1976-77			
Direct investment		*Portfolio investment and institutional loans*	*Total*	*Direct investment*		*Portfolio investment and institutional loans*	*Total*
Undistributed income	*Other direct investment*			*Undistributed income*	*Other direct investment*		
PRIMARY PRODUCTION							
5	6	39	50	23	35	—9	49
—6	14	28	36	—11	32	—2	19
81	—76	12	17	—24	—104	32	—96
. .	—4	—2	—6	(a)	—1	(a)	3
16	—14	8	10	(a)	—1	(a)	28
22	—24	6	4	51	—51	58	25
119	*—98*	*90*	*111*	*39*	*—89*	*78*	*27*
MANUFACTURING							
102	—7	30	124	119	20	—27	112
2	—7	—39	—44	7	30	21	57
120	—14	122	228	221	58	116	395
7	—1	—5	1	10	—13	—5	—8
—6	23	5	22	7	13	39	59
6	4	15	25	3	7	—11	—1
230	*—2*	*128*	*356*	*367*	*115*	*133*	*615*
OTHER INDUSTRIES (b)							
165	—6	—57	102	174	12	10	197
4	—2	16	18	9	89	81	179
66	36	10	113	50	237	27	314
18	1	. .	20	(a)	7	(a)	73
7	54	1	62	(a)	25	(a)	117
—4	—25	10	—19	20	—1	167	30
256	*59*	*—20*	*294*	*253*	*371*	*285*	*909*
TOTAL							
272	—7	12	277	316	68	—27	357
. .	4	5	10	4	151	100	255
267	—53	144	358	246	191	175	613
25	—3	—8	14	28	—7	47	68
16	63	14	94	47	37	120	204
24	—45	30	9	18	—44	81	54
605	*—41*	*198*	*762*	*659*	*396*	*496*	*1,551*

INCOME RECEIVABLE ON AUSTRALIAN DIRECT INVESTMENT IN FOREIGN ENTERPRISES, BY TYPE OF INCOME (SA MILLION)

Year	Undistributed income		Distributed income			
	Branches	Subsidiaries	Remitted profits of branches	Dividends of subsidiaries	Interest	Total
1967-68	2	18	6	19		45
1968-69	—9	21	5	24		41
1969-70	—3	20	7	24	1	49
1970-71	—7	26	9	26	2	56
1971-72	—7	37	7	32	2	71
1972-73	—10	83	16	34	2	125
1973-74	—3	103	18	67	1	187
1974-75	—12	40	23	60	3	113
1975-76	2	63	22	46	5	138
1976-77	—10	100	33	59	7	190

(a) Details of income receivable in Australia are not available on either portfolio investment and institutional loans or on Australian holdings of foreign government securities.

INCOME RECEIVABLE ON AUSTRALIAN DIRECT INVESTMENT IN FOREIGN ENTERPRISES BY COUNTRY (a) (SA MILLION)

Year	EEC		New Zealand	USA and Canada	Papua New Guinea	ASEAN	Other countries	Total
	UK	Other						
UNDISTRIBUTED INCOME								
1967-68	..	(b)	8	..	5	(b)	(c)6	20
1969-69	—2	(b)	9	1	—3	(b)	(c)6	12
1969-70	3	..	6	1	1	3	4	17
1970-71	3	..	9	2	—2	2	5	19
1971-72	2	..	7	2	7	2	10	30
1972-73	9	..	9	2	(b)	—1	(d)54	73
1973-74	13	..	19	2	(b)	3	(d)62	99
1974-75	5	—7	15	2	—7	5	14	28
1975-76	11	2	18	5	22	—2	9	65
1967-77	18	—3	37	5	16	4	14	90
DISTRIBUTED INCOME ON DIRECT INVESTMENT								
1967-68	3	(b)	9	1	4	(b)	(c)8	25
1968-69	3	(b)	8	..	7	(b)	(c)11	29
1969-70	7	..	8	..	8	2	7	32
1970-71	8	..	8	(b)	9	3	(e)	37

(a) See footnote (a), Table above.
(b) Not available; included in 'Other countries'.
(c) Includes Other EEC and ASEAN.
(d) Includes Papua New Guinea.
(e) Includes USA and Canada.

Year	EEC UK	EEC Other	New Zealand	USA and Canada	Papua New Guinea	ASEAN	Other countries	Total
1971-72	7	..	7	1	15	2	8	41
1972-73	10	..	12	1	14	5	10	51
1973-74	12	..	16	..	(b)	2	(d)56	87
1974-75	12	..	14	2	(b)	4	(d)54	85
1975-76	13	..	16	3	(b)	11	(d)30	73
1976-77	15	..	17	3	24	13	27	100
				TOTAL				
1967-68	3	(b)	18	1	9	(b)	(c)14	45
1968-69	2	(b)	16	2	4	(b)	(c)17	41
1969-70	9	..	13	1	10	5	11	49
1970-71	12	..	17	(b)	7	5	(e)13	56
1971-72	9	..	14	3	23	4	18	71
1972-73	19	..	21	3	(b)	4	(d)78	125
1973-74	25	..	35	2	(b)	6	(d)118	187
1974-75	17	—7	29	4	(b)	9	(d)61	113
1975-76	24	2	34	8	(b)	9	(d)61	138
1976-77	33	—3	54	8	40	17	41	190

(a) See footnote (a), Table above.
(b) Not available; included in 'Other countries'.
(c) Includes Other EEC and ASEAN.
(d) Includes Papua New Guinea.
(e) Includes USA and Canada.

LEVEL OF AUSTRALIAN INVESTMENT IN FOREIGN ENTERPRISES, BY TYPE OF INVESTMENT AND COUNTRY, AT JUNE 1977 (SA MILLION)

Country	*Direct investment* Corporate equities (a)	Branch liabilities to head office	Inter-company indebtedness	Borrowings	*Portfolio investment and institutional loans* Corporate equities (a)	Borrowings	*Totals* Corporate equities (a)	Other
EEC-								
United Kingdom	61	14	25	10	5	5	66	55
Other	16	(b)	4	7	..	..	16	(c)11
New Zealand	139	64	18	30	18	5	157	118
USA and Canada	45	20	9	52	31	26	76	107
Papua New Guinea	126	86	41	26	2	1	128	154
ASEAN	69	7	18	38	1	..	70	63
Other countries	79	(d)83	21	46	20	29	99	(e)177
Total	535	274	136	209	77	66	613	685

(a) Paid up value only.
(b) Not available; included in 'Other countries'.
(c) Branch liabilities to head office included in 'Other countries'.
(d) Includes Other EEC.
(e) Includes branch liabilities for Other EEC.

Austria

Dr. Heinz H. Löber *

A. TAX INCENTIVES FOR INVESTMENTS ABROAD

In Austrian tax law there are no specific incentives for investments in developing countries. There are, however, provisions governing all investments abroad.

1. Preferential Treatment of Foreign Investments

According to section 6 para. 7 Income Tax Act 1972, under certain conditions a preferential treatment for investments abroad by Austrian residents is granted. The preferential treatment consists of a partial value depreciation (Teilwertabschreibung) of 90% of the original purchase price and is granted for the following investments:

(a) Holdings in a foreign stock company acquired in connection with the establishment or with a capital increase of such company;

(b) Holdings in foreign partnerships acquired on the occasion of the establishment or a considerable increase in the business activity of such partnership;

(c) Granting of loans to foreign stock companies on the occasion of the establishment or a considerable increase in the business activity of such company.

The law requires that the foreign stock companies and partnerships be of a legal form comparable to those under Austrian law. Furthermore, the amount of the holdings have to be at least 25 per cent of the stated share capital of the stock company or at least 25 per cent of the assets of the partnership. A holding of at least 25 per cent in the company concerned is also required in case of a loan granted to such company.

The above mentioned 'considerable increase in business activity' is defined by the law as an increase by at least 50 per cent of the stated share capital or the assets of a company.

Finally, section 6 para. 7 Income Tax Act 1972 applies only to investments in such foreign companies that trade, install or service goods manufactured in Austria.

2. Allowance for Export Sales

Section 123 Income Tax Act 1972 provides for an allowance of certain

* Heller, Löber & Bahn, Vienna.

percentage amounts of accounts receivable earned by Austrian resident companies from export sales or services. This operates as a tax deferral in that presently 15 per cent of the face amount of such receivables may be depreciated until full payment is received by the creditor, at which time the allowance becomes taxable income. This position will be in force until 1979.

3. Tax Relief for Dividends in Absence of Tax Convention

An Austrian resident, be it an individual or a company, is normally subject to liability for personal income tax and corporate income tax, respectively, on world wide income, whether or not remitted to Austria.

Whereas the Income Tax Act applies to individuals, the Corporate Income Tax Act applies to corporations and other legal entities. However, the same basic principles underlie the two acts. Section 8 para. 2 Corporate Income Tax Act explicitly refers to the income concept and the profit concept, respectively, as developed by the Income Tax Act.

Under the concept of Corporate Income Tax Law an Austrian resident company's profits are taxed in the hands of the company itself, but are also subject to further tax liability if distributed as income to shareholders. To mitigate that effect of economic doubletaxation a lower rate for distributed profits was introduced. Distributed profits are therefore taxed with only half the normal tax rate. Such distributed profits – which are considered part of the taxable income of the recipient of those dividends – are also subject to a withholding tax at a standard rate of 20 per cent. If the recipient is subject to Austrian tax liability this withholding tax is credited against its own tax obligation. As far as Austrian non-residents are concerned this source-tax is only repaid if a double-taxation convention so provides. Under most double taxation conventions, however, this source-tax is at least partly repaid.

No such dividends tax has to be paid where an Austrian resident company holds directly 25 per cent or more of the share capital of another resident company and where dividends are paid by virtue of that holding. Those dividends are left out of account when the recipient company is taxed (section 10 para. 1 Corporate Income Tax Act). With effect from January 1, 1973 the same rule applies when a resident company has a holding of at least 25 per cent of a company resident abroad. Thus dividends paid by a foreign subsidiary to its resident parent company are not taxable to the recipient. It should be noted that this so-called holding-privilege is not acorded to Austrian branch offices of foreign companies.

4. Double Taxation Conventions

Austria has concluded double taxation conventions with 31 countries (including 14 developing countries), of which 28 were in force at the end of 1977. These conventions, which normally follow closely the OECD-Model Convention, also provide tax incentives for investments in developing countries though inclusion of a credit for taxes spared. Thus, an Austrian resident may credit against its Austrian tax obligation not only the tax it has actually paid abroad but the tax it would have had to pay if there had been no local tax incentives for the Austrian investment.

B. EXPORT PROMOTION SYSTEM

One of the reasons why there are so few provisions on tax incentives for investments in developing countries in Austrian tax laws is probably the existence of an elaborate export promotion and insurance system. So far, the following main guarantee-systems were and are used:

(a) Guarantees relating to the proper execution of an export contract (delivery-performance-guarantees);
(b) Guarantees relating to the maintenance of existing rights out of export business or investments (political-risks-guarantees);
(c) Guarantees relating to changes in the exchange rate between the Austrian Shilling on one side and foreign currencies on the other side;
(d) Guarantees relating to the financing of exports and investments abroad.

Exports promotion is available to any Austrian enterprise, i.e. an enterprise or corporation registered or incorporated in Austria, irrespective of any foreign (even wholly-owned) participation. Under this export promotion system credits, as well as guarantees for such credits, for investments abroad and particularly in developing countries are available to Austrian enterprises.

The export promotion system is managed by several institutions such as the 'Entwicklungs- und Erneuerungsfondgesellschaft mbH' and the 'Österreichische Kontrollbank AG', an institution comparable to the US-Eximbank. Those institutions are generally owned by the State and by Austrian banks, respectively.

C. TAX INCENTIVES FOR INVESTMENTS AT HOME

1. The Austrian tax law contains several provisions for the promotion of investments at home:

(a) Accelerated Depreciation (Vorzeitige Abschreibung)

Accelerated depreciation is granted under section 8 Income Tax Act in the form of an initial allowance in addition to straight-line depreciation on the purchase price or manufacturing costs of the qualifying depreciable asset. It applies to the year in which the qualifying asset is put into operation. The date an order is placed or the date of payment is not material. The book value of the asset is reduced by the allowance taken.

An accelerated depreciation is granted in the year of acquisition, in most cases at the rate of 50 per cent for movable property. The Income Tax Amendment of July 12, 1974 continued, with few exceptions, the allowance of accelerated depreciation for immovable property previously granted at a rate of 25 per cent of production or purchase costs. Under a more recent Tax Changes Act of March 31, 1976 (Abgabenänderungsgesetz 1976) accelerated depreciation for immovable property was again allowed at a rate of 50 per cent of the building costs, but solely for the calendar years 1976 and 1977. This has been regarded as an economic incentive favouring the construction industry in a recessionary period. It should be noted that accelerated depreciation is restricted to assets used in a permanent establishment located in Austria. For certain business ventures such as for prevention of environmental pollution, tax law has established additional incentives in the form of special accelerated depreciation rates.

(b) Investment Reserve (Investitionsrücklage)

Under section 9 Income Tax Act enterprises may deduct up to 25 per cent of their profits and allocate such deductions to an investment reserve account (Investitionsrücklage) for subsequent investment in future periods. The reserve must be used within 4 years for the purchase of business assets. It may not be set up to the extent that accelerate depreciation or an initial investment allowance (Investitionsfreibetrag) is being claimed. If therefore, an accelerated depreciation or an initial investment allowance is claimed by the taxpayer in the same year, the reserves are taxed to that extent.

(c) Initial Investment Allowance (Investitionsfreibetrag)

Under section 10 Income Tax Act 1972, in addition to regular depreciation, enterprises may deduct 20 percent of the costs of acquisition or the costs of production of assets (movable or immovable) to be used in a domestic permanent establishment (Investitionsfreibetrag). If the assets are sold or transferred to a permanent establishment situated abroad within five years of their acquisition, the amount deducted becomes taxable. For certain assets no initial investment allowance is available.

(d) Tax-free Reserves (Nicht entnommener Gewinn)

Individuals or partnerships which carry on a trade or business and do not avail themselves of the accelerated depreciation provisions or the investment reserves and which keep a regular set of books may place the lower of 50 per cent of undistributed profits or 15 per cent of total annual profits in a tax-free reserve account. If the reserve fund is kept for a period of five years it will be permanently tax-free and treated as business capital. If the business is sold the reserve fund will be added to taxable income in the year of the sale.

(e) Reinvestment of Capital Gains

In most tax systems, business enterprises are taxes on capital gains accruing to them for the disposal or realization of assets used in their business.

Under Austrian law (section 12 Income Tax Act) if an enterprise sells an asset the excess profit over the book value is taxable. However, such amounts of profits may be deducted from the production or purchase costs of other fixed assets acquired in the same year. Such transfer of hidden reserves (Ubertragung stiller Rücklagen) is only permissible if, in the case of movable assets, they were held for 7 years (prior to 1975, 10 years) and, in the case of immovable property such property was held for 15 years (reduced from 20 years prior to 1975).

2. It should finally be noted that apart from tax incentives for investments in Austria there are several funds and institutions granting either investment credits or guarantees for such credits. The main purpose of those institutions is to promote investments in less developed regions of Austria as well as in branches of the Austria economy that are either less developed or have run into difficulties.

Belgium

Dr. R. D. de Broglio *

Successive Belgian governments have consistently welcomed foreign investment and have adopted numerous measures to stimulate it. Thanks to this attitude and its location, Belgium has been chosen as European headquarters by many multinational companies. In practice there is presently freedom from exchange control for virtually all purposes.

Belgium provides incentives to attract investment to 'special development areas', principally in areas such as East and West Flanders, Limburg and southern Belgium. These incentives take the form of government guarantees, noninterest bearing loans, property rating rebates, additional depreciation allowance, and reduced taxes.

FOREIGN INVESTMENTS

A. Internal Law

The various measures introduced by successive Belgian governments to encourage foreign investment into Belgium have not been matched by any significant action to encourage investment from Belgium into less developed countries.

The strength of the Belgian economy is to a very large extent the result of the high level of exports which the country has achieved over the past twenty years. In view of the limited amount of natural resources the future prosperity of Belgium depends on this level of exports being maintained. However, Belgium has been somewhat slower than for instance France or West Germany in recognizing that foreign investment is a necessary element in the opening up of new markets for its exports and can thus have a beneficial effect on domestic unemployment rather than simply absorbing funds which could be used for internal investment.

That this view is gaining offical recognition is evidenced by the proposed setting up of the Fonds de la Cooperation au Developpement which will be a government body providing finance for joint projects in developing countries. Regrettably the draft law under which such fund was to be established lapsed with the dissolution of the last parliament and will now have to be reintroduced.

The present position is therefore that there are no fiscal provisions specifically designed to encourage external investment and the only positive measures taken in this direction are:

1. Agreement of the Office National du Ducroire to underwrite political risks in developing countries.

* Clifford-Turner & Co., Brussels.

2. Participation by a government holding company in the Societe Belge d'Investissement International SA.

The Office National du Ducroire is a public body operating under State guarantee which provides export credit insurance. It will insure foreign investments in developing countries provided the investments promote the economic and social expansion of that country and is of a nature to promote economic relations between Belgium and that country. The cover is limited to a maximum of 90%.

The Societe Belge D'Investissement International SA (SBI) is a semi-official financial organization specializing in the medium and long-term financing of business ventures outside Belgium. It is owned as to 55% by a government holding company and as to 45% by the private sector notably the larger banks and industrial concerns specializing in overseas business. Its shareholding reflects its dual purpose – to promote the general economic interests of Belgium and host countries whilst at the same time being financially profitable. It receives no special government subsidy for support and thus the financing it provides must be made on commercial terms. Funds are usually loaned in Belgian francs and so it is the Belgian market conditions which affect interest rates. The financing is not limited to loan capital but may take the form of minority equity participation, convertible debentures, guarantees, performance bonds or equity/loan blends. The amount of capital which the SBI is willing to provide to suitable projects is generally in the range of 10 to 50 million Belgian francs.

As regards the taxation of profits, there is at present no group relief, i.e. consolidation for tax purposes of group profits and losses. Each company is taxed separately whether incorporated in Belgium or elsewhere. Belgian companies are subject to corporation tax (currently 48%) on their world-wide income subject to any relief affected by double tax treaties. Foreign companies having an establishment in Belgium, but whose registered office, principal establishment or seat of management is outside Belgium, are liable to non-resident tax (currently 54% except where reduced by double tax treaty) on profits realized in Belgium but will not be liable for withholding tax upon distribution of these profits. Dividends received by one Belgian company from another are deductible from taxable income to the extent of 95% if the shares are held throughout the fiscal year in question. In the case of a financial holding company the deduction is limited to 90 per cent. A company is deemed to be a financial holding company if more than half its assets comprise shares in other companies but for this purpose shareholdings of more than 75% can be excluded.

The standard rate of withholding tax on dividends is 20 per cent but this may be reduced by double tax convention.

B. Tax Treaties

Substantial benefits are granted to investment in designated developing countries through income tax treaties. Within the past five years, Belgium has signed conventions with, among others, Brazil, India, Indonesia, Israel, Malaysia,

Morocco, and Singapore. In these double tax treaties Belgium in effect exempts from tax income from the foreign permanent establishment and dividends from permanent holdings held by Belgian companies in subsidiaries in the country of the treaty partner. Also, as in the treaty with Israel, Belgium grants a credit for taxes spared on interest and royalties. Where a developing country wishes to impose a high withholding tax, Belgium has agreed to a rate above the OECD model, unlimited in some cases.

Canada

James Scott Peterson *
Robert Anthoine **

Tax Incentives for Investment at Home

The general federal corporate tax rate is 46 per cent before an abatement of 10% for the income tax levied by each of the ten Canadian provinces at general rates which range between 10% and 15%. Accordingly, the combined general federal-provincial tax rate usually ranges between 46 and 51 per cent.

Reduced Rates of Taxation

There are a number of provisions, however, which reduce the effective rate of Canadian income tax on certain types of Canadian source income, thereby encouraging certain types of domestic investment.

Active Business Income of Canadian Controlled Private Corporations

The combined federal-provincial tax rate applicable to the active business income of a Canadian controlled private corporation is approximately 25 per cent subject to specific annual and total business limits. Generally a Canadian controlled private corporation is a Canadian resident corporation whose shares are not listed on a stock exchange in Canada and which is not controlled, directly or indirectly, by non-residents, by public corporations or by any combination thereof.

Only the first $ 150,000 of active business income earned in Canada by a Canadian controlled private corporation for a particular taxation year qualifies for the reduced rate of tax subject to a total business limit of $ 750,000 of retained Canadian active business income. The total business limit can be preserved to a degree by the payment of taxable dividends to shareholders.

Associated Canadian controlled private corporations which include Canadian controlled private corporations under common control are not individually entitled to the reduced rate of taxation to the full extent of the annual and total business limits discussed above but are rather required to allocate these limits among themselves and claim the reduced rate of tax accordingly.

* McMillan, Binch, Toronto.
** Winthrop, Stimson, Putnam & Roberts, New York.

Canadian Manufacturing and Processing Income

The combined federal-provincial tax rate applicable to the income earned by a corporation from the manufacturing or processing in Canada of goods for sale or lease is approximately 40 per cent subject to being further reduced to approximately 20 per cent where the corporation is a Canadian controlled private corporation whose manufacturing and processing income qualifies for the small business deduction discussed above. However, the reduced rate of taxation is not applicable where the corporation's Canadian manufacturing and processing revenue is less than 10 per cent of its total Canadian active business revenue. Manufacturing and processing does not include farming or fishing, logging, construction, or certain oil, gas, mineral and other energy related operations.

Other Tax Incentives

In addition to the above reductions in the combined general federal-provincial tax rate, Canada provides tax based incentives in the form of investment tax credits and favourable tax treatment of certain types of expenditures, for the purpose of encouraging certain types of domestic investment.

Investment Tax Credits

A taxpayer may reduce his tax payable for a particular taxation year to the extent of the lesser of his investment tax credit and $ 15,000 plus one-half of the amount by which his investment tax credit exceeds $ 15,000. A taxpayer's investment tax credit is equal to the aggregate of 5% of his capital cost of qualified property and 5% of his expenditures for scientific research with respect to his business in Canada. This rate is increased to between 7% and 13% for qualifying investments that are made in prescribed slow growth regions. Qualified property comprises new prescribed buildings and machinery and equipment which are acquired for use or leased for use in Canada in the manufacturing and processing of goods for sale or lease, logging, farming or fishing, the storing of grain, or certain oil, gas and mineral operations.

Investment tax credits claimed by a taxpayer in respect of depreciable and non-depreciable property reduce the capital cost for capital allowance purposes and the adjusted cost base thereof respectively in the amount of the investment tax credit claimed. Qualified expenditures with respect to which a taxpayer claims an investment tax credit are not also deductible by the taxpayer in the computation of his income.

Employment Tax Credit

Similarly a taxpayer may reduce his tax payable for a particular taxation year by the amount of his employment tax credit which comprises employment credits earned up to March 31, 1981 pursuant to an agreement between the employer taxpayer and the Canadian government entered into prior to March 31, 1980 and which provides for the employment of new eligible workers in eligible employment. The employment tax credits vary in amount with the area of employment, the larger credits being granted with respect to eligible employment in slow growth areas.

Scientific Research

Generally Canada permits a taxpayer to deduct scientific research expenditures of a current and also of a capital nature made in Canada with respects to a business carried on in Canada. Amounts deducted with respect to capital expenditures are considered to have been claimed by the taxpayer as capital cost allowance for the purposes of determining the tax consequences on the disposition of the property acquired by the expenditure. As indicated above scientific research expenditures qualifying for an investment tax credit are not also deductible.

The federal government has recently announced that it intends to permit a taxpayer for taxation years ending after 1977 and before 1988 to deduct in computing its Canadian source business income an extra allowance equal to 50% of the amount by which its qualified current and capital expenditures on research in Canada exceed the average of such expenditures made by the taxpayer during a prescribed base period.

Manufacturing and Processing Equipment

Capital cost allowance with respect to depreciable property used or leased for use in Canada in the manufacturing or processing of goods for sale or lease can be claimed over a two year period on a straight line basis. For these purposes manufacturing and processing does not include the activities referred to in the discussion respecting the tax treatment of Canadian manufacturing and processing income.

Resource Industry

In an attempt to encourage expansion of the Canadian oil, gas and mineral industry Canada has adopted a system which generally permits a taxpayer to deduct certain types of expenditures on a current basis. However, as discussed below, the proceeds of disposition of resource properties are similarly treated on account of income.

Expenditures made by a taxpayer subsequent to May 6, 1974 in connection with the exploration or development of Canadian oil, gas or mineral resources are treated on a pool basis and are accordingly classified collectively as Canadian exploration expense and Canadian development expense, respectively. A taxpayer's cumulative Canadian exploration expense which is calculated by adding and subtracting several specified amounts essentially represents the Canadian exploration expense incurred to date by a taxpayer less amounts previously deducted or deductible by him with respect to his cumulative Canadian exploration expense. A taxpayer's cumulative Canadian development expense which is similarly calculated essentially represents prior Canadian development expense less prior deductions with respect to cumulative Canadian development expense and also proceeds of disposition from the disposition of a Canadian resource properties.

A principal business corporation, which is a corporation whose principal business relates to the gas, oil or mineral sector, may deduct in calculating its income the lesser of the positive amount, if any, of its cumulative Canadian exploration expense and its income calculated ignoring deductions with respect to its cumulative Canadian development expense and depletion which are discussed below. A taxpayer who is not a principal business corporation may deduct in calculating his income the whole of his Canadian exploration expense incurred after May 25, 1976 and before 1979. Otherwise he can deduct the greater of 30% of his cumulative Canadian exploration expense and his Canadian resource income.

All taxpayers are permitted to deduct 30% of their cumulative Canadian development expense in calculating their income.

Canada also permits a taxpayer to claim a depletion allowance with respect to Canadian oil or gas wells, mineral resources, and processing of ore from a mineral resource to the prime metal stage or its equivalent. Generally the allowance is in the amount of the lesser of 25% of the taxpayer's 'resource profits' for the particular year and the taxpayers 'earned depletion base', all as defined by regulation. In addition a taxpayer may deduct a resource allowance in calculating his income from Canadian oil or gas wells or mineral resources in the amount of 25% of his 'resource profits'.

As indicated above, the proceeds of disposition from the disposition of a Canadian resource property reduce the taxpayer's cumulative Canadian development expense. Any negative amount is included in income subject to the application of a reserve where the proceeds are payable over time.

Canada affords less favourable tax treatment with respect to foreign resource properties. Foreign exploration and development expense may be deducted by a taxpayer in calculating his income to the extent of the greater of 10% thereof and his income from foreign resource property. A taxpayer must include in his income the whole of his proceeds of disposition from the disposition of foreign resource property subject to the application of a reserve where the proceeds are payable over time.

Machinery, equipment, structures (including buildings) and certain other property acquired for the purpose of gaining or producing income from a mine are depreciable on a declining balance basis at a rate of 30%.

Additional Tax Incentives for Investment in Small Canadian Businesses

Canada has recently enacted measures to further encourage taxpayers to invest in Canadian controlled private corporations and to encourage families to maintain certain types of incorporated small businesses.

As a rule Canadian resident individuals and corporations can only deduct allowable capital losses realized on the disposition of capital property from taxable capital gains realized thereon. In addition an individual may deduct up to $ 2,000 of any excess against his income from other sources. However, Canadian resident individuals and corporations may now generally deduct the whole of any excess allowable capital loss realized from an arm's length disposition of shares or debt of a Canadian controlled private corporation from their income from other sources in the year of disposition. Any unused portion thereof may be carried back 1 year and carried forward 5 years and deducted from taxable capital gains and other income earned in those years.

Ordinarily inter vivos transfers of shares and also transfers of shares on death between family members other than spouses give rise to proceeds of disposition equal to the fair market value of the shares. Where the shares have increased in value since the time of their acquisition a taxable capital gain will be realized. However up to $ 100,000 of taxable capital gains can now be deferred on family transfers of shares of Canadian controlled private corporations which use all or substantially all of their assets in manufacturing, processing, mining, logging, construction, farming or fishing, selling or leasing tangible personal property, or other prescribed business carried on in Canada.

Dividends from Canadian Corporations

A Canadian resident public corporation can receive taxable dividends from a taxable Canadian resident corporation on a tax free basis. However, a Canadian resident private corporation is required to pay a refundable tax of 25% of the amount of taxable dividends received by it from corporations which are not connected with it. This tax is refunded to the recipient corporation on the basis of $ 1.00 for every $ 4.00 of taxable dividends paid by it. If the Canadian resident private corporation and the payor corporation are connected the refundable tax which the recipient is required to pay is a proportion of the tax, if any, refunded to the payor corporation on the payment of the taxable dividends. This tax is also refunded to the recipient corporation on the payment of taxable dividends in the manner discussed above.

Whether the Canadian resident private corporation and the payor corporation are connected is determined by certain considerations respecting control and ownership of shares.

In computing his income a Canadian resident individual is required to include 3/2 of the taxable dividends received by him from taxable Canadian corporations. The federal tax rate is applied to this amount and the resulting federal tax payable is then reduced by 3/8 of the taxable dividend. The applicable provincial tax rate is applied to this reduced amount. The end result is that the individual generally receives a tax credit slightly in excess of 1/2 of the taxable dividend received.

A significant feature of the Canadian tax credit mechanism is that unlike France, Germany and the U.K., Canada does not impose any corporate equalization tax to match the individual shareholder tax credit upon the distribution by Canadian corporations to their resident shareholders of profits that have borne no Canadian corporate income tax, for example, because they have been received from the exempt surplus of foreign affiliates.

Dividends paid by a Canadian resident corporation to a non-resident is subject to a withholding of tax of 25% subject to being reduced by Treaty.

TAX INCENTIVES FOR FOREIGN INVESTMENT

Canada provides tax incentives for investment in developing countries through the adoption of income tax treaties. Canada negotiates these separately with each of its treaty partners.

No Treaty

In the absence of a treaty, the general Canadian tax regime with respect to foreign source income is as described below. Note that a resident Canadian corporation generally means a corporation either incorporated in Canada after April 26, 1965 or, if incorporated earlier, carrying on business in Canada in any year after April 26, 1965, or having its central control and management in Canada, and that such a resident corporation is taxed on its worldwide income.

Foreign Branch Income

Foreign source business income of a foreign branch of a Canadian corporation will currently be subject to Canadian tax at the usual rates, with a credit for the foreign taxes paid on the branch income. The effective rate of income tax will be the higher of the Canadian rate or the foreign rate.

Dividend Distributions

The tax consequences of the distribution of dividends from non-resident corporations depends upon whether the recipient is a Canadian resident corporation or individual and whether the payor is a foreign affiliate of the recipient. A foreign affiliate of a Canadian resident is defined as a non-resident corporation in which the Canadian resident has a 10 per cent or greater interest, direct or indirect, in any class of shares.

Dividends received from foreign corporations by Canadian resident individuals and by Canadian resident corporations where the payor is not a foreign affiliate are included in income and are subject to full Canadian tax. A foreign direct tax upon the dividend distribution, usually a gross withholding tax, is allowed as a credit against the Canadian tax. However, in the case of Canadian resident individuals the credit is limited to 15 per cent of the dividend. Any additional foreign tax is deductible by the Canadian resident individual in computing his income from the shares.

The taxation of dividends received from a foreign affiliate depends as indicated above upon whether the recipient is a Canadian resident corporation or individual and also upon whether the amounts being distributed are from the exempt surplus, taxable surplus or pre-acquisition control surplus of the foreign affiliate. The concept of exempt surplus is limited to foreign affiliates resident in countries listed in the regulations and will be discussed later. The taxable surplus of a foreign affiliate resident in a listed country includes its net earnings for 1976 and subsequent years derived from an active business carried on by it in countries which are not listed in the regulations whereas the taxable surplus of a foreign affiliate resident in an unlisted country includes its active business income from all sources. In each instance taxable surplus also includes the foreign affiliate's net foreign accrual property income after 1975. The meaning of foreign accrual property income is discussed below. The term pre-acquisition control surplus is a residual category covering amounts not included in taxable surplus or exempt surplus.

Inter foreign affiliate dividends enter into the same surplus pot of the recipient foreign affiliate as that of the payor foreign affiliate. Dividends are deemed to be paid out of the various surplus pots of a foreign affiliate in the following order: exempt surplus, taxable surplus and pre-acquisition control surplus.

All dividends received by a Canadian resident individual from a foreign affiliate are subject to full Canadian tax. As indicated above, the individual may claim a foreign tax credit for a maximum of 15 per cent of any foreign income tax allocable to the dividend plus a deduction from the dividend income of any such tax in excess of 15 per cent. No credit is allowed for the foreign tax paid by the distributing foreign affiliate on the earnings out of which the dividend was paid.

Dividends received by Canadian resident corporations from a foreign affiliate are subject to tax to the extent paid out of taxable surplus, and a credit against the Canadian tax is given for both the direct withholding tax applicable to the dividend and the foreign tax applicable to the earnings out of which the dividend was paid. The credit formulas are somewhat more complicated than the equivalent US formulas, but the objective is similar in seeking to achieve neutrality by taxing the corporate recipient on the distribution at the Canadian effective rate of corporate tax. Distributions paid out of pre-acquisition control surplus to Canadian resident corporations are generally not taxable but reduce the tax basis of the shares. If the recipient of the dividend is a Canadian resident private corporation the refundable tax discussed above is applicable with respect to amounts credited in respect of dividends paid out of taxable surplus and also with respect to the full amount of dividends paid out of pre-acquisition control surplus.

Foreign Accrual Property Income

Superimposed upon the foreign affiliate structure are provisions similar to the US subpart F income provisions, under which the participating percentage of the foreign accrual property income (FAPI) of every share owned by a Canadian resident in the capital of a controlled foreign affiliate must be reported as income in the year in which earned or received by the controlled foreign affiliate provided the FAPI of the controlled foreign affiliate for the particular year exceeds $ 5,000. FAPI is generally the controlled foreign affiliate's net income from property and non-active business including net taxable capital gains from the disposition of property not used in connection with an active business but exclusive of dividends received by the controlled foreign affiliate from other foreign affiliates of the Canadian resident. A deduction from income is permitted with respect to the underlying foreign tax applicable to the FAPI.

Adjustments are made, including application of foreign tax credits, to prevent the FAPI from being taxed again at the time of actual distribution in the form of dividends out of the controlled foreign affiliate's taxable surplus. A controlled foreign affiliate is defined as a foreign affiliate of the taxpayer which is controlled directly or indirectly by the taxpayer, or by the taxpayer and not more than four other Canadian residents, or by a related group of which the taxpayer is a member.

Treaty in Force or Near Conclusion

The incentive for direct private investment in foreign countries is provided through a combination of the internal law and the tax treaty program. Under internal law, dividends paid to Canadian resident corporations out of the exempt surplus of foreign affiliates are first includable in gross income, but are then fully deductible in computing net income; hence, they escape Canadian income tax. However, where the recipient of the dividend is a Canadian resident private corporation the refundable tax discussed above is applicable. The term exempt surplus is defined to mean the net earnings of an affiliate resident in a country listed in the regulations, derived from carrying on an active business in Canada or in a listed country through a permanent establishment. To be listed, a country must have concluded an income tax convention with Canada or general agreements must have been reached on the contents thereof. The net effect of these rules is that through the negotiation and ratification of income tax treaties, Canada applies the 'exemption method' to foreign business income and will thus give effect to any tax holiday provision contained in the law of a developing country in which a foreign affiliate is conducting an active business.

The Canadian tax regulations designate, as of July 1, 1978, 49 countries within the favoured network. Many of the treaty partners are developing countries, most of which grant some form of tax holiday to foreign investment.

Denmark

Svend Oppenhejm *

A. INCENTIVE TO INVEST AT HOME

In Denmark there are no special rules that privilege investments in certain parts of the country, except from a few special rules concerning Greenland according to which Danes working in Greenland under certain circumstances are free of paying taxes.

B. INVESTMENTS ABROAD

Denmark has no tax concession to private investments in developing countries.

Denmark is following the global income principle i.e. that a Danish company is assessed according to its complete taxable incomes, no matter where in the world they have been earned. The foreign income is assessed according to Danish rules for assessments and the income tax is assessed according to Danish tax rules.

For companies the assessed income tax can be reduced or fully remitted if the taxable income includes incomes from activity abroad, profits from foreign subsidiary companies or in case the company has paid taxes to the foreign country.

1. Reliefs for Foreigners

Reliefs for foreigners can only be granted for certain companies (companies incorporated and private companies). Reliefs can be granted after an application for it. The conditions are, that it can be proved that a part of the taxable income of the company arises from a net income earned by activities abroad. The assessed income tax will then be reduced with one half of the tax amount which proportionally correspond to the above mentioned part of the income.

2. Double Taxation Agreements

According to law no. 74 of March 31. – 1953 the government is authorized to grant reliefs in the liability of paying taxes and duties. Reliefs are granted under the condition, that mutual agreements are existing with foreign countries,

* Oppenhejm & Prangen, Copenhagen.

so that double taxation can be avoided. Double taxation agreements between Denmark and other states are based on the Exemption – or Creditprinciple.

The Exemption-principle is realized by conferring exclusively taxation on the source-country (the country where the income has been earned) or the domicile-country (the country where the receiver of the income is living). The opposite part of the contracting states in that case will grant fully renunciation of yield of taxes of the Exemption – income in question.

The Credit-principle retains the taxation-access of the contracting states according to the respective national laws and the double taxation, that by these reasons would take place is in the principle obviated as follows:

The domicile-state gives credit in the tax assessed on an income included under the agreement with an amount equal to the tax which the source-state has assessed on the income in question. In a number of agreements of the credit type maximum limits for the rights of taxation for the source-country are fixed.[1]

3. Taxation Act Paragraph 33

This provision implies a credit principle according to which the unilateral reliefs are granted in Danish income taxes in those cases where an income received from abroad has been assessed in the source-country. This principle has its self-contained significance where the incomes in question sources from states with which Denmark has no agreements.

In cases where an agreement on double taxation with the source-state has been entered, the credit according to § 33 never can exceed the claim of taxation according to the agreement on double taxation.

4. Reliefs for Subsidiary Companies

In cases where the taxable income of a company includes profits from subsidiary companies abroad, a relief can be granted on the following conditions:

An application must be presented to the tax authorities. The source-company must have been the possessor of minimum 25% of the share-capital during the whole income year in question.

The relief is granted in the income tax of the source-company for the year in which the profit has been received.

If the income tax has been reduced with reliefs for activity abroad or according to Exemption- and Creditagreements, the relief is granted the thus reduced income tax.

1. The following is added by the Reporter: As an alternative to providing tax incentives to investment by exempting from Danish tax certain categories of foreign source income under the exemption with progression technique, in some treaties Denmark provides for credit against Danish tax for certain spared taxes, as in the case of the treaties with Kenya and Tanzania.

France

J. C. Goldsmith *

INTRODUCTION

Internal tax law contains a number of types of tax incentives.

Besides tax incentives provided in favour of under-developed metropolitan areas or overseas departments ('Départements d'Outre-Mer' or DOM), several measures have been provided to encourage investment in certain types of operations or fields of activities, such as investment in immovable property, scientific research or pollution control.

Most tax incentives concern companies or enterprises. In most cases, they are subject to prior agreement by the Finance Ministry. However, several measures are also provided for individuals.

From a general point of view, incentives are realized by way of exemption, total or partial, permanent or temporary, from corporation tax or from personal income tax. Others are realized by way of reduction of registration duties which would normally have been applicable.

Investments made abroad, particularly in developing countries, may benefit from tax incentive provisions contained either in internal tax law or in certain tax treaties concluded by France providing sparing or matching credit clauses.

I. TAX INCENTIVES AT HOME

A. Companies or Enterprises

1. Regional Development

a) Regime of Government Grants

Investment in under-developed metropolitan areas is encouraged by way of cash subsidies or investment premiums.

Through the application of general tax rules, these grants or subsidies would be included in taxable income.

This is the reason why Art. 42 (Septiès) of the General Tax Code ('Code Général des Impôts' – CGI) provides a special favourable system for grants and premiums for equipment received from the Government.

Normally, these subsidies do not have to be included in the taxable profits of the financial year of their payment.

Subsidies used for the acquisition of depreciable assets must be added to the

* Goldsmith, Delvolvé & Associés, Paris.

results of each of the following financial years to the extent of the depreciation recorded on the assets during those financial years.

If the assets acquired are not depreciable, the subsidies are taxed in equal instalments over the ten years following their payment. If the contract granting the Government subsidy contains a clause of non-transferability of the assets acquired with the grant, the subsidies are taxed by equal instalments during the duration of this clause.

b) Creation of Local Industrial Activity and Employment

Enterprises which create industrial activity in certain under-developed areas, or extend or transfer their activities to these areas, may be totally or partially exempted by local authorities with the consent of the Ministry of Finance, from business tax ('Taxe Professionelle') (Art. 1473 bis – CGI). They may also benefit from a reduction of registration duty (Art. 697 CGI) and from special depreciation rates.

i) The exemption from business tax may be granted, for a period up to five years, to enterprises in connection with:

- the creation or extension of industrial or research installations in developing areas,
- the reconversion of industrial installations,
- the decentralization of industrial enterprises, located in the Paris or the Lyon areas,
- the creation in certain towns or areas of hotels or tourism establishments having at least 200 rooms or of holidays villages providing at least 100 beds,
- the regrouping or conversion of enterprises favouring economic difficulties.

ii) Acquisition of immovable property made in the course of such operations may benefit from a reduction in the Registration duty from 16.6% tot 4.8%.

iii) Special depreciation rates are provided by Art. 39 quinquiès D CGI for industrial or commercial buildings erected for the purpose of such operations. This special depreciation, at the rate of 25% of the cost of such buildings, is deductible from the trading results of the financial year during which they are built. This measure is applicable until December 31, 1980.

c) Incentives in the Paris Region

The Government attempted to discourage the establishment of new offices in the Paris region, by imposing a special tax whose rate ranges from 200 to 500 FF per m² of the new offices. (Law of August 2, 1960).

2. Overseas Departments [1]

i) Permanent Rules

Profits recorded by companies located in overseas departments are only liable to corporation tax on 2/3 of the amount of such profits (Art. 217 bis CGI).

Exemption from income tax is also granted for profits arising from the production of certain types of crops for the first ten years of such production (Art. 76 bis CGI).

ii) Temporary Rules

The following tax incentives were to have expired on December 31, 1977 but have been extended until December 31, 1980 by the Finance Law for 1978.

a) Total or partial exemption from corporation tax for up to 8 years (10 years for mining companies set up in Guyana) is provided, subject to agreement by the Ministry of Finance, in favour of activities creating local employment (Art. 208 quater CGI).

b) Exemption from corporation tax, or from income tax, is also provided in favour of profits arising from industrial or agricultural activities when these profits are reinvested in activities essential for the development of overseas departments. (Art. 238 bis E-1 CGI).

This exemption is also granted on profits arising from other sources when invested in companies carrying out activities deemed to be essential for the departments. (Art. 238 bis E.II CGI).

Prior agreement from the Ministry of Finances is required to obtain this exemption.

c) Industrial or commercial profits realized in France may benefit from corporation tax exemption if invested in overseas departments in the same field, or in hotelry activities. (Art. 238 bis H CGI).

Prior agreement from the Ministry of Finance is required, which may be granted only if investments amount to over 1 million FF and create more than 20 jobs.

d) Research and mining companies, and also forestry or agricultural companies, with the consent of the Ministry of Finance, may benefit for a period of 25 years from special rules which exempt profits from corporation tax if invested in similar activities. (Art. 1655 bis CGI).

e) Registration duty of 1% is reduced to 0,25% for contributions in cash

1. Martinique, Guadeloupe and dependancies, Guyana, Réunion.

or in kind made to companies whose activities take place in the overseas departments. (Art. 833 CGI).

3. Tax Incentives for Certain Types of Operation

a) Creation of Companies or Enterprises

i) Newly formed companies or private enterprises, created between June 1, 1977 and January 1, 1981 may benefit from a reduction by 1/3 of profits liable to income or corporation tax, provided that their turnover does not exceed 30 million FF and their staff, 150 employees (Law of December 21, 1977 – Art. 15).

ii) The same companies may be exempted from corporation tax on profits recorded during the year of their creation and the two following years, provided that the untaxed profits are reinvested. (Art. 19 Law of Finances for 1979).

This exemption may not be cumulated with that described above.

b) Winding-up of Companies

In order to facilitate the winding-up of dormant companies or companies obliged to stop activities, a special regime may apply with prior agreement from the Ministry of Finance:

- captital gains arising from liquidation are subject to corporation tax, reduced to 15%,
- distribution to shareholders of these capital gains is subject to a 15% flat rate tax.

This regime only applies to French companies which have been liable to corporation tax for at least the last 5 years, and the winding-up of which will tend to facilitate reorganisation of production and the economic market (Art. 239 bis – CGI).

c) Restructuring of Companies

i) The favourable regime provided for mergers of companies liable to corporation tax was to have expired on December 31, 1977 but has been extended until December 31, 1980 by the Law of Finance for 1978.

The main aspects of this regime are the following:

- capital gains realized on assets brought by the absorbed company to the absorbing company are exempted from corporation tax, whereas under the normal system, such capital gains would be liable to tax at the rate of 50% or 15%. However, the absorbing company must restore to the taxable results of the five following financial years the capital gains recorded on depreciable assets (Art. 210 A – CGI).
- The distribution by the absorbing company of shares to the shareholders of

the absorbed company in remuneration of assets is not taxable, unless distribution of dividends paid on the merger bonus is made by the absorbing company.

- The losses recorded by the absorbed company may be transferred to the absorbing company with the consent of the tax authority.
- Exemption from corporation tax of the capital gain resulting from the writing-off by the absorbing company of its participation in the absorbed company (Art. 210 a 1-2° al.).
- Registration duty at a rate of 1,2% is due from the absorbing company on the merger bonus, which may be incorporated into the share capital without registration duty.

ii) The same regime is applicable for divisions of companies provided that the prior consent of the Ministry of Finance has been obtained (Art. 210 B – CGI). This consent is only given when the operation is in the interest of the economy.

iii) The same regime is also applicable in case of transfers of part of a business. Consent is not necessary when the transfer is of a complete branch of activity and if the transferring company binds itself to keep the shares remunerating the transfer for 5 years and to compute the future capital gain on these shares from the net book value of the assets transferred.

d) Improving the Structures of Enterprises

i) According to Art. 697 CGI, the acquisition of immovable properties for reconversion or the regrouping of industrial activities, or the creation of professional training centres, may benefit, with the consent of the Ministry of Finance, from a reduction to 4.8% of the registration duty. The same applies to the acquisition of goodwill ('fonds de commerce') when such acquisition tends to facilitate the adaptation of an enterprise's structure to the economy. (Art. 721 – CGI).

ii) The ordinance of February 4, 1959 granted certain tax advantages in favour of small and medium-sized groups. Enterprises which wish to benefit from this regime must set up a subsidiary having the object of investigating possible markets and the promotion of sales of their products. The subsidiary must conclude an agreement with the Ministry of Finance by which it binds itself to pursue the economic programme elaborated by the parent enterprises.

The tax advantages are:

- the possibility given to the subsidiary's associates of recording a depreciation of the amount of their subscriptions in the subsidiary's share capital (Art. 39 quinquiès C, 93 ter – CGI);
- exemption from taxation of capital gains recorded on the sale of the subsidiary's shares, provided that the amount of sales are used for the acquisition of the same type of shares within one year (Art. 40 quinquiés) – CGI).

e) Pollution Control

Exceptional depreciation of 50% of the cost of industrial installations for water purification and for the control of atmospheric pollution may be recorded before December 31, 1980 in respect of factories constructed before January 1st, 1976 by companies or enterprises during the financial year in which the construction of such installations takes place (Art. 39 quinquiès (e) and (f) – CGI).

f) Scientific Research

Exceptional depreciation of 50% of their cost may be recorded by enterprises constructing buildings destined for scientific research, in the year of their completion. (Art. 39 quinquiès) A CGI).

The same applies to subscriptions of shares of companies created for scientific research. (Art. 39 quinquiès A.II CGI).

g) Investments in Fixed Assets

Companies which are subject to the regime of compulsory profit sharing ('participation des salariés aux fruits de l'expansion') may create a special reserve equal in amount to 50% of the sums blocked on behalf of their employees in the reserve for profit sharing. This reserve is exempt from corporation tax if used to acquire fixed assets and if it is not distributed to shareholders before the reserve for profit sharing has been distributed to the employees. (Art. 237 bis A.III CGI).

h) Investments in Immovable Property

Many tax incentives have also been provided in favour of de developments of investments in immovable property:

i) 'Sociétés Immobilières d'Investissement (Companies for Investment in Immovable Property). Created by the Law of March 15, 1963, these companies must have a capital of at least 50,000,000 French Francs, dividend into shares. Their company rules must be agreed by the Ministry of Finance. They must have the sole object of renting buildings in France, at least 3/4 of whose floor-space is given over to private housing.

Such companies may benefit from exemption from corporation tax in respect of the rents collected.

Dividends distributed by such companies do not give rise to the 'avoir fiscal' (tax credit) and, if distributed to shareholders outside France, are not subject to the 25% withholding tax (Art. 139 ter – CGI).

Private individuals are liable to personal income tax on dividends distributed by these companies, but they are entitled to be taxed on only 80% of dividends distributed from January 1st, 1967 provided that they are collected before January 1st, 1981. (Art. 159 quinquiès CGI).

When the shareholders are companies liable to corporation tax, dividends collected are liable to tax in the normal way.

Transfers of shares are exempted from death duties, unless the shares have been subscribed or acquired before September 19, 1973.

ii) 'Sociétés Immobilières de Gestion' (Companies for Management of Immovable Property). These companies, created by the Law of March 15, 1963, benefit from the same tax advantages described above, and under the same conditions. However, they must be limited liability companies ('SARL'), and no minimum share capital is required except the 20,000 French Francs prescribed by French company law.

iii) 'Sociétés Immobilières Conventionnées – SIC' (Companies Recognized by the Government for Investment in Immovable Property). These companies were created by the Ordinance of September 24, 1958. They and their shareholders benefited from tax advantages, most of which were withdrawn at the time of the creation of the 'Sociétés Immobilières d'Investissement' (see above). The temporary regime which remains in force concerns the shares of SIC acquired by enterprises before July 1st, 1964, and fully paid up before January 1st, 1966:

- exemption for 25 years for dividends when the shareholders did not avail themselves of the exceptional depreciation allowed by the Ordinance of 1958 (Art. 43 bis – CGI),
- exemption in respect of the capital gains recorded on sales or reimbursements of SIC's shares within the limit of the exceptional depreciation of 25% (or 50% as it may be) recorded on such shares. (Art. 40 sexiès – CGI).

iv) 'Sociétés Immobilières pour le Commerce et l'Industrie' – SICOMI. This type of company was created by an ordinance of september 28, 1967.

They must be share companies ('Sociétés Anonymes') or limited liability companies ('Sociétés à Responsabilité Limitée') and have the sole object of renting industrial and commercial buildings. Their company rules must be agreed by the Ministry of Finance.

SICOMI are exempt from corporation tax on rents collected, and from tax on capital gains recorded on the sale to the tenant of their building at the end of a lease. The dividends distributed do not benefit from the 'avoir fiscal' (Art. 158 quater – CGI).

Incorporation of SICOMI incurs a reduced registration duty of 0.6% on immovable assets brought to the company (Art. 810 IV b – CGI), except when the operation is liable to VAT, and a fixed duty of 300 FF on other assets, instead of 1% (Art. 830 b – CGI).

Acquisition of immovable properties for immediate leasing incurs a registration duty at the rate of 0.6% (CGI, Art. 698), except when the sale is liable to VAT. The acquisition of buildings made under a lease-back agreement incurs a registration duty reduced from 13.8% to 4.80%.

i) Investments in Stockholding: 'Sociétés Mobilières d'Investissement'

Investment companies and similar corporations may take advantage of a special regime which avoids double taxation on income arising from stockholding at the time of payment and at the time of distribution:

The investment companies concerned are:

- ordinary investment companies,
- the national investment company,
- companies with variable share capital ('SICAV') at present, the most important.

Similar companies are:

- companies for regional development,
- financial companies for the development of overseas territories,
- companies for the financing of gas and petrol research.

From a general standpoint, these companies, the creation of which is in principle subject to prior agreement by the Ministry of Finance, are entitled, under certain conditions, to exemption from corporation tax on the profit arising from their stockholdings and from tax on capital gains on sales of stocks (CGI, Art. 207-2, 208-1).

The creation of such companies incurs a reduced registration duty of 300 French francs.

j) Financing of Telecommunication Equipment

The law of December 24, 1969, created the 'Sociétés agréées pour le financement des télécommunications' (Companies for the financing of telecommunication) for the purpose of improving the financing of telecommunication equipment under prior agreements concluded with the postal services. Their company articles must be agreed by the Ministry of Finance.

Such companies are entitled to exemption from tax in respect of the profits and capital gains realized on leasing operations concluded with the Postal Administration, and for the part of their net profit arising from renting their buildings (CGI, Art. 208 – 3 quinquiès).

They also benefit from exemption from various property taxes. The creation of such companies incurs a registration duty reduced to 0.6% (CGI, Art. 810 IV b) on contributions of immovable properties.

k) Loans Granted to Employees

Enterprises which grant loans to their employees in order to enable them to create their own enterprise may create a special reserve equal to the half of the sums lent subject to a limit of 75.000 FF per employee.

This reserve must be restored in three instalments during the 5th, 6th and 7th financial year following that in which it is recorded. (Law of Dec. 30, 1977, Art. 18).

1) Miscellaneous

Amongst the tax incentives provided for certain kinds of operations, must be added the following examples which may be considered as 'negative'.

i) The Law of October 29, 1976, prohibited for the calendar year 1977 wage increases for taxpayers earning more than 288,000 FF per year, and limited to a percentage increases of remuneration paid to taxpayers earning between 216,000 and 288,000 FF.

The amount of the increase which exceeded these limits was not deductible form the taxable results of the company paying the wages.

ii) In order to curb the increase of pornographic films and films considered to be violent, such films are subject to a special tax regime. As well as being taxed at the highest rate of VAT (33.1/3%) and being subject to a higher tax on seats (1,5 times the normal rates) the profits are subject to a special levy at the rate of 20% of results liable to corporation tax or income tax. Furthermore, films produced abroad are liable to a tax of 150,000 or 300,000 FF.

iii) The erection of buildings should be made under certain conditions determined by the town planning authorities, for instance coefficients of land occupation, of total surface area to be constructed and so on.

If the developpers wish to erect buildings exceeding these coefficients (under certain limits), they will be liable to taxes computed on the excess ('Participation pour construction en surdensité', CGI, Art. 1635 quater and 'Versement pour dépassement du plafond légal de densité', Law of December 31, 1975).

iv) In order to curb the clearing of woods or forests, the law of Dec. 24, 1969, created a special tax ranging from 3.000 FF to 6.000 per hectare cleared, with a penalty of 50% if prior authorisation has not been obtained.

v) Failure to build parking space for cars when erecting a building entails a special duty which may not exceed 15,000 FF. per space (Law of December 31, 1976, Art. 69 II).

B. Agricultural Activities

Several measures have been passed to benefit farmers in order to improve investments, to favourise certain types of crops and to facilitate the commercialisation of their products.

a) The following are exempt from corporation tax:
- Agricultural cooperatives and syndicates,
- Mutual agricultural audit banks,
- Associations constituted for an exploitation in common.

b) Farmers may deduct from their taxable profits, under certain conditions, an amount equal to 125% of interest paid each year on loans granted for the purchase of immovable property. This special deduction of 25% must be restored to the taxable results of the years following that of the last deduction (CGI, All-III, Art. 38 sexdeciès F).

c) Usually, the acquisition of immovable property for agricultural purposes entails a registration duty at the reduced rate of 11.8%.

This rate is reduced to 4.8% for acquisitions which tend to improve the profits of the exploitation, particularly when such acquisitions unable the farmer to exploit an area equal to that deemed by the law to be the minimum viable ('Surface minimum d'exploitation') (Art. 702 CGI).

The 11.8% rate is reduced to 0.6% when the properties bought had been previously rented to the buyer for at least two years, provided that the buyer binds himself personally to exploit the properties for the next five years (CGI, Art. 705).

d) Bequests of forests and shares of associations for forestry development are exempt from death duties to the extent of 3/4 of their value (Art. 793 - 1 3e, and 2-2e CGI).

e) Agricultural properties let on long term leases are also exempted from death duties to the same limit (CGI, Art. 793-2 3e).

This only applies to that part of the transferred property which does not exceed one and a half times the minimum viable surface area (see above).

C. Tax Incentives for Private Individuals

These tax incentives present the possibility for tax payers domiciled in France of deducting from their net taxable income, under certain conditions, expenses or charges which normally would not have been deductible.

These deductible expenses are:

a) Deductible expenses relating to the tax payer's principal residence:

- interest paid on loans for the purchase, construction or major repairs of the residence. The deductions are limited to the first 10 yearly payments,
- expenses of re-surfacing of the residence,
- expenses made to economize heating.

The total amount of such deductible expenses is limited to FF. 7.000, plus 1.000 for each of the taxpayer's dependants.

b) Interest on Government loans granted to French citizens repatriated from countries on their becoming independent.

c) Gifts and contributions to scientific, educational or cultural institutions up to a limit of 1% of the net taxable income (1.5% for gifts made to the Fondation de France).

d) Premiums of less than 1.500 FF. per year for certain types of life insurance contracts. Between 1.500 FF., and 5.000 FF., only the half the premium is deductible.

e) A recent law, that of July 13, 1978, encourages private investment in companies.

This law provides that the excess of purchases of shares over sales during a calendar year may be deducted from the taxable income up to a limit of 5.000 FF plus 500 FF for the two first dependent children and 1.000 FF for the third and above.

If, during one of the four following calendar years following the first deduction, the amount of sales exceeds the amount of purchases, the difference must be added to the taxable income.

In other words, this system provides an exemption from income tax for income invested in shares up to a limit of 5.000 FF per year and remaining invested for 4 years.

This regime is applicable until December, 31, 1981.

II. FRENCH INCENTIVES FOR INVESTMENT ABROAD

These measures are of two kinds:

The first encourages French exports or facilitates the development or the implantation abroad of French companies. They are characterized by tax advantages in France provided by internal tax law.

The second is provided through tax conventions, in order to offer advantages for private investments in developing countries. Most of these conventions are concluded with former French colonies and overseas territories ('Territoire d'Outre-Mer' or TOM). There are also certain conventions concluded with other countries which provide tax sparing clauses and matching credit clauses.

A. Tax Incentives for Investments Abroad in Internal Law

Under the territoriality principle, profits liable to corporation tax are those realized in France and those for which taxation is attributed to France by tax treaties. Therefore, if profits made outside France are not taxable in France, losses realized abroad may not be offset against profits taxable in this country.

However, there are five exceptions:

1. Investigation and Prospecting Expenses

Investigation and prospecting expenses incurred by an enterprise situated in France to research the possibility of setting up abroad a sales office or an information office, together with expenses incurred by such offices during the first three financial years, may be deducted from the French enterprise's taxable results during the said financial years.

The sums deducted by application of the above rule must be restored in equal instalments to its taxable results during the first five financial years after the fourth financial year following the creation of the office, unless dispensation is granted by the Ministry of Finances (CGI - Art. 39 Octiès).

2. Commercial Establishment Abroad

French companies or enterprises which invest abroad in the setting up of a sales outlet, or of an information office, may create a special reserve, deductible from taxable results.

i) If the investment is made in the EEC, this reserve may not exceed the smaller of the following two sums:

- the losses recorded during the first five years of management of the establishment or office, or
- the capital investment during the same period.

The deducted amounts are added back to the taxable results in five instalments, from the sixth financial year following the first investment.

ii) For other countries excluding tax havens, the reserve may equal the capital investment.

This regime is subject to prior approval from the Ministry of Finance. (CGI - Art. 39 Octiès A-I).

3. Industrial Establishment Abroad

French companies or enterprises which make an industrial investment in one of the countries listed by the Ministry of Finance may create a deductible reserve amounting to at least half the investment. This reserve will be taxed in five equal instalments from the sixth financial year following the first.

The investment regime is also subject to prior approval. (CGI, Art. 39 Octiès A - II).

4. Special Tax Regimes

With the consent of Ministry of Finance (which is rarely given), French companies may take into account the results of activities performed both in France and abroad for the determination of total profit liable to French corporation tax. (CGI, Art. 209 quinquiès).

The first system is the global profit regime ('Bénéfice Mondial') by which taxes paid abroad are deductible from French corporation tax, and the second, the consolidated profit regime ('Bénéfice Consolidé'), in which French companies may include in their taxable results their shares in the results of their foreign subsidiaries. (CGI, App. II Art. 103).

5. Provision for Medium Term Loans

Enterprises which make sales abroad in respect of which they grant medium term loans may constitute a special reserve exempt from tax, up to a limit of 10% of such loans. (CGI Art. 39 I, 5e, 7e al.).

B. Tax Incentives Through Tax Treaties

1. Treaties with Tax Sparing Clauses

Several treaties concluded by France and developing countries provide tax sparing clauses, the purpose of which is to avoid the neutralization of incentives resulting from the reductions in the countries concerned of the withholding tax on interests or dividends paid to French residents. This is the case, for instance, of treaties concluded with Brazil (September 10, 1971) for dividends and interest, with Morocco (May 29, 1970) for interest.

2. Treaties with Former Colonies

Most of the former French colonies in Africa benefited from special tax treaties when they became independent.

The first such treaty was concluded with Madagascar (Sept. 29, 1962) which provisions have been followed, with certain modifications, in subsequent treaties.

From a general point of view, and to simplify, this system is characterized by:

- the sharing of taxation between France and the contracting state concerned of dividends and interest distributed by a company having a permanent establishment in the other state;
- the application of a standard reduction ('décote') of 25 per cent on tax due in the contracting state in dividends from profits earned in the other state. In other words, dividends, are deemed to have been subject to a withholding tax of 25% in the country of source, whatever may be the amount of the withholding tax actually levied by this country.

As a consequence, if the withholding tax actually levied in the country of source is less than 25%, the tax reduction will constitute a tax incentive. Otherwise, should the withholding tax in fact paid amount to 25%, the tax reduction will only operate as an ordinary tax credit.

Federal Republic of Germany

*Reinhard Poellath**

I. APPLICABLE LAW

This paper[1] attempts to describe the relative impact of German taxation of investment in developing countries (less developed countries - LDC) as contrasted with investment at home or in more developed countries (MDC). Investment will be understood to mean primarily investment by a domestic corporation in a foreign corporation actively producing or distributing goods or services[2] with an emphasis on contributions to capital and a side look at loans and licencing. In accordance with the enumeration in § 6 of the German Act on Tax Measures to Promote Private Capital Investment in Developing Countries (LDC Tax Act)[3], LDC's shall be considered to include countries such as Greece, Portugal and Spain, the OPEC countries and some East European countries like Romania or Yugoslavia. The taxes covered – all of them, in principle, on worldwide income or capital – are mainly corporate income tax (corporation tax)[4], with a glance at individual income tax (income tax)[5], local trade tax[6] and net worth tax[7], all of them partly modified by the LDC Act and the Tax Act on Investment Abroad[8] and on International Tax Relations[2] as well as by the extensive German tax treaty network.[9]

2. PRESENT LAW ON TAX PREFERENCES FOR LDC INVESTMENTS

The German incentive and relief provisions affect investment by German taxpayers in an LDC both in respect of the initial investment decision and the subsequent income (or loss) resulting from the investment made.

- The major tax privileges in this context relate to the deferral of domestic income through the LDC Investment Reserve (below B. II).
  A German taxpayer investing in an LDC may set up a reserve in the amount of 40%, 60% or 100% of the funds or assets invested. This reserve decreases his German domestic income; it is written back to income – barring special instances, in particular, a failure or sale of the investment – after 6 years over a period of another 6 or 12 years.
- Other special rules avoid realization of profits on transfer of assets, either through roll-over of book value for contributions in kind to an LDC investment (below B. III) or through tax-free reorganization of LDC subsidiaries or incorporation of LDC branches (below B. IV).
- There are less prominent benefits for current income or losses from LDC subsidiaries or branches (below B. V) and related interest and royalty income (below B. VI).

* Attorney at Law, Munich.

1. For foot-notes 1 to 118, see pages 100 up to and including 106.

– Most of these special provisions cover profits as well as other, particularly net worth and municipal trade, taxes (below C).

Parliament adopted 1979 amendments retroactive to 1 January 1979 subject to State approval.[3] The changes brought out by these amendments for years 1979 onwards are specifically referred to below.

A new § 9 added to the Act provides for a compilation of data by the Federal Office of Statistics from information returns to be filed by taxpayers benefitting from the Act. This serves to prepare a Government report by end 1982 when the Act is to be reviewed again.

The discussion will first address some economic aspects of German investment in LDC's including least developed countries (LLDC's) (A) and then turn to a comparison of German taxation of German investment domestically, in MDC's and in LDC's, under profits (B) and other taxes (C).

A. ECONOMIC IMPORTANCE OF GERMAN INVESTMENT IN LDC'S AND TAX TREATMENT THEREOF

Germany's direct investment in LDC's is about 30% of her total investment abroad. The figures vary widely for different countries and industries (see below I). Germany grants a number of tax (and non-tax) reliefs and incentives for investment in LDC's. The revenue loss, the tax cost, to the Treasury of these tax benefits is almost negligible if compared with the tax expenditure to promote domestic investment in particular areas such as Berlin (see below II.1). The individual investor in a LDC, though, may benefit substantially (see below II.2). There is reason to believe that the impact of the German tax incentives on German LDC investment – while obviously difficult to assess – is probably not too important (see below III).

I. German Direct Investment in LDC's

At mid 1978, accumulated German direct investment[10] abroad since 1952 totaled about Deutschmarks (DM) 54.87 bill., of which 27.14% (end 1975: 27.3%) in LDC's (excl. Arab countries and Mideast oilcountries 2.59%; end 1975: 2,0%) and 67.8%, i.e. almost all of the remainder, in European and North American MDC's. Far more than 1/2 of the investment dates back no longer than to 1970, and less than 10% existed in 1960. Recent annual overall net increases were in the 10% range p.a., the compounded 1976 through mid 1978 increase was + 30.66 above end 1975.[11]

1. German Investments in LDC's per Country

The LDC share in total German direct investment abroad rose from 29.3% at end 1975 to 30.16% at end 1977; at mid 1978, it was down to 29.73%. Excl.

Arab countries and Mideast oilcountries, LDC's have fared worse, up from 27.3% (end 1975) to 27.83% (1976), but then down again to 27.61% (1977) and 27.14% (mid 1978).
Federal Bank figures [12] show the MDC share in all German direct investment abroad to have increased from 70.6% (1972–1974) to 76.4% (1975–1977) with a corresponding reduction of the LDC share from 27.9% to 21.8%. Most of this relative loss for LDC's is attributable to Spain which accounted for most of the 16.9% share of European LDC's in 1972–1974 which – partly due to the termination of tax benefits for investment in tourism at end 1973 – went down to 3.9% in 1975–1977. Conversely, the non-European LDC share rose from 11% to 17.9% (incl. American LDC's: 7% to 14.8% with Brazil: 6.2% to 9.5%). The OPEC countries received a fairly steady 1.5% to 1.8%.

The percentage increase of German investment [11] (31. Dec. 1975 = 100) ranks LDC's in the following order:

Investment mid 1978 (end 1975 = 100)	*Country*	*Investment mid 1978 (mio DM)*
General		
132.79	all LDC's (incl. Arab countries + Mideast oilcountries)	16,309.2
130.66	all countries	54,865.3
130.18	all LDC's (excl. Arab countries + Mideast oilcountries)	14,885.6
129.68	all LLDC's	38,521.4
117.93	21 LLDC's	167.7
Individual LDC's		
633	Saudi Arabia	36.1
289	Philippines	40.2
247	Egypt	162.3
241	Korea (South)	47.9
240	Hongkong	127.6
229	Taiwan	39.2
217	Tunisia	55.2
208	Morocco	53
204	Iran	453.8
(176	USA	7,428.3)
174	Yugoslavia	107.2
168	Singapore	173.6
163	Trinidad and Tobago	103.6
163	Mexico	754.9
155	Algeria	210.3
151	Indonesia	118.8
150	UAE	46
147	Brazil	4,215

Investment mid 1978 (end 1975 = 100)	*Country*	*Investment mid 1978 (mio DM)*
147	Netherlands Antilles	1,046.8
141	Israel	591.7
134	Ivory Coast	48.1
(132	Canada	3,816.6)
128	Malaysia	50.3
126	Nigeria	216.3
124	Kenia	74.9
(123	Japan	339.8)
122	Panama (excl. Canal Zone)	246.8
122	Venezuela	92.8
120	Peru	117.1
118	Portugal	437.5
116	Greece	331.5
116	Zaire	79.6
114	Colombia	134.3
113	Liberia	158.1
110	Lybia	355.3
107	Spain	3,048.2
102	Turkey	139.5
102	Chile	100.7
101	Argentina	600.4
100	Bermuda	59.2
100	Pakistan	57.7
99	India	176.4
Individual LLDC's		
1,060	Gambia	5.3
591	Sudan	6.5
178	Malawi	10.3
108	other 18	145.6

2. Least Developed Countries (LLDC's)

From the 30 LLCD's enumerated in § 6 LDC Tax Act according to the UN classification, 21 are separately shown as recipient countries in the mid 1978 Government statistics.[11] They accounted for just 0.29% of all German direct investment abroad and for about 1% of such investment in LDC's and LLDC's together.

Their 1976 through mid 1978 overall net increase was particularly poor, viz. + 18% (see schedule above).

Thus, the relative importance of German investment in LLDC's even went down in 1976 through mid 1978, from 1,24% of total German investment in LDC's to 1.11% (excl. Arab countries and Mideast oilcountries).

3. German Investments in LDC's per Industry

German investment in LDC's has taken place mainly in a few important industries (in bill. DM):

Industry (investor)	*accumulated LDC investment end 1977*	*in % of total (MDC + LDC)*	*accumulated LDC investment end 1971*
chemical (excl. oil)	2.579	27.5	1.384
electrical	1.738	30.9	0.692
cars, trucks	1.416	42.3	0.850
machinery	1.082	26.8	0.493
iron, steel	0.695	17.1	0.397

Apart from mineral oil production and processing (accumulated end 1977 = DM 1.423 bill. = 41.7% of total), there also were banking and insurance (1.404 = 25.9%), hotels (0.983 = 93.8%) and real estate (0.843 = 52.9%). Hotels, real estate and – in industry – car manufacturing stand out for their high ratio of LDC investment to total investment abroad.

4. German Source Funding of LDC Investments

A sample survey 13 established the following ratios of German source funding of LDC investments by German companies in the five major industries above (in % of total funds invested)

	below 30%	*30–70%*	*above 70%*
chemical			
iron, steel,	52.4	26.8	20.7
non-ferrous	68.4	21.0	10.5
electrical	42.5	38.2	10.1
cars, trucks	70.0	25.0	5.0
machinery	58.3	27.7	13.2

German source funds only entitle to the main tax benefit discussed below, the LDC investment reserve.

5. Trade [14]

The export sales figures for the industries listed above have increased even more than their LDC investment and in a different order of industries. Still, Germany's trading with non-oil LDC's had a continuous import surplus: DM 0.2 bill. (1976), DM 2.9 bill. (1977) and DM 1.4 bill. (1978). Imports from non-oil LDC's increased more than average to about 10% of total German imports (+ 2.5 points since 1970). This is largely due to higher imports of commercial goods, finished and in process, (up from DM 1.84 bill. in 1970 to DM 8.41 in 1976), but mostly from just a few countries such as Hongkong, Taiwan, South Korea, India and China excl. the poorest LDC's. Total 1978 non-oil imports were down — 1%, exports up + 5%.

6. Royalties from LDC's

Still, the importance of LDC's for German investment abroad may exceed the range indicated by the above figures. Thus, it is known that the amount of royalties paid or received by a country varies depending on whether or not the licensor holds shares in the licencee.[15] In 1972 and 1973 about 1/4th of German gross royalty receipts came from LDC's.[16] The 1973 overall net deficit of DM 871.3 mill. was composed of a net deficit against MDC's of DM 1,022.8 mill.[17] and net surpluses from LDC's of DM 134.8 mill.[18] and from socialist countries (DM 16.7 mill.).

II. Tax Revenue Loss and Tax Relief Effect from German LDC Investment Tax Incentives

1. Revenue Loss for German Treasury

Germany grants a number of tax incentives to promote German investment in LDC's. The major provision is § 1 of the LDC Tax Act resulting in a deferral of taxes on profits, and in final savings of net worth tax, for up to 12 or 18 years. The estimated revenue loss from taxes deferred or foregone under this provision has been DM 200 mill. in 1973, DM 180 mill. (1974), DM 220 mill. (1975), DM 200 mill. (1976), DM 220 mill. (1977) and DM 240 mill. (1978). The additional revenue loss from the amended 1978 Act is estimated to amount to another DM 35 mio. p.a. About 40% thereof is borne by the Federal Treasury.[19] For 1975 through 1978, this is roughly 2.5–3% of total German tax expenditure to promote commerce and industry (excl. transportation) and less than 5% of the tax expenditure for Berlin investment incentives or for all domestic regional development tax incentives.[20]

2. Tax Relief Effect for Investors

The tax relief resulting from the investment reserve under § 1 LDC Tax Act may be indicated as the discounted cash value of taxes deferred.[21] For the 40% reserve to be written back to taxable income over 6 years this cash value is about 11% of total investment; the corresponding figure for the 100% reserve for investment in least developed countries is about 27.5%. If restoration to income is spread over 12 rather than 6 years these values are increased to 14% or 35%, respectively.

Higher cash values may be obtained if loans rather than equity are used to a larger or lesser extent (leverage).

According to the 1971 corporation tax statistics [22], the initial allowance and the reserve under the earlier version of § 1 LDC Tax Act were made use of by 79 corporations with a total benefit of slightly below DM 100 mill. 47 of them (with taxable profits above DM 1 mill. each) obtained about 70% of the benefit with almost all of the rest going to integrated companies or companies in, or almost in, a loss position.

III. Tentative Assessment of Impact of German Tax Incentives on German LDC Investment

There is little or no clear-cut evidence on the actual effect of the German tax incentives for German LDC investment. The above figures suggest some tentative conclusions which tend to assess the actual effects of the tax incentives as not too important.

1. Ratio of German Investment in LDC's and MDC's

In 1976 and 1977, when the LDC Tax Act incentives should have been fully known and available to investors, the LDC share in total German investment abroad increased but marginally. The considerable differences in the increases per country and per industry may be interpreted as indicative of predominant non-tax motivation, the non-tax situation in any given country and industry being different while the tax incentives would seem to be very much alike.

A similar conclusion might be drawn from the difference in shares of LDC investment (in absolute figures) in total investment abroad in different industries. LDC's obtained the highest shares in the hotel business and in the real estate – both meanwhile largely eliminated from the investments eligible for incentives under the 1975 version of the LDC Tax Act. In this field, where syndicated tax shelters were frequent, the tax incentives appear to have had considerable effects.

The LDC shares for manufacturing industries tend to be the lower the more capital-intensive the investment in the particular industry may be assumed to be. This could be in line with the Act's higher tax benefits bestowed upon labor-intensive projects. Still, the basis on which tax benefits are computed is capital invested. And it is reasonable to assume that the higher share in labor-intensive industries rather reflects non-tax motives for investing in a IDC.

2. Least Developed Countries

The LDC Tax Act more than doubles the incentive for investing in LLDC's. But German investment there is almost negligible. So, the incentives have certainly not been sufficient to overcome adverse non-tax considerations.

3. Tax Treaties

The existence of a tax treaty with the recipient LDC country may be another tax factor to be considered.[9] An existing or expected tax treaty may influence the investment decision; conversely, existing or expected German investment is a good reason to negotiate a treaty. Germany has concluded or negotiated treaties with most of the countries listed above II.1, and in particular with all but three of the top ten countries on the list. And the treaties with four of them (Tunisia, Singapore, Trinidad and Tobago, Brazil) date back to about the time of the rise in investment posted in that list. Brazil though, is a good example for a country with sizable German investment before concluding the treaty.

4. Investment Motives Stated by Investors

According to a recent survey, the two major reasons for German investors to invest in LDC's are an attempt to secure markets (29%) and to circumvent trade barriers (19%) whereas other reasons potentially involving tax and similar considerations come only second together with other arguments.[23]

These findings have been supplemented by another sample survey.[24] Whether or not an investment is made may also depend on the availability of guaranties (against expropriation, war, transfer restrictions and similar risks) under German domestic law and some 45 investment promotion treaties entered into by Germany by end 1977. More than one fifth of the DM 16 bill. invested in LDC's benefitted from these specific Federal guaranties, 3/4 thereof in Brazil, Israel, Lybia, Liberia, Argentina, Iran, Yugoslavia, Singapore, Spain, Indonesia and Greece.[25]

5. Tentative Conclusion

The tax incentives for LDC investment granted by domestic German law together with the protection afforded by a German tax treaty with a recipient LDC are important factors to be considered in making an investment decision. But from a global point of view and from the evidence we have, it is not apparent that these tax considerations have actually gone very far in stimulating German investment in LDC's over and above investment in MDC's or at home and in excess of LDC investment for non-tax reasons.

B. TAXES ON PROFITS

I. Domestic Situation

1. General Rules

(a) *Corporation tax* [26] is levied on resident [27] corporations at a statutory rate of 56% on retained earnings (business profits and capital gains). The effective rate depends on, inter alia, the direct or indirect foreign tax credit, exempt foreign intercompany dividends etc. On distributions at any time, the tax is increased or decreased, respectively, to 36%, fully creditable to the corporate or individual resident shareholder.
The 36% rate is levied on all distributions. Income that has suffered no (or less than 36%) 1977 or later German corporation tax is assumed to be distributed last (hifo principle). Where such income is determined to have been distributed, prior benefits from tax reduction (such as foreign tax credits) or tax exemption (such as foreign inter-corporate dividends from LDC's or from treaty MDC's) are wiped out by the German version of the précompte mobilier, i.e. the tax increase to 36%.

There is no credit for German corporation tax on distributions made to non-residents. However, they receive a refund of the précompte if any. Credit relief for foreigners is not expected to be readily brought about by DTA revisions.

Example 1: Flow of income from non-treaty LDC subsidiary S through German parent P to resident shareholder R

Taxable income of S		130
(assumed) LDC tax thereon	./.	30
dividend received by P		100
German trade tax: exempt		—
German corporation tax ./. indirect tax credit (see below V.2)		—
amount of P's retained earnings after income taxes		100
This effective exemption is lost on distribution of the LDC income: 36% German corporation tax ('distribution burden' creditable to resident shareholder; refundable to non-resident and other shareholders not eligible for credit)	./.	36
gross distribution by P		64
25% German withholding tax	./.	16
cash distribution by P		48

taxable income of R cash received	48	
+ gross-up for creditable corporation and	+ 36	
withholding taxes	+ 16	
taxable income	100	
./. tentative personal income tax thereon (assumed rate 50%)	50	
+ dividend tax credit	+ 36	
+ withholding tax credit	+ 16	
tax refund to shareholder		+ 2
R's income after income taxes		50
Tax in % of pre-tax income of 130:		61.5%

The additional tax burden above the (assumed) 50% burden on domestic earnings is due to international double taxation effectively unrelieved on the shareholder level.

A non-resident shareholder would receive a 48 cash dividend plus refund of the 36 précompte (less withholding tax), which had fallen due on distribution of earnings previously exempt while retained.

The German 'imputation' system does not treat a cross-border flow of profits on a quite equal footing with purely domestic situations.

Relief from international double taxation is secured while foreign earnings are retained: either they are exempt from German tax or foreign tax is deductible from German tax by way of the direct or indirect foreign tax credit. These reliefs are not channeled through to the shareholder on distribution. There is no harm in that as long as the German corporation has enough fully taxed domestic earnings available for distribution, i.e. earnings from any post-1976 year having borne 'new' German corporation tax. Thus, a German corporation will have to make sure to have a proper 'tax mix' of earnings available for distribution.

(b) *Personal income tax* is levied at 22–56% (plus church tax) on world-wide income of individuals (including partners) subject to full credit relief for corporation tax on dividends received and (under national law) a direct tax credit and (under DTA's) an exemption of foreign branch profits.

(c) *Trade tax rates* of 15–22,5% on world-wide income of domestic (local) branches are reduced to about one half of statutory rates because they are deductible from taxable corporate or personal income.[28] Income from foreign branches and subsidiaries is exempt.

2. Special Rules for Investment at Home

Incentives to promote investment at home are equivalent to disincentives against investing abroad.

(a) Apart from straightline depreciation for all assets and declining balance depreciation [29] for movable tangibles, there are numerous initial allowances of rather limited applicability [30] for domestic [31] investment.

(b) In addition, there are regional investment incentives.[32] Investment in Berlin is promoted by reduced VAT rates on value added in Berlin, considerable reductions of corporation and income tax liabilities, initial allowances up to 75%, tax credits for loans to Berlin banks, and tax-free outright cash grants of 10% of cost acquisition or production of depreciable fixed assets, of 25% of production facilities and of 30% of R & D cost, none of which reduce depreciable bases. Investments in eastern border zone: districts entitle to initial allowances of 30% or 50% for immovable or movable fixed assets, respectively; alternatively, approved investments in this area and in other development areas covering a large part of Germany entitle to cash grants of 7.5% of cost.

(c) The same cash grants of 7.5% of cost are meant to promote a limited number of other investments, including R & D, power plants and power distribution, or, previously, anticyclical investment ordered between 11/30/1974 and 7/1/1975.

This is the general background for the incentive and relief measures in favour of private investment in LDC's, particularly under the LDC Tax Act discussed below.

II. LDC Investment Reserve

The main feature in the catalogue of tax measures under the LDC Tax Act is the investment reserve of 40%, 60% or 100%, respectively, of capital invested.

1. Investment in MDC's

Under general rules, shares acquired on original issue or from a shareholder are entered into the acquiring shareholder's books at cost. They may be written down to lower going concern value [33] if the taxpayer can show such lower value to be applicable, for example, in the presence of sustained losses. Initial losses incurred during the first three to five years of a new business, however, do not suffice.

Valuation at cost also applies to shares in foreign companies irrespective of 'abstract' risks involved in such investment, such as the risk of expropriation, exchange restrictions, or generally difficult market conditions. There are very few departures from this, such as the special write-downs for investment in foreign corporations by the German mineral oil industry.[34]

2. Investment in LDC's

An investor may set up a reserve reducing German business profits in the amount of 40% (or 60% or 100%) of funds directly invested in a LDC provided such funds are applied to investment in certain assets in certain industries.

The LDC investment reserve [35] constitutes, on the one hand, a proper reserve not otherwise available, providing for risks involved in investing in a LDC, and, on the other hand, a tax deferral incentive to invest there.

Example 2: LDC Investment Reserve

Assume a German parent corporation P subscribing all of the share capital of 100 of its Brazilian manufacturing subsidiary S. P contributes 100 of funds to S partly derived from a loan which P has received from a German bank. S uses the funds to invest in elegible fixed assets.

Under § 1 LDC Tax Act, P may set up a 40% reserve in its balance sheet at year end sheltering income from German tax:

Shares in S 100	LDC reserve 40

The 40 reserve will be restored to income after 6 years over another 6 years (or, perhaps, over 12 years).

The subsequent text will discuss the main features of the reserve, its creation and its write-back to income:

A German taxpayer (see a) invests in an LDC subsidiary, partnership or branch (b). The funds invested originate in an MDC business (c) and are used for the acquisition or production of certain assets of an active LDC business (d). The investor may set up a reserve of 40 or 100% of the capital invested (e) to be charged against taxable domestic profits. There are certain time (f) and accounting restrictions (g) and a so-called loss clause against tax shelter operations (h). After 6 years, the reserve must be restored to income over another 6 years (i) or 12 years if the investment is considered particularly effective to combat LDC unemployment or if the investment relates to raw materials or energy and receives Government approval. Early restoration to income is required when the conditions for its set-up are no longer fulfilled, when the investment is liquidated or when its book value is written down (k).

(a) Eligible Investors

Corporate and individual taxpayers alike qualify for relief, including non-residents running a business within Germany whose funds (possibly borrowed) are used for investing in an LDC.[36]

To be eligible for the reserve,

- there must be a transfer of funds to a qualifying LDC investment (below b);
- the funds transferred must originate from qualifying sources (below c) and
- they must be invested in the LDC in qualifying assets (below d).

(b) Eligible Investments

aa) Legal Format of Investment. Investment may be in LDC subsidiaries, partnerships or branches including certain loans to a subsidiary. The Act expressly enumerates [37]:

(i) shares in LDC corporations acquired on incorporation or increase of capital (no. 1),

(ii) loans to LDC corporations in connection with their incorporation or a substantial business extension [37] if no amortisation is due on such loans before six years *and*
   - at the time of granting the loan, the lendor directly or indirectly holds a minimum of 15% of the lendee's capital (5% in mining companies since 1979) or
   - the lendor receives no fixed interest but only shares in the lendee's profit, or
   - the lendee produces goods under the lendor's industrial property rights, copy-rights, plans, models, procedures or industrial or commercial know-how or distributes goods under the lendor's trademark to a not unsubstantial extent for at least six years after having received the loan (no. 2),

(iii) participations in LDC partnerships for the purpose of founding or substantially extending the business (no. 3), and

(iv) business assets transferred to an LDC business or establishment of the taxpayer for the purpose of its foundation or substantial extension [38] (no. 4).

Where the LDC law does not permit investments of the types above the reserve is applicable to legal structures similar to a participation in an LDC business.[39]

Corporate shares are shares in the capital of associations which are treated as corporations under German tax law. This treatment may differ from foreign law for certain associations such as Spanish partnerships which, under Spanish tax law, are subject to corporation tax.[40] Acquisition of shares not fully paid in qualifies for relief to the extent of subsequent contributions to capital on such shares. It is questionable whether capital increases out of corporate funds (without distribution) are eligible.[41]

Loans to corporate lendees qualify unless reimbursed within six years.[42] Conversion of loans into capital within such period is tantamount to early amortisation [43]; but, since 1978, there would be an exception to this if the loan is so converted into equity within 3 years in fulfillment of a contractual obligation of the lendor.

Businesses or establishments within the meaning of no. 4 of § 1 (3) of the Act are those which are not part of an LDC corporation or partnership.

Like investments under § 1 (8) of the Act refer in particular to joint ventures in Rumania or Yugoslavia and other countries whose laws do not allow for full private ownership of means of production.

The 1978/79 amendments would grant the tax relief under the Act also to investments made not directly but through an LDC corporation if the investor holds more than 25% of the capital of such corporation.

bb) New Investments, not Acquisitions. Qualifying investments must be original, new investments in an LDC active business.[44]

Original investments are made when the taxpayer sets up a new business rather than acquiring an existing one. This requires that the substance of the business be new, not just its form; for instance, it is not sufficient that a new partnership takes over, and continues to run, an existing business. A derivative investment is sufficient only in one instance, viz. when the taxpayer acquires shares in an LDC corporation from the German Company for Economic Cooperation (Development Company) [45], a funding vehicle of the Federal Republic to promote incorporation and extension of German enterprises in LDC's.

cc) LDC Business Location and Activity. LDC's are the countries enumerated in § 6 of the act.[46]

The business must be situated in an LDC, either in the country of residence or in another LDC, but not in an MDC.[47] The business must be active exclusively or almost exclusively

- in manufacturing or distributing goods (except arms and military supply [48]),
- in mining,
- in rendering commercial services except producing or running tourist industry facilities and except letting or renting-out assets including the letting of the use of rights, plans, models, or know-how, or
- in agriculture and forestry.[49]

All activities performed by a corporation are considered commercial even if they were otherwise categorized as non-commercial, e.g. certain consulting services. The exclusion of the tourist business is due to a change of the Act, on account of general criticism as well as to forestall further widespread use particularly for hotel tax shelter operations, tourist business, however, is not excluded from the general loss reserve under § 3 of the Foreign Investment Act (below V.1.b).

Commercial services to be rendered through exploiting commercial ships or aircraft in international traffic must be approved by the Federal Ministry of Economic Cooperation in agreement with the Federal Ministry of Traffic determining that the investment is worth of being promoted in view of development and traffic policies.[50]

(c) Origin of Funds Invested

Investments may be made out of the taxpayer's own funds or out of loans granted to him; they may also be in fixed or current assets owned by him. The administration maintains that loans, however, may not be received from LDC lendors, not even from OPEC countries or the like.[51] It is in dispute, too, whether capital increases out of reserves of the LDC corporation qualify. In any case, the funds or assets must be those of a domestic business, i.e. a West German or West Berlin business. In the instance of a non-resident taxpayer, such business need not always constitute a permanent establishment. But only a permanent establishment would subject its owner to German tax as a non-resident taxpayer qualifying for relief. The LDC investment must be held by the German business.

(d) Use of Funds Invested

The investor may transfer to the LDC investment
- either assets
- or, usually, money (funds).

Assets transferred to the LDC must be either depreciable fixed assets or business land or inventory items (raw materials. supplies, goods in process or finished goods). Agricultural or forestry land (whether or not owned by corporations) does not qualify according to a Finance Ministry ruling.[52]

Alternatively, funds transferred must be used to acquire or produce such assets before the end of the business year subsequent to the business year of transfer. Inventory items qualify only to the extent that there is an increase in inventory held by the LDC business at the end of the business year subsequent to that of the transfer over and above the inventory at the end of the preceding business year.[53]

Investments in LDC banking and insurance institutions qualify for the reserve only to the extent that funds transferred have been used by the end of the subsequent business year to grant loans running at least six years to LDC businesses to finance LDC business investment or acquisition of LDC shares [54], or to the extent that such funds have been by such sime to comply with LDC statutory requirements to deposit funds at the LDC national bank. This special treatment requires approval by the Federal Ministry of Economy in agreement with the Federal Ministry of Economic Cooperation determining that the investment is particularly worth of being promoted in the light of development policy.[55]

(e) Amount of Reserves

The reserve is equal to 40% of the funds invested in the LDC. It is 100% for investments in least developed countries enumerated in § 6 of the Act acc. to UN classifications (see Appendix).[56] Under the 1978/1979 amendments, there is a 60% reserve for investments relating to raw materials or energy, with Ministry approval.

(f) Time When Reserve Is Set Up

The reserve may only be set up in the business year in which the funds invested have been transferred to the LDC business. In the instance of money remitted to the LDC this is at the date when the recipient is in a position to dispose of the amounts remitted.[57] If the acquisition or production of assets financed out of funds transferred has not been fully accomplished by the end of the business year subsequent to that of the tranfer [58], such funds are eligible for the reserve to the extent that they have been used for advance payments on cost of acquisition or production.[59]

In the instance of transfers of fixed assets or inventory items the relevant date is when the assets are actually handed out to the LDC recipient, which generally is the date of delivery through the LDC customs authorities.[60]

(g) Accounting Requirements

The creation or liquidation of a reserve must be shown in the taxpayer's books.[61] The reserve must appear both on the tax and the commercial balance sheets.[62]

(h) Loss Clause

The creation of the reserve may not result in, or increase, an overall loss [63] of the German business. This loss clause has been added to many incentive provisions to prevent their use for tax shelter operations [64] but it applies to any and all firms, and business organizations continue to fight this clause. The activities of partnerships and corporations constitute one business and give rise to one business result (profit or loss).[65] The business results of corporations filling consolidated returns are determined severally.[66]

(i) Ordinary Restoration to Income: 6 Years

Ordinarily, reserves may be carried in the taxpayer's books for six years. At the end of the 7th year, they shall be restored to income in annual installments of a minimum of 1/6 of the total amount, i.e. over a period of not more than another six years. Thus, reserves will have been fully written back to income at the end of twelve years after their creation.

Restoration to income is spread over 12 years if the investment is particularly

- effective in creating jobs or
- since 1979: worth being promoted in respect of cooperation in the fields of raw materials or energy.

In both instances, the approval of the Ministries of Economy and of Economic Cooperation is necessary.

(j) Special Job-Creating Effect: 12 Years

Where the investment has had a special job-creating effect [67] restoration to income after the initial six years' period may be spread over twelve years rather than another six years. The reserve will then have been fully liquidated at the end of 18 years after its creation.

The special job-creating effect is assessed on the basis of circumstances prevailing after the end of the forth year after the creation of the reserve. It must must be certified by the Federal Ministry of Economic Cooperation in agreement with the Federal Ministry of Economy on a showing by the taxpayer that investment was in enterprise with a particular job-creating effect thus capable of counteracting LDC unemployment.

The Federal Ministry of Economic Cooperation has issued guidelines on the conditions to be fulfilled and on the approval procedure.[68]

aa) How to Measure Creation of Jobs. There is a special job-creating effect where the LDC business' total payroll is at least equal to 35% of value added by the LDC business.

Payroll includes salaries and emoluments paid, social security contributions, old age benefits and subsidies, but only to the extent that they have been paid to, or for the benefit of, LDC nationals. Thus, payments to MDC supervising, teaching or other personnel are not taken into account.

Value added by the LDC business is the excess of business turnover over cost of goods and supplies. Business turnover is the sum of business receipts (excluding turnover tax) except for receipts from ancillary transactions, rentals and other services which are not part of business turnover (such as broker activities, consideration received for abstention from, or toleration of, acts, etc.). Increases or decreases of goods in process or finished goods on hand at beginning and end of year are taken into account.

Costs of goods and supplies used or consumed in producing such business turnover include costs of acquisition of raw materials and supplies and of services rendered by third parties. Cost of transportation, freight in, etc. must be included, costs allocable to items outside business turnover must be excluded. Again, increases or decreases of stock on hand at beginning and end of year are taken into account.

Cumulative turnover taxes need not be excluded from turnover if they are excluded also from cost of goods or supplies used or consumed. Excises may be excluded if they have also been excluded from cost of goods and supplies used or consumed or if they have arisen in the business itself.

In principle, the relevant rules for this computation are based on German tax law provisions except special incentive and relief provisions.

In short, the Guidelines try to contrast value added by local labor to value added by capital. Payroll must be in excess of roughly one half of cost of capital (depreciation, interest, rentals, etc.) and profits. Only direct effects on employment are taken into account, measured by payroll paid or incurred by the business itself, not indirect effects through an increase in the demand for labor employed in third parties' businesses in the LDC. This might induce vertical integration where it penalizes division of labor between different businesses. Conversely, highly integrated businesses with high capital cost at one stage of production (e.g. mineral extraction) may be excluded from preferential treatment even if they require a very high labor input on some later stage (e.g. labor intensive processing of raw materials) since all these stages are lumped together within one business.

The relevant data are those of the fifth year after the reserve has been set up. The approval may be, but need not be, revoked if the 35% minimum ratio of payroll is later found to have been absent originally or in the sixth or seventh business year after the reserve has been set up.

bb) Approval Procedure. The approval procedure [69] is similar to that for the approval of investment in ships and aircraft [70] or in banking and insurance institutions [71] or, since 1978, in energy and raw materials-related fields.

Proof by the taxpayer requires submission of balance sheets and profit and loss statements (in notarized translation) certified by a state-approved independent accountant or a comparable organisation.

The first applications for approval may be filed after 12/31/1978, i.e. the fifth year after the 1975 act entered into force.

(k) Early Restoration to Income

A taxpayer may elect to write the reserve back to income before the end of the 6 years period or at annual amounts higher than 1/6th or 1/12th, respectively, which may be adventageous for him where he could not otherwise use losses carried forward.

Irrespective of ordinary restoration to income reserves must be liquidated in some instances where the conditions for their creation are no longer fulfilled.

The reserve is fully liquidated when the LDC corporation or business is no longer exclusively or almost exclusively active in a field enumerated in § 1(2)(1) last clause.[72]

A reserve is also liquidated to the extent that shares in an LDC corporation are sold or withdrawn from business property and incorporated into the taxpayer's private property.[73] The reserve is equally liquidated to the extent that business assets of an LDC corporation or business are sold or incorporated into the taxpayers private property or transferred to an MDC. If they are transferred from an LDC of group 1 to a group 2 LDC 6/10th of the reserve are restored to income. There is no such restoration if such business assets have been replaced by the end of the subsequent business year.

There is a similar restoration to income if a taxpayer has availed himself of the preferential treatment for loans given by banking or insurance institutions or amounts deposited by them at the LDC national bank [74] if such loans are reimbursed or assigned or incorporated into private property or transferred to an MDC (unless to the extent that new eligible loans are given) or such deposits are repaid. There is a restoration of 6/10th in the case of transfers from a group 1 to a group 2 LDC.

Amounts restored to taxable income are subject to corporation or income tax at regular rates, even if there was a sale of the business otherwise eligible for preferential capital gains treatment.[75]

Write-downs of investments from book-value to lower going-concern value must be charged against the reserve, i.e. the reserve is liquidated proportionately.[76] For the same reason, the administration asserts an incomptability between the reserve and current expensing of lowpriced assets.[77]

3. Relative Importance of LDC Preferences

As pointed out above (A.III), the discounted present value of the investment reserve is in the range of 10% to 15% of the amount invested in an LDC. The much higher tax benefits to be obtained for investments in LLDC's appear to have not been attractive enough to overcome business considerations arguing against such investment; German direct investment in LLDC's has been quite negligible. The effects from the anti-unemployment provision remain to be seen.

It is true, though, that the tax incentives for investing in LDC's are more substantial than those for domestic (or MDC) investment with the possible exception of the Berlin incentives.

Tax benefits from the reserve may be very much reduced, potentially to nil, where the investment fails: sustained losses give rise to the loss deduction or reserve for investment abroad in general (below V) and, finally, to the write-down of the investment as such to be charged against the investment reserve. Thus, § 1 LDC Tax Act enhances the after-tax profitability of an already profitable operation but does little or nothing to reduce the risk of losses or total failure.

III. Realisation of Profits or Roll-over to New Investment

As a rule, investment abroad may only be made out of taxed earnings, i.e. usually out of after-tax funds; if assets are transferred abroad undisclosed reserves contained in these assets are liquidated and taxed in most cases.

1. Investing in an MDC

a) As a general rule, there is realisation of profits and losses in the amount of the difference between market and book values if assets are contributed to a domestic or foreign subsidiary in exchange for such subsidiary's shares [78] or if assets are transferred to a foreign branch in a treaty country.[79] There is no realisation of profits contained in assets transferred before the entry into force of a DTA if after the transfer Germany concludes a treaty with the recipient country.[80]

b) In the case of investment in an MDC (or an LDC), the tax liability resulting from realisation of undisclosed reserves of assets transferred is spread over a period totaling 10 years by means of a reserve in the amount of profits realised on transfer of depreciable fixed business assets.[81] Such reserve shall be liquidated in not more than 5 installments of one fifth each beginning in the fifth year after the investment has been made and the reserve set up. The relief is available for contributions to capital of foreign corporations, partnerships or branches as long as they are engaged in active business.[82] There is early restoration to income on sale of shares aquired [83] or on sale of assets transferred to partnerships or branches and on certain similar transactions.

2. Investing in an LDC

Alternatively to the general provision mentioned above – that applies to investments both in MDC's and LDC's – there is a particular deferral [84] for contributions of depreciable fixed assets to LDC investments. Lower book value of depreciable assets contributed to a foreign corporation is rolled over to shares aquired in exchange for the assets, to be shown in het taxpayer's books at the book value of the assets transferred. The undisclosed reserves would thus be liquidated on a sale or exchange of the shares under normal rules.

In the instance of a transfer of depreciable assets to an LDC partnership or branch in a treaty country, profits realised on transfer may be disregarded (exempt) for German tax purposes provided the assets transferred will be retained in the LDC partnership or branch for at least 3 years.[85] This results in a final saving of German tax since a later sale or exchange of the assets by the LDC recipient partnership or branch will produce branch profits exempt from German tax under the treaty.[86]

Example 3: Roll-over of Book Value to LDC Investment

Assume a German parent company P subscribing all of the share capital of 100 of an LDC manufacturing subsidiary S. P contributes to S, in consideration for shares, machinery at a book value to P of 10.

Under § 3 LDC Tax Act, P may roll-over the book value of 10 from the assets contributed to the shares received in its balance sheet:
shares in S 10

The unrealized profits contained in that book value may become subject to tax, for instance, when P sells the shares to a third party.

a) Eligible Investment

Investment entitles to the roll-over relief if the assets are transferred to an LDC corporation, partnership, branch or business of a type, in the manner, and for the activities discussed above for the LDC investment reserve.[87] Like investments, particularly in socialist LDC's, also qualify.[88]

Where both § 1 and § 3 of the LDC Tax Act apply, the LDC investment reserve under § 1 is computed on the basis of the book value rolled over under § 3.[89]

Assets transferred must be depreciable fixed assets in the hands of the recipient, including intangibles.[90] It is doubtful, though, whether constructive contributions to capital qualify, too, resulting for instance from licencing a patent held by the German parent to its LDC subsidiary at a lower than arm's length royalty prescribed by LDC regulatory bodies. The German field auditors are understood to be disposed to some leniency in such LDC cases where, otherwise, they would have to adjust the royalty charged.

b) Contributions in Kind

Assets qualifying for roll-over must be contributed to the foreign corporation, partnership, branch or business as a contribution in kind. Thus, they must be capable of being contributed under German (tax) law.[91]

This requirement may cause problems in the case of intangibles.[90] Intangibles such as patents, trademarks or know-how may be contributed as such. Since R & D costs paid or incurred on self-produced intangibles must be currently expensed [92] shares received in exchange for the intangibles contributed are entered into the contributor's books at a (rolled-over) book value of nil.

If, however, the German investor retains the intangible as such and only contributes the right to use such asset this will probably not qualify as a contribution in kind.[93]

The investor could obviously contribute money from which the recipient LDC corporation etc. could purchase or rent the intangibles or the right to use them. Such contribution of monetary items, though, would not give usually rise to a § 3 roll-over but may qualify for a § 1 reserve, also in a case where the money is not contributed but lent.

Difficulties arise particularly in the case of intercorporate technology transfers where the LDC of which the transferee is a resident permits neither full payment and/or deductibility of royalties for the use of the technology transferred nor the contribution to capital of such technology. In such cases, it is felt that the LDC Tax Act reliefs should be available because there is a like investment in the sense of § 3 (4), § 1 (7) LDC Tax Act. Under the prevailing doctrine, however, it appears there is no such relief; this deficiency has frequently been sought to be remedied.

3. Relative Importance of LDC Preferences

The roll-over relief under § 3 LDC Tax Act is of limited applicability restricted to contributions in kind, excluding re-investment of sales proceeds. To a large extent, it analogizes LDC investments to a purely domestic situation and to the reserve under the Tax Act on Investment Abroad. LDC investment is treated more generously insofar as the tax deferral from roll-over may be indefinite; in some cases it may amount to a final tax saving.

IV. Incorporation of Branch or Sale of Shares

Restructuring the original investment may lead to a realization of profits, such as on merger of corporations or on incorporation of a branch or partnership.

1. Restructuring an MDC Investment

Reorganization may be tax-free under the specific provisions of the Act on Taxation of Mergers 1977 which is also applicable to holdings in foreign corporations etc. including LDC corporations.[94] It does not permit the tax-free export of domestic undisclosed reserves to a foreign entity. Whether the limited roll-over provision of § 6 b Income Tax Act may also be applicable to transfers abroad had been in dispute [95]; the situation has now been clarified by § 4 Foreign Investment Act making roll-over applicable to a reinvestment in a foreign corporation of the profits from the sale of shares in another corporation.

2. Restructuring a LDC investment

§ 4 LDC Tax Act provides for a roll-over of undisclosed reserves from foreign branch assets or from shares in a foreign corporation to domestic or foreign depreciable movable fixed assets. It defers domestic profits [96] from the disclosure of hidden reserves on

- incorporation of a foreign branch or partnership [97]
  and
- on sale of branch assets or of shares in a corporation, partnership or branch [98],

provided such corporation, partnership, branch or business in an LDC investment within the meaning of this term under § 1 LDC Tax Act.[99]

The incorporation or other transfer must have been caused by the situation in the LDC, for instance by legal requirements imposed upon the taxpayer or by a purely factual situation.

The roll-over of book values may be effected either in the year of realization of profits or in a later year. In the latter case, profits realized may be entered into a reserve to be charged against the cost of acquisition or production of eligible new assets within two years; otherwise the reserve must be written back to taxable income.[100]

If a taxpayer elects in favour of the deduction or reserve under § 4 LDC Tax Act he must forego the tax relief under § 34 Income Tax Act granting a tax rate of 1/2 of the ordinary rate for extraordinary gains from the sale of a business or branch.[101]

Example 4: Roll-over of Book Value ot Restructured Investment

Assume a German parent corporation P holding an equity stake in an LDC subsidiary S with a book value to P of 10 and a market value of 50. The book value of shares may be, for instance, the book value of assets contributed by P to S (see above Example 3) and rolled over under § 3 LDC Tax Act.

Assume LDC regulations requiring P to sell its share in S to a third party for 50.

Under § 4 LDC Tax Act, P deducts its profit of 40 (50 ./. 10) from the cost of, say, machinery acquired by P within the next two years.

Thus, the depreciable base of P's new assets is reduced by 40 and P's profit of 40 from the sale of the LDC shares will become subject to tax over the new assets' useful life.

3. Relative Importance of LDC preferences

The roll-over under § 4 LDC Tax Act is of very limited applicability. It goes beyond the roll-over in a purely domestic setting under § 6 b Income Tax Act inasfar as the assets or shares sold need not have been held by the taxpayer for any minimum period; § 6 b Income Tax Act would require a minimum holding of 6 years. In part, this reflects the fact that book values of LDC investments may contain undisclosed reserves by reason of other tax preferences under § 1–3 LDC Tax Act or the like, right from the beginning of the investment. Similarly, § 6 b Income Tax Act would require that depreciable assets sold have a minimum useful life of 25 years, a restriction not contained in § 4 LDC Tax Act.

On the other hand, § 4 permits roll-over only to depreciable movable fixed assets, not to immovables or buildings. Most importantly, taxes are only deferred where disclosure of hidden reserves has been caused by the LDC situation, not where the taxpayer freely decided to sell the assets or shares; in the latter case he may also retroactively lose benefits obtained earlier on original investment as discussed above.

V. Treatment of Current Income or Loss

There are by far less, and less important, special provisions for LDC investment in respect of the German taxation of the current return therefrom. None of them is contained in the LDC Tax Act.

1. Current Income from MDC Investment

As a rule, German tax is deferred on retained earnings of foreign corporations; such earnings are only taxed on a 'remittance basis' when distributed except for certain 'Subpart F' income.[102]

a) Dividends

Dividends received are taxable to the German shareholder as part of the shareholder's world-wide income unless there is a specific exemption. To relieve international double taxation there is a direct credit[103], subject to a per country limitation[104], for foreign taxes (particularly withholding taxes) on intercorporate and portfolio dividends. In addition, there is an indirect credit for intercorporate dividends from non-Subpart F foreign corporations.

Alternatively, the taxpayer may forego the tax credits and apply for lump sum taxation of 25% of dividends received[105], an election which is rarely made.

German treaty law generally reduces foreign withholding taxes and incorporates the domestic direct tax credit provisions in the DTA. In lieu of the indirect credit, however, there is an exemption for intercorporate dividends, which often is restricted to dividends from non-Subpart F corporations, particularly in the case of LDC's and some other treaty partners.

b) Losses

Foreign losses would not usually be relevant for German tax purposes, except in determining the tax rate on other income.

Retained foreign corporate earnings are not subject to German tax because of deferral; foreign branch profits (and losses) are usually exempt under German DTA's.[106]

The Foreign Investment Tax Act, however, introduced German tax relief for foreign losses. At the taxpayer's election foreign branch losses may be set off against domestic profits including carry-forward and carry-back of losses; correspondingly, subsequent foreign branch profits will be taxable in Germany up to the amount of losses for which the election was exercised (recepture).[107]

Foreign corporate losses sustained by a subsidiary entitle the parent to a reserve in proportion to its share in the subsidiary's capital with a minimum direct holding of 50%. Only initial losses suffered in the first five years after acquisition of the original holding or of additional shares of at least 5% of nominal capital qualify for relief. The reserve must be written back to taxable income within 5 years; early restoration to income is required to the extent that there are subsequent profits, a write-down to lower going-concern value, a sale or like transaction, or a failure to comply with the detailed requirements of proof.[108]

2. Treatment of Current Profits or Losses from LDC Investment

There are but few deviations from these rules for the taxation of current income from investment in an LDC.

Intercorporate LDC dividends are effectively exempt already under domestic law, i.e. even in the absence of a treaty.[109] The law deems the foreign LDC tax on the subsidiary and eligible for the indirect tax credit to be equal to the amount of German tax due on the dividends received.

In the instance of foreign corporate losses the minimum holding in an LDC subsidiary is 25% rather than 50% to entitle the parent to the 5 years reserve.[110]

Example 5: Treatment of Current Losses and Profits

a) Parent's Loss Reserve

Assume a German parent corporation P holding 25% of the shares of an LDC company S. S sustains annual losses of 20 in each of the first 5 years after its incorporation.

P may set up a loss reserve of 5 (= 25% of 20) annually totalling 25 at the end of the 5th year.

b) Restoration of Loss Reserve to Income

Assume S showing a profit of no more than 20 in each of the following 5 years (= years 6 through 10).

P has to write back to its taxable income the 25 reserve by annual installments of 5 leaving nil at the end of the 10th year.

c) LDC Subsidiary's Dividends Received by Parent

Assume S showing and distributing a profit thereafter. S's dividends received and retained by P are effectively exempt from German corporation tax in P's hands, irrespective of whether S is situated in a treaty country or not.

When P distributes these dividends received from S, the exemption ends: P pays a 36% corporation tax fully creditable against its shareholders' personal income tax (see Example 1, above B.I.1.a).

VI. Interest and Royalties

Intercorporate interest [111] and royalties [112] flowing from an LDC subsidiary to its domestic parent are taxed largely as any other income. The direct tax credit available for dividends received applies as well to interest and royalties. Under domestic law, there are no special rules for intercorporate payments. Intracorporate payments, however, between a foreign branch and its domestic head office are disregarded for German tax purposes if they relate to items other than goods; thus, interest or royalties (in excess of allocable costs) charged by the head office to the branch do not reduce branch profits.

In its treaties [9], Germany has not always been successful to reduce foreign withholding taxes, particularly not so against LDC treaty partners.

Subject to exceptions, particularly for bank loans and for certain approved loans and licences, the German treaty rates which LDC's are (in %; first figure = interest / second figure = industrial royalties): Brazil (15/15 / trade mark 25), Ecuador (15/15), Egypt (15/0), Greece (10/0), India (full domestic rates), Iran (15/10), Israel (15/5), Jamaica (12,5/10), Liberia (20/10), Morocco (10/10), Malta (10/10), Pakistan (20/0), Romania (10/10), Singapore (10/10), Spain (10/5), Sri Lanka (full/half domestic rates), Thailand (25/15), Trinidad and Tobago (15/10), Tunesia (10/15), Zambia (10/10).

Thus, the foreign withholding tax on gross income may not always be fully creditable against German tax under the per country limitation. In contrast to this, Germany has made wide use of the fictitious [113] credit for tax spared particularly by an LDC. In the case of Brazil, the German tax sparing credit amounts to 20% on interest (withholding tax treaty rate 15%), to 20% for technology royalties (treaty rate 15%) and to 25% for such royalties if they are non-deductible expenses of the licensee and if the latter is a 50% or more subsidiary of the licensor.

The Brazilian example also shows that Germany has not been able to rule out LDC restrictions on the deductibility of intercorporate royalties.

C. NET WORTH AND OTHER TAXES

The special German tax provisions relative to LDC investment concentrate on profits taxes.

The profits and capital tax exemptions for intercorporate holdings in foreign non-Subpart F corporations also apply to net worth tax [114] and municipal trade tax on profits and capital.[115] The Foreign Investments Tax Act reliefs and reserves are also taken into account for purposes of municipal trade profits tax.[116]

All of the special LDC Tax Act reliefs discussed above are taken into consideration in establishing profits subject to municipal trade tax [117]; the investment reserves under § 1 (1) and § 2 LDC Tax Act reduce the assessable value of the business particularly for net worth tax.[118]

APPENDIX

§ 6 LDC Act, containing the definition of Developing Countries, reads (1979 version):

(1) Developing countries within the meaning of this Act are the following countries and territories:

Group 1:
Afghanistan, Bangla Desh, Benin, Bhutan, Botsuana, Burundi, Cape Verde, Central African Empire, Comores, Ethiopia, Gambia, Guinea, Haiti, Laos, Lesotho, Malawi, Maledives, Mali, Nepal, Niger, Ruanda, Somalia, Sudan, Tansania, Tschad, Uganda, Upper Volta, West Samoa, Yemen (Arab Republic), Yemen (Democratic Republic).

Group 2:
Algeria, Angola, Antiqua, Argentina, Bahamas, Bahrain, Barbados, Birma, Bolivia, Brazil, Brunei, Camerun, Chile, Colombia, People's Republic of Congo, Costa Rica, Cyprus, Dominica, Dominican Republic, Djibouti, Ecuador, Egypt, Equatorial Guinea, Fidchi, Gabun, Ghana, Grenada, Greece, Guatemala, Guinea-Bissau, Guyana, Honduras, Iceland, India, Indonesia, Irak, Iran, Israel, Ivory Coast, Jamaica, Jordan, Kenia, Republic of Korea, Kuweit, Lebanon, Liberia, Lybia, Madagascar, Malaysia, Malta, Mauretania, Mauritius, Mexico Morocco, Mosambik, Nauru, Nicaragua, Nigeria, Oman, Pakistan, Panama, Papua-New Guinea, Paraguay, Peru, Philippines, Portugal (excluding territories outside Europe), Qatar, Rumania, El Salvador, Sao Tomé and Principe, Saudi-Arabia, Senegal, Seychelles, Sierra Leone, Singapore, Spain (excluding territories outside Europe), Sri Lanka, Sta. Lucia, St. Kitts-Nevis-Anguilla, St. Vincent, Suriname, Swasiland, Syria, Taiwan, Thailand, Togo, Tonga, Trinidad and Tobago, Turkey, Tunesia, United Arab Emirates, Uruguay, Venezuela, Repub lic of Vietnam, Yugoslavia, Zaire, Zambia.

(2) Developing Countries of Group 2 within the meaning of this Act are also countries outside Europe which have attained independence after December 31, 1978.

Note:
Classification as a least developed country under the Act may be revised in accordance with UN classifications.

1. Based on material published up to March 1979.
English language papers on German tax treatment of investments in LDC's include Anthoine, Tax Systems of Major Capital Exporting Countries: An Examination of Incentives for Private Investment at Home and in Developing Countries, 32 Tax Law Rev. 323, 337-343 (Spring 1977). Byran, Developed Nations Tax Law and Investment in LDC's: A Comparative Analysis, Columbia J. of Transnat'l Law (July/1978). OECD, Investing in Developing Countries, 3rd rev'd ed., Paris 1975, pp. 53-62 (also deals with investment guarantees and other non-tax issues); Raedler, Germany: The New Tax Law Concerning Investments in Developing Countries and its Impact on Business, 1975 Intertax 25-28; for a more general view see Raedler, Measures Taken By the Government of the Federal Republic of Germany to Encourage Investment in Industrial Projects in Developing Countries, 1970 Management Int'l Review 93-109.
Publications in German include Flick-Husmann, Das neue Entwicklungsländer-Steuergesetz, Cologne 1975, Pp. XVI, 118; Goltz, Förderung privater Kapitalanlagen (Direktinvestitionen)

in Entwicklungsländern – Garantie-, Finanzierungs- und Steuerhilfen sowie Investitionsschutz, Ausl. Wirtschafts- und Steuerrecht, Bd. 52, BfA, Cologne; Kirchner (DEG), Steuerliche Behandlung von Erträgen und Verlusten aus Investitionen in Entwicklungsländern, Cologne 1976; Raupach, in Herrmann-Heuer, EStG, § 6, EntwHilfeStG (Jan. 1973) to be rewritten by the author hereof in forthcoming release; Treskow, Förderung ausländischer Direktinvestitionen in Entwicklungsländern durch Steuervergünstigungen, Goettingen 1977, Pp. XXIX, 187.

2. Certain passive or 'tainted' income of foreign corporations controlled by German residents holding more than 50% of the corporation's capital is taxable to the German shareholders if it exceeds 10% of corporate gross income or DM 120,000 provided such income is not taxed abroad at a minimum rate of 30%. The relevant provisions of the Foreign Tax Relations Act of Sept. 8, 1972, similar to Subpart F of the US IRC, shall be disregarded hereinafter.

3. Gesetz über steuerliche Massnahmen zur Förderung von privaten Kapitalanlagen in Entwicklungsländern (Entwicklungsländer-Steuergesetz) of 13 February 1975, BGBl. I 493 = BStBl. I 163, now amended by 1979 Act retroactive to II/1979, BT-Drs. 8/1857 and 8/2501 of Jan. 24, 1979. The first incentive provisions for LDC investment were § 34d Income Tax Act, § 19b Corporation Tax Act, both of 1961 permitting a reserve of 1/3 of approved investment in depreciable fixed assets to be restored to income after three years over five years. For investments in LDC's after 12/31/1962, the then Development Aid Tax Act granted an initial allowance of 15%, a six years reserve of 50% of the balance (60% for treaty countries for which the initial allowance was excluded) and a roll-over provision for contributions in kind. The act was extended for another five years period commencing 1/1/1968 with a somewhat larger scope and for another year with certain restrictions until 12/31/1973.

The present version, renamed LDC Tax Act, had originally applied to investments made before 12/31/1978. The main changes as against the earlier versions include:

- no initial allowance
- a six years' reserve of 40% (100% for least developed countries = LLDC), restorable to income over another six years
- the extension of the restoration period to twelve years for investments with a particular job-creating effect
- no incentives for investments in the tourist industry.

The 1978/79 amendments

- made the Act indefinite,
- extended the write-back period of the § 1 reserve to 12 years for least developed countries (LLDC's) and for energy related investments,
- increased to 60% the amount eligible for the reserve,
- reduced the minimum share-holding to 5% for loans to mining subsidiaries,
- made the benefits available for investments made through 25% LDC holding companies, and
- subjected the tax payers to statistical reporting requirements.

Some further reaching proposals by business organisations and others (e.g. to reintroduce the initial allowance) were not adopted.

The list of LDC's under § 6 LDC Tax Act has been reproduced in the Appendix.

4. Corporation Tax Act 1977 of 8/31/1976 (Körperschaftsteuergesetz); for an English translation with commentary see Ault/Rädler, The German Corporation Tax Reform 1977, Deventer/Frankfort 1976; see also Ault, Germany: The New Corporation Tax System, 1976 INTERTAX 262-275; Frommel, The New German Imputation System and Foreign Investors 21 British Tax Review 269-288 (1976).

5. Individual Income Tax Act of 4/5/1974, as amended (Einkommensteuergesetz), containing also the provisions on determination of corporate income. The statutory rates from 22% to 56% are increased by church tax rates of 8 to 10% of income tax liability. The top rate applies to income brackets above DM 130.000 (single) or DM 260.000 (married couple filing joint return).

6. Trade Tax Act of 8/15/1974 (Gewerbesteuergesetz). The tax is levied by each municipality on income and capital of local branches of domestic or foreign enterprises located on the municipality's territory, including shares held by that branch. The local rate multipliers are determined annually by the Town Councils, usually 300-450%, resulting in a tax rate

on profits (plus certain interest on long-term debt, rentals, etc.) of 15-22,5% and on capital of 0,6-0,9%. The tax liability is deductible in arriving at taxable corporate or personal income. In some parts of Germany, there is a municipal payroll tax, too.

7. Net Worth Tax Act of 4/17/1974 (Vermögensteuergesetz) with 1978 rates of 0,7% for corporations and of 0,5% for individuals (not deductible from taxable income).

8. Act on Tax Measures Concerning Investments Abroad by the German Industry of 8/18/1969, as amended (Auslandsinvestitionsgesetz).

9. Germany has entered into DTA's with most industrialized countries and with many LDC's, viz. Brazil (1975), Cyprus (1974), Egypt (1959), Greece (1966), Iceland (1971), India (1959), Iran (1968), Israel (1962), Jamaica (1974), Korea (1976), Liberia (1970), Malta (1974), Morocco (1972), Pakistan (1958/1963/1970), Poland (1972), Romania (1973), Singapore (1972), Spain (1966), Sri Lanka (1962), Thailand (1967), Trinidad and Tobago (1973), Tunisia (1975), Zambia (1973). Draft DTA's have been negotiated or signed with Argentina (1978), Ecuador (1977), Egypt (1977), Indonesia (1977), Israel (1977), Kenia (1977), Malaysia (1977), Mauritius (1978), Portugal (1977), Sri Lanka (1977), Turkey (1974). Negotiations are under way with Bangladesh, Birma, Chile, Gabun, India, Ivory Coast, Lybia, Mexico, Philippines, Poland, Thailand, Turkey, Yugoslavia.
See Krabbe, German Tax Treaty Policy, INTERTAX 226-232 (1976).

10. Direct investment figures may be misleading in that they have been established for the countries first receiving the funds invested even if these funds are only channelled through to another country. Thuis, for instance, the Brazilian subsidiary of Bayer, second largest outside the EC of this chemical firm, is held through the Canadian Bayforin holding.

11. These and the following data, mostly rounded, are taken from, or computed on the basis of, the figures published by the Federal Minister of the Economy, Runderlaß Aussenwirtschaft Nr. 11/78 betreffend IV 1; Vermögensanlagen Gebietsansässiger in fremden Wirtschaftsgebieten, of April 11, 1978, in Federal Gazette No. 83, pp. 2-3, of May 3, 1978 and Nr. 22/78 of Oct. 9, 1978, ibid. No. 201, pp. 1-2 of Oct. 24, 1978. They reflect foreign investments by residents declared under §§ 55, 56 of the Aussenwirtschaftsverordnung. See also Kraegenau, Internationale Direktinvestitionen, 1973-1975, HWWA-Report Nr. 42, March 1977, pp. 57 et seq., 62. This paper uses the most recent 1976 and 1977 figures. The present LDC Tax Act was adopted in 1975. It is difficult to estimate when this and earlier versions of the Act may have started and ended to have some influence, if any, on investment decisions; so, any choice of figures would be somewhat arbitrary.
The LDC definition is that of the DAC of OECD, which may differ from the UN definition on which § 6 of the LDC Tax Act is based.

12. Monatsberichte der Deutschen Bundesbank, Oct. 1978, pp. 31-36.

13. Survey conducted by Fikentscher/Moritz, RIW/AWD 26-31 (1978). The survey covered 203 investors of which 52.7% returned the questionnaire submitted to them.

14. Sources: Süddeutsche Zeitung, 6.10.1977; VWD, ibid., 6.12.1977; Handelsblatt No. 118 of 23.6.1977; Government figures, VWD/NfA (yy) 10.11.77; Federal Economy Ministry, HB 28.12.1978; Economist, July 22, 1978, p. 85; DIW, SZ 1.9.1978, Stat. Fed. Office, SZ 3.3.1979.

15. The 1975 net deficit from royalties paid by German enterprises in which foreigners held substantial participations was ⁒ DM 1,342 mill (of which 691/electrical). Their royalty receipts totalled only DM 41 mill (of which 6/electrical). In contrast to this, the net royalty surplus of German enterprises without such participations by foreigners was + DM 307 mill after deduction of royalties paid by them of DM 410 mill.

16. The subsequent figures for industrial royalties in 1972 and 1973 are the detailed figures last published by the Federal Bank (Bundesbank) in Monatsberichte der Deutschen Bundesbank, Oktober 1974, pp. 26-38. German gross royalty receipts in 1973 from LDC's included royalties paid by Brazil and Spain, amounting to DM 56 Mill. (10% of total receipts/3rd largest licencee country) and to DM 30 Mill. (5%/6th), respectively.

17. The only MDC's from which Germany's balance of royalties obtained a net gain were Japan (+ DM 94.3 mill.), Italy (37.8), Austria (15.1), South Africa (12.9), including in this list Portugal (4.7) and non-EC/EFTA European MDC's (3.4).

18. Germany's net surplus from LDC's included net gains from Brazil (56.3), Spain (29.3), Mexico (13.6), Argentina (6.1), Asian LDC's (14.1), other Latin American LDC's (6.6), other European LDC's (2.9) and African LDC's (1.5).

19. Source: 5th and 6th German Tax Expenditure Budgets of Oct. 22, 1975, BTDs. 7/4203

p. 212, and of Nov. 17, 1977, BTDs. 8/1195, p. 226.
20. ibid. pp. 238, 28, 212 and n. 32.
21. The figures have been taken from the computations (with comparisons with prior law) by Rädler, Germany: The New Tax Law Concerning Investments in Developing Countries and its Impact on Business, 1975 Intertax 25-28, using for discount a 8% interest rate. The effective cash value will depend on many factors, for instance, the ratio between retained and distributed foreign source earnings particularly under the new German imputation system discussed below B.I.1.a, text accompanying n. 26. Similar computations of discounted cash value may be found in Flick-Husmann, Das neue Entwicklungsländer-Steuergesetz, Cologne 1975, pp. 26, 29; Müller-Dott, Mit dem Entwicklungsländer-Steuergesetz verbundene Steuerersparnis, Der Betrieb 1975, 762-763. Goltz, 1979 Betrieb 636, claims the tax relief to be worth 17-43% in cash and 24-59% in liquidity.
22. Federal office of statistics, Finanzen und Steuern, L 6 I, Körperschaftsteuer 1971, Dec. 1975.
23. Survey conducted by IFO-Institut für Wirtschaftsforschung, Munich; source: Süddeutsche Zeitung 5/7/77, p. 33.
Other arguments include lower cost (14%), financial incentives (7%) and higher profits (5%).
24. See also the survey above n. 13 and Steinmann/Kumax, SZ No. 192 of Aug. 23, 1977, p. 8.
25. Kitterer, in: Chamber of Commerce, Munich, IuH p. 26 (5/1978); Goltz, ibid. (n. 21).
26. For an English explanation of the Act, see publications cited above n. 4.
27. Branch profits accruing to foreign corporations are taxed at 50%.
28. See also Rädler, Model Computations of Tax Burden of a German Subsidiary or Branch, INTERTAX 14-18 (1978).
29. Up to twice of straight-line with a 20% ceiling.
30. For coal and mineral mining, environmental protection, ships, R&D, etc.; §§ 75 et seq. Income Tax Regulations.
31. There is considerable doubt whether these initial allowances also apply to foreign investment; see Herrmann/Heuer, Kommentar zur Einkommensteuer und Körperschaftsteuer, EStG § 7 Annot. 54.
32. Berlin-Förderungsgesetz of 2/18/1976, as amended; the other incentive reliefs are derived from the Zonenrandförderungsgesetz of 8/5/1971, as amended, and the Investitionszulagengesetz of 2/24/1975, as amended.
33. Going-concern value (Teilwert) is a specific German tax law concept. For practical purposes it may largely be equated with replacement market value. Conceptually, it is that part of the total price paid by a hypothetical purchaser of the taxpayer's business that would be allocable to an individual asset or a group of assets or liabilities.
34. See decree of Finance Ministry of Lower Saxony of 4/10/1975 – S 2741 – 36-31 2, 28 (1) Betrieb 908-909 (1975). This decree largely puts foreign investments on an equal footing with domestic investments by the oil industry.
35. See § 1 LDC Tax Act.
36. See below c).
37. See § 1 (3) LDC Tax Act.
38. Substantial extension has been interpreted to require an increase by fore than 1/4 of total business asset value; Flick-Husmann, ibid., p. 40.
39. See § 1 (8) LDC Tax Act aiming particularly at Romania and Yugoslavia.
40. See generally Rädler/Raupach, Deutsche Steuern bei Auslandsbeziehungen, München-Berlin 1966, pp. 17-24. Spanish partnerships are advocated not to consitute corporations for German tax purposes; see Federal Ministry IV C 6 – S 1301 – Spanien – 20/75 of March 19, 1975, no. 5, 31 (58) FR 325 (1976); Krabbe, Qualifikationskonflikte bei ausländischen Personengesellschaften, 22 RIW/AWD 135-139 (1976).
41. See Herrmann/Heuer, ibid., § 6 EntwHilfeStG Annot. 4; Flick/Husmann, ibid., p. 38, and 33 (60), FR 1, 2 (1978); doubted by – g –, 28 (55) FR 239-240 (1973).
42. See § 1 (3) last sentence LDC Tax Act.
43. See Flick/Husmann, ibid., p. 40; occasionally the Tax Administration has taken the contrary position, see Reimann, BB 1357, 1358 (1978), and the Bavarian ruling 31-S 1981-26/2-72 215, DIHT-Steuerinformation of Sept. 28, 1978.
44. The same criteria of what is a new investment apply to domestic investments eligible

for tax grants etc.; see Federal Ministry of Finance IV B/2-S 1981-45/70 of 3/24/1971, StEK EntwHilfeStG Nr. 12, per 2, issued under the pre-1975 version of the Act; see also Federal Ministry of Finance 2/12/1970, BStBl. 1970 I 226; contra Marber, Zur Gründung von Personen- bzw. Kapitalgesellschaften, Betrieben und Betriebstätten, 23 (2) Betrieb 2053 (1970).

45. See § 2 LDC Tax Act. The DEG company has available an equity capital of DM 1 bill.

46. See Appendix to this paper.

47. Federal Ministry of Finance of 3/24/1971, ibid., per 3.

48. Military equipment of any kind, see Upper Finance Directorate Düsseldorf S 1981 A-St 113 of 6/20/1975, 28 (2) Betrieb 1772 (1975) = Cologne S. 1981-14-St 111 of 7/23/1975, StEK EntwHilfeStG Nr. 21.

49. The enumeration in § 1 (3) of the act itself has replaced earlier administrative rulings; see Finance Ministry Northrhine-Westphalia S 1981-13-VB 2 of 5/12/1976, 29 (1) Betrieb 1085 (1976).

50. § 1 (3) (2) LDC Tax Act; see text accompanying n. 70 below.

51. This also applies to pre-payments made by customers to the taxpayer for such assets; Schönnenbeck, BB 757 (1978).

In general, see Federal Ministry of Finance 3/24/1971 ibid. (n. 40), issued under pre-1975 Act; see also Schönnenbeck, Fragen zum Entwicklungsländer-Steuergesetz, 28 Betrieb 2105-2107 (1975); Reuter, Entwicklungshilfe mit Mitteln eines inländischen Betriebs, 14 DStR 252-254 (1976); Flick/Husmann, 33 (60) FR 1, 2 (1978).

52. IV B2-S 1981 – 30/78 of April 27, 1978, 31 Betrieb 960 (1978) = BB 648 (1978) contra –vi–, 33 (60) FR 431 (1978).

53. See § 1 (5) LDC Tax Act; where LDC Law permits (or requires) the contribution in kind of intangibles such as patents or know-how such depreciable intangibles qualify for relief; see Decree BdF IV B 2 – S 1981 – 2/78 of 26.1.1978, (1978) AWD/RIW 208, and text accompanying n. 90 below.

54. See § 1 (6) LDC Tax Act; loans by the banking or insurance institute must be given to enterprises active in the fields enumerated in § 1 (2) (see above text accompanying n. 49).

55. § 1 (6) (1) LDC Tax Act; see text accompanying n. 17 below.

56. See § 6 (1) Group 1 LDC Tax Act, reproduced in the Appendix to this paper.

57. See Federal Ministry of Economy and Finance F/IV B 2-1981-102/71 of 4/24/1972, STEK EntwHilfeStG Nr. 16 = Ministry of Finance Northrhine-Westphalia S. 1981-18-VB 2 of 5/4/1972, 27 (54) Finanz-Rundschau 262 (1972). See now § 1 (4) of the 1978 version.

58. § 1 (5) LDC Tax Act; see above d).

59. Federal Ministry of Economy and Finance 2/28/1972 – F/IV B 2-S 1981-12/72, 25 (1) Betrieb 462, 463 (1972) = Decrees Schleswig Holstein, Hamburg, Kiel, StEK EntwHilfe-StG Nr. 15 b; see also Eggesiecker, 23 RIW/AWD 402-404 (1977).

60. See Federal Ministry of Economy and Finance 4/24/72 = Finance Ministry Northrhine-Westphalia 5/4/1972, ibid., n. 56 above. For the similar situation at 12/31/1972 see Zitzmann, 27 Betriebsberater 396-397 (1972) referring to Federal Ministry of Economy and Finance 2/28/1972, ibid. (n. 59 above).

On deadline problems see Zitzmann, ibid.

61. See § 1 (1) last sentence; the former provision that there was no relief at all where books were found deficient has been dropped.

62. See Decrees Northrhine-Westphalia S 2195 – 6 VB1 of 8/3/1966 = Schleswig Holstein S 2195 – 31 of 8/22/1966 = Kiel S 2195 A – St 11/111 of 8/29/1966, STEK EntwHilfeStG Nr. 5 = Decrees 1965 Bremen/Essen/Hamburg/Schleswig-Holstein/Northrhine-Westphalia/ Kiel, STEK EntwHilfeStG Nr. 2.

63. See § 1 (7) LDC Tax Act.

64. See Böger/Raupach, in Rädler/Raupach, Handbuch der steuerbegünstigten Kapitalanlagen, Cologne 1973, pp. 191 et seq.

65. See Title 19 (4) Trade Tax Guidelines; Böger/Raupach, ibid., p. 201.

66. See Federal Ministry of Economy and Finance F/IV B 5/S 2755-42/71 of 12/30/1971, no. 28, BStBl. 1972 I 2, 8; Flick/Husmann, ibid., p. 59-60; – HWS – Anwendung der Verlustklauseln in Organschaftsfällen, 28 (55) Finanz-Rundschau 43 (1973).

67. See § 1 (1) (4) LDC Tax Act.

68. See Guidelines for the certification of special job-creating effects of 1/24/1975, BStBl. 1975 I 168 with Appendix (Computation Form); see Husmann, 13 DStR 658-660 (1975);

Rosenthal, 30 (57) Finanz-Rundschau 195-197 (1975); the Guidelines are largely based on the terminology used for tax audit purposes, see Compendium of terms to be used in tax audits, Federal Ministry of Finance IV B 7 – S 1401-25/74 of 11/11/1974, BStBl. 1974 I 994.
69. See Rosenthal, ibid., 83-85.
70. See § 1 (1) (2) LDC Tax Act; see text accompanying n. 50 above.
71. See § 1 (6) (1) LDC Tax Act; see text accompanying n. 55 above.
72. See above text accompanying n. 49.
73. See § 5 (2) (1) LDC Tax Act. Withdrawal from business into private property results in realisation of undisclosed reserves; as a rule, private capital gains are not taxable in Germany.
74. See § 1 (6) LDC Tax Act; see above text accompanying n. 55.
75. Recapture; see Federal Ministry of Finance of 3/24/1971, ibid. (n. 44), per 5 with reference to Supreme Tax Court decision IV 40/62 U of 8/20/1964, BStBl. 1964 III 504.
76. See § 5 (1) (1) LDC Tax Act; this does not apply if lower going concern value is for the sole reason that a loan has been given interest-free; see also above n. 33.
77. See Federal Ministry of Economy and Finance IV B 2 – S 1931 – 31/72 of 5/8/1972, StEK EntwHilfeStG Nr. 17; contra Bätterhausen/Eggesiecker, Zur Zulässigkeit der Kumulation von Bewertungsfreiheit für geringwertige Wirtschaftsgüter und steuerfreier Rücklage nach dem Entwicklungsländer-Steuergesetz, 30 (57) Finanz-Rundschau 213-214 (1975).
78. See Supreme Tax Court decision BFH I 175/60 U of 10/11/1960 BStBl. 1960 III 492 (taxable exchange); I R 38/70 of 10/30/1973, BStBl. 1974 II 255 (incorporation of branch); realisation of profits may be avoided under the special merger rules but not for contribution of individual assets.
79. On realisation of profits on transfer to treaty countries see BFH I 266/65 of 7/16/1969, BStBl. 1970 II 175; BFH I R 55/66 of 4/28/1971, BStBl. 1971 II 630; BFH I R 261/70 of 10/13/76, 1977 Finanz-Rundschau 124; there is no realisation on transfer to non-treaty countries, BFH VI 137/59 U of 9/30/1960, BStBl. 1960 III 489; the same realisation requirement applies to a situation where a taxpayer transfers assets from a business falling under one category of income (for example a commercial firm) to a business falling under another category (for example professional services), see BFH IV 72/65 of 3/16/1967, BStBl. 1967 III 318.
80. See BFH VIII 3/74 of 12/16/1975, BStBl. 1976 II 246.
81. See § 1 (1) Foreign Investment Act.
82. The enumeration of activities is similar to that applicable to the LDC Tax Act Reserve; see above text accompanying n. 49.
83. For another roll-over provision applicable to merger and reorganization situations see below IV.
84. See § 3 LDC Tax Act dating back to earlier similar earlier provisions since 1963.
85. The reserve may be continued if the assets are retained during the original three year's period in a corporation to which the partnership or branch have been transformed. On the violation of the three years' holding period profits are adjusted for the first and subsequent years in which the reserve for the asset sold has been set up; see § 175 (1) no. 2 Tax Code 1977.
86. There is no realisation of profits on transfer to a non-treaty country unless there is a change of categories of income; see above n. 79.
87. See above B.II.2.
88. See § 3 (4), § 1 (8) LDC Tax Act and above.
89. See § 3 (2) LDC Tax Act.
90. See § 3 (3) LDC Tax Act; see Decree above (n. 53).
91. If an asset is capable of being contributed only under German but not under LDC law its contribution to capital may be alike investment in the sense of § 3 (4), § 1 (7); see above n. 88.
92. See § 5 (2) Income Tax Act; § 153 (3) Stock Corporations Act; on contributions in kind of self-produced know-how under LDC Tax Act see Müller, 25 Betrieb 1552-1553 (1972).
93. Uses have been held to be incapable of being contributed in a domestic setting; see BFH I 139/59 S of 11/8/1960, BStBl. 1962 III 338; I 203/61 S of 3/9/1962, BStBl. 1962 III 338; I R 41/66 of 2/3/1971, BStBl. 1971 II 408. The tax administration did not acquiesce in these holdings in respect of foreign corporations (Finance Ministry Lower Saxony S 2741-37-312 of 2/25/1970, Betrieb 1970, 469) but appears to deny constructive contributions

of uses now relying on profit adjustments under § 1 Foreign Tax Relations Act (equivalent to sec. 481 IRC) instead. For non-contributability Döllerer, Verdeckte Gewinnausschüttungen und verdeckte Einlagen bei Kapitalgesellschaften, p. 119; contra Meilicke/Meilicke, Nutzungsüberlassung von Gegenständen als offene oder verdeckte Einlage bei Kapitalgesellschaften in Handels-, Bilanz- und Steuerrecht, 30 Betrieb 927-933 (1977).

94. See Flick, Keine Gewinnrealisierung bei Einbringung von Entwicklungsländergesellschaften, 13 DStR 217-218 (1975).

95. See Herrmann/Heuer, ibid., § 6 Annot. 8.

96. There are no domestic profits, viz. no profits taxable in Germany, where a foreign branch is incorporated and the branch profits resulting therefrom are exempt under the usual German DTA provisions.

97. See § 4 (1) LDC Tax Act; see also n. 78 above.

98. See § 4 (2) LDC Tax Act.

99. See § 1 (3), (8) LDC Tax Act and above text accompanying n. 37, 49.

100. See § 4 (1) last clause LDC Tax Act, § 6 b (3) – (5) Income Tax Act.

101. See § 4 (3) LDC Tax Act.

102. See n. 2 above.

103. See § 34 c Income Tax Act; § 26 (1) Corporation Tax Act.

104. § 68 c Income Tax Regulations.

105. See State Decrees of 7/8/1959, BStBl. 1959 II 109, and of 11/26/1970, BStBl. 1970 I 1074.

106. Often confirmed by case law, e.g. BFH I R 150/73 of 2/25/1976 BStBl. 1976 II 454.

107. See § 2 Foreign Investment Tax Act.

108. See § 3 Foreign Investment Tax Act.

109. See § 26 (3) Corporation Tax Act.

110. See § 3 (1) Foreign Investment Tax Act.

111. Rädler, Tax Treatment of Interest flowing from developing countries, XXI Canadian Tax Journal 28-34 (1973).

112. German Chamber of Industry and Commerce (Deutsche Industrie- und Handelskammer), Hohe Hürden für Lizenzen, 1975; Menck, Steuerliche Förderung des Transfers von Patenten und Lizenzen in Entwicklungsländer, 1976 Intertax 209-219 (with summary in English).

113. Credit for tax deemed paid; see Krause, Steuerliche Massnahmen der Industriestaaten zur Förderung von Investitionen in Entwicklungsländer unter besonderer Berücksichtigung der fiktiven Anrechnung ausländischer Steuern, 1979 Intertax 99-105.

114. § 102 (2) Valuation Act; see also above n. 7.

115. § 9 no. 7 Trade Tax Act; § 12 (3) no. 4 Trade Tax Act; see also above n. 6.

116. § 5 Foreign Investment Tax Act.

117. § 7 (1) LDC Tax Act.

118. § 7 (2), (3) LDC Tax Act; the reserve is taken into account for taxes on capital even if disallowed by the loss clause of § 1 (7) for profits taxes.

Italy

Giuseppe Bisconti *
Bruno Gangemi *

I. BRIEF OUTLINE OF THE ITALIAN INCOME TAX SYSTEM

A. General

For a better understanding of the subject matter we shall briefly outline the Italian Income Tax system as it results from the 1974 tax reform, limiting the analysis to those taxes which are relevant to this report, *i.e.*, the Corporate Income Tax and the Personal Income Tax. Consequently, we will not consider the Local Income Tax (which applies only to income produced in Italy) nor the Tax on Increase in Value of Real Estate (which applies only to real estate in Italy).

(1) Corporate Income Tax ('Imposta sul reddito delle persone giuridiche'), governed by Presidential Decree No. 598 of September 29, 1973 as subsequently implemented and/or amended (hereinafter referred to as 'Decree No. 598'), is assessed at a flat rate of 25% on income of corporations ('Societa' per Azioni'), limited liability companies ('societa' a responsabilita' limitata'), partnerships limited by shares ('societa' in accomandita per azioni'), cooperative enterprises ('societa' cooperative'), mutual insurance companies and other public and private entities engaged in commercial, financial and industrial activities and having their registered office or administrative headquarters or principal object in Italy. The Corporate Income Tax is assessed on all income of any nature from all sources ('worldwide' or 'residence' tax principle).

Foreign companies of any type are subject to Corporate Income Tax with regard to the income from their permanent establishments in Italy as well as to income from real estate and interest income from sources located in Italy.

(2) Personal Income Tax ('Imposta sul reddito delle persone fisiche'), governed by Presidential Decree No. 597 of September 29, 1973 as subsequently implemented and/or amended (hereinafter referred to as 'Decree No. 597'), is assessed on a progressive scale (from 10% on income of up to Lire 3,000,000 to 72% on income exceeding Lire 550,000,000) on the income of individuals. Income from sole proprietorships as well as income attributable to partners of informal partnerships ('societa' semplici'), general partnerships ('societa' in nome collectivo') and limited partnerships ('societa' in accomandita semplice') is subject to Personal Income Tax.

Personal Income Tax applies to Italian residents on income from all sources either in Italy or abroad ('worldwide' or 'residence' tax principle).

* Studio Legale Bisconti, Rome.

Non-residents are subject to Personal Income Tax only with respect to income produced in Italy. For tax purposes, residents are those individuals who are registered in Italian population registries or maintain the principal seat of their business in Italy or reside in Italy for more than six months in a calendar year.

B. Computation of Foreign Source Income

Article 14 of Presidential Decree No. 600 of September 29, 1973 which establishes the accounting records required for business enterprises, provides that taxpayers subject to corporate income tax and individual entrepreneurs, who carry out commercial activities through permanent establishments abroad, are required to record separately in their books the operational items which relate to their foreign permanent establishments, computing separately the operating results of each such establishment.

Except for the above-mentioned provision, there are no other specific rules concerning the computation of foreign source income. Consequently, taxable income from sources outside Italy is calculated, and income taxes are assessed, in accordance with general rules on income and corporate taxation. As a rule, Corporate and Personal Income Taxes apply on the aggregate income, irrespective of the nature and source of same. In particular, business income is computed on the basis of the Profit and Loss Statement which all entrepreneurs, whether subject to Personal Income Tax or to Corporate Income Tax, are required to attach to their annual tax return.

Business income produced abroad through a permanent establishment is taxable in Italy irrespective of whether or not it is remitted to Italy. Business income of a foreign subsidiary of an Italian company (or of a foreign company owned by Italian shareholders) is taxable in Italy at the time it is distributed.

With regard to losses incurred abroad, if same are incurred by a subsidiary of an Italian Company, such losses are not deductible by the parent company; the negative results of the foreign subsidiary may be reflected in the balance sheet of the Italian company by writing down the value of the stock in the foreign subsidiary. If the losses are incurred by a foreign branch of an Italian company, they are deductible and the Italian company can carry said losses forward for five years.

Interest on loans, fees for technical, administrative and management services as well as royalties for licenses concerning patent rights, know-how, trademarks etc., are components of business income.

Dividends are also included in business income but are not subject to Local Income Tax.

C. Tax credit

Income taxes assessed by foreign countries on income produced in such countries and which is subject to Personal or Corporate Income Taxes in Italy are, in principle, allowed as tax credits in accordance with the provisions which will be hereinafter examined in detail.

II. LACK OF ANY SPECIFIC TAX INCENTIVES FOR INVESTMENT IN DEVELOPING COUNTRIES

Italian income tax laws do not provide for any incentives for investment in developing countries, neither in the form of depreciation or other special allowances, tax-free reserves, etc., nor in the form of exemption from, or reduction of, income taxes on income from such foreign sources.

In this regard, it should be noted that various tax incentive methods have been and are widely utilized by the Italian Government to channel investments into Southern Italy as well as to facilitate the industrialization of other areas in Italy. For instance, income derived from new plants of Italian or foreign companies located in Southern Italy for a period of ten years is exempt from Local Income Tax (otherwise levied at the rate of approximately 15%) and is subject to Corporate Income Tax at a lower rate (12½% instead of 25%).

It is necessary however to mention some tax benefits provided for by Law No. 227 of May 24, 1977, concerning the insurance and financing of credits relative to exportation of goods and services as well as to work contracts to be carried out abroad, even though such benefits are not specifically destined to developing countries. For example, under article 32 of the aforementioned law, interest on bonds issued abroad by foreign entities in favor of Italian banking institutions in connection with financing granted by the latter is exempt from the 30% withholding tax which, as a rule, would otherwise apply to said interest. Interest on bonds and similar securities issued by Italian banking institutions in connection with export financing is exempt from the 10% withholding tax which would otherwise apply. Promissory notes or similar instruments issued in Italy or abroad in favor of Italian entrepreneurs or banking institutions in connection with export financing are exempt from stamp duty tax. The normal stamp duty tax rate is respectively 8 per 1,000 and 5 per 1,000 for promissory notes payable in Italy or abroad. Moreover, the guarantees relating to export financing are exempt from the 0.25% registration tax. In addition, insurance and reinsurance of the export financing is exempt from the insurance tax which applies at 2% of the premiums. The above benefits apply provided the financing relates to exportation of Italian goods or to projects, engineering, work contracts and services performed abroad by Italian entrepreneurs.

Equivalent benefits were available to Italian exporters under Law No. 131 of February 28, 1967. It may be of interest to note that the amount of financing that benefitted from the provisions of Law No. 131 from January 1, 1970 through December 31, 1976 has been Lire 4,725 billion of which Lire 3,438 billion were utilized in relation to exports to developing countries.

III. ANALYSIS OF THE PRESENT TAX CREDIT SYSTEM

A. General

As hereinabove mentioned, the 1974 tax reform has adopted the worldwide tax principle, abandoning the principle of territoriality previously in force for several decades. As a rule, with minor exceptions concerning complementary tax for individuals and excess profits tax for companies, under the old tax system, only income produced in Italy was subject to taxation. The worldwide tax principle in most cases is mitigated by the adoption of a built-in system for the prevention or lessening of double taxation on income from foreign sources. From among the various methods, Italy has elected the 'credit' method.

Aside from the provisions contained in the large number of treaties for the avoidance of double taxation to which Italy is a party, the credit system is, at present, the only unilateral relief available. However, with regard to developing countries, this method turns out to be wholly insufficient.

B. Present Tax Credit System

Article 18 of Decree No. 597 and Article 9 of Decree No. 598 provide that, if income earned abroad is included in the computation of the taxable base, taxes finally paid abroad upon such income shall be recognized as credits against personal income tax or corporate income tax to the extent to which the foreign taxing country grants a tax credit for income of the same nature earned in Italy, but in any event in an amount not greater than two-thirds nor lower than 25% of that part of the Italian tax (i.e. personal income tax or corporate income tax on worldwide income) which is proportional to the ratio between foreign source income and aggregate income. If the foreign country does not grant a tax credit, a credit shall be allowed but in an amount not exceeding 25% of said proportion.

If income is produced in more than one foreign country, the credit shall be applied separately with respect to each country.

The credit must be claimed in the tax return relating to the year in which the foreign taxes have been finally paid, or the right there to shall be forfeited. If the tax due in Italy for the year in which the foreign income was included in the taxable base has already been settled, a new settlement shall be prepared taking into account any increase in foreign source income and the credit shall be applied to the annual return in which it was claimed. If the period of limitation for assessment has already expired, the credit shall be limited to that part of the foreign tax proportional to the part of foreign source income subjected to tax in Italy. If the credit is greater than the amount of tax determined for the year in which the credit is allowed, the taxpayer shall be entitled to a refund of the excess.

The wording of the above provision seems prima facie to mirror the tax credit clause included in the income tax codes of most of the countries which adopt the residence principle of taxation.

However, as the credit is allowed only for taxes 'finally' paid abroad, the Italian taxpayer is faced with the problem of determining what 'finally paid' means in the foreign taxing country. If 'finally paid' means that the tax is no longer subject to assessment by the tax authorities (i.e., that the period of limitations has run or the court decision on that tax case is no longer subject to appeal) the credit against the Italian taxes may be delayed for a substantial period of time.

Furthermore, with specific regard to developing countries, it can be noted that:

(i) the tax codes of the developing countries seldom embody a tax credit clause which, in view of their limited investment abroad, would not have any practical meaning;

(ii) the Italian tax credit system, limited up to two-thirds of the Italian tax which is proportional to the ratio between foreign source income and aggregate income, would be a very limited incentive in all the cases in which the foreign corporate income tax rates are higher than 25%;

(iii) several developing countries offer income tax benefits to foreign investors. The tax credit method, as presently adopted, in the absence of a 'tax sparing' provision, obviously nullifies the benefits received abroad by an Italian investor.

IV. TAX TREATIES

Among the large number of tax treaties to which Italy is party, the only ones with developing countries are the treaty with Egypt, the treaty with Trinidad and Tobago and the treaty with Zambia.

The treaty with Egypt, signed on March 26, 1966, does not provide any specific incentives for Italian investment in Egypt.

On the contrary, Article 22, paragraph 4, of the treaty with Trinidad and Tobago, signed on March 26, 1971, provides that the Italian tax authorities in calculating the credit relative to Trinidad and Tobago taxes, shall include the taxes which have not actually been paid by virtue of a temporary exemption granted in that country. A similar tax sparing clause is included in the treaty between Italy and Zambia, signed on October 27, 1972, but not yet ratified. Article 22, paragraph 3, of said treaty provides that for tax credit purposes 'Zambian tax payable' shall be deemed to include any amount which would have been payable as Zambian tax, but for an exemption or reduction granted under the Pioneer Industries (Relief from Income Tax) Act, 1965, or any other Zambian law of similar purpose and effect.

One should also mention Article 19, paragraph 2, of the treaty between Italy and Israel signed on April 22, 1968 and Article 22, paragraph 2, of the treaty between Italy and Greece signed on March 19, 1965 which provides for tax sparing clauses similar to the one contained in Article 22 of the above-mentioned treaty with Trinidad and Tobago.

V. CONCLUSIONS

It appears that the 1974 tax reform, by adopting the worldwide tax principle, has worsened the tax position of Italian investment in developing countries, as compared with the tax position resulting from the prior territoriality tax principle.

The tax credit system, as adopted, does not represent a sufficient relief. On the contrary, it may nullify the benefits granted by developing countries to foreign investors.

The negative consequences which may derive from the present method have been repeatedly pointed out in the course of Parliament hearings devoted to the discussion of the tax reform.

In particular, the Honourable Pandolfi, present Italian Minister of Finance, pointed out the advisability to exclude, under particular circumstances, from the taxable base the income produced abroad 'for reasons of economic policies especially in relation to developing countries'.

The lack of any specific tax incentive to Italian investment abroad, if compared with the tax incentives granted to investment in Southern Italy, is due to the fact that the Italian tax system substantially reflects the economic policy of the Government which is aimed to encourage the industrialization of Southern Italy.

Japan*

Gary M. Thomas **

I. TAX PATTERN IN GENERAL

A. Taxation of Residents and Domestic Corporations

Japan imposes its income tax upon Japanese residents and domestic juridical persons (corporations and other legal entities) upon their worldwide income (*Income Tax Law* (Law No. 33 of 1965; hereinafter, 'ITL'), art. 7(1); *Juridical Persons Tax Law* (Law No. 34 of 1965; hereinafter, 'JPTL'), art. 5). A resident of Japan is an idividual who has his domicile in Japan or who has resided in Japan continuously for one year or more (ITL, art. 2(iii)). A domestic juridical person is a juridical person with its head office, office or main office within Japan (JPTL, art. 2(iii)). The terms 'head office" and 'main office' are not defined in the tax law, but the Japanese tax officials interpret this to refer to the formal head office stated in the articles of incorporation of the juridical person. (However, some scholarly concern exists as to whether a foreign corporation with no substantial office outside of Japan may be considered to be a domestic corporation).

Though Japan taxes its residents and domestic juridical persons on their worldwide income, in order to avoid double taxation the tax law allows a foreign tax credit to be taken for foreign income taxes assessed against the foreign source income of such residents or domestic juridical persons determined under Japanese source rules (ITL, art. 95; JPTL, art. 69(1)). In addition, an indirect credit is allowed for the foreign corporate income taxes assessed upon the profits underlying the dividends distributed by foreign subsidiaries to their Japanese corporate shareholders (JPTL, art. 69(4)).

As a general rule, the non-Japanese source income of foreign subsidiaries of Japanese shareholders is not subject to Japanese income taxation until distributed as dividends to shareholders in Japan. However, under legislation enacted in 1978, the undistributed income of certain foreign subsidiaries of Japanese shareholders established in prescribed low-tax countries will be attributed (in pro rata shares) to and included in the gross income of the Japanese shareholder (*Tax Special Measures Law* (Law No. 29 of 1957; hereinafter, 'TSML'), arts. 40-4 and 66-6).

Individuals are taxed upon their personal income according to progressive rates which range from 10 percent to 75 percent (ITL, art. 89). The 50 percent tax bracket (incremental rate of 50 percent) is reached at a taxable income level of 15 million yen ($69.767 at $1/Y215).

* This study is part of a larger work on Japanese law that Mr. Thomas is writing for the Harvard International Tax Program and Mr. Thomas reserves the right to use this therein.

** Baker & McKenzie, Tokyo.

The Japanese corporate tax burden is comprised of three taxes, the juridical persons tax (national corporate tax), the inhabitants tax (prefectural tax), and the business activities tax (prefectural income tax).

The Juridical Persons Tax standard rate is 40 percent (JPTL, art. 66). However, under the split-rate integration system effective in Japan, a reduced rate of 30 percent is applicable with respect to that income earmarked for dividend distribution (TSML, art. 42).

The Inhabitants Tax is imposed by each prefectural or municipality within a range prescribed in law. The maximum rate (used in major metropolitan areas) is 20.7 percent of the juridical persons tax amount. *(Local Tax Law* (Law No. 226 of 1950; hereinafter, 'LTL'), arts. 51 and 314-6).

The Business Activities Tax is also imposed according to rates imposed by local governments within a prescribed range. The maximum rate (used in major metropolitan areas) is 13 percent (LTL, art. 72-22). The Business Activities Tax is imposed upon corporate income for the previous year and is a deductible expense for purposes of computing the current year's taxable corporate income.

The overall tax rate imposed upon large corporations is approximately 54 percent (adjusted for the deduction of the business activities tax) where no dividends are distributed. If all profits are distributed as dividends, then this burden is reduced to approximately 43.5 percent.

B. Taxation of Nonresidents and Foreign Corporations

Nonresidents and foreign juridical persons are taxed only upon their domestic (i.e. Japanese) source income determined according to Japanese source rules (ITL, art. 7(1)(iii); JPTL, art. 9). Non-residents are individuals other than residents, whereas foreign juridical persons are juridical persons other than domestic juridical persons (ITL, art. 2(1)(v); JPTL, art. 2(v)). A foreign corporation is thus one which is established outside of Japan. Because the rules for nonresidents and foreign corporations are similar, for the sake of brevity only the rules applicable to foreign corporations will be discussed herein.

Japanese source income is determined according to a set of specific rules generally similiar to US rules (*see,* JPTL, art. 138).

However, the tax base (the scope of domestic source income taxable) for foreign corporations depends upon the nature of the contracts of such corporations with Japan. Japanese domestic tax law applies a permanent establishment concept similar to that found in the OECD Model Convention, with some important exceptions.

In accordance with the force of attraction doctrine applicable under domestic law, if a foreign corporation has a fixed place of business-type of permanent establishment in Japan, it will be subject to the full corporate tax rates on a net basis in Japan on the total amount of its Japanese source income (JPTL, art. 141(i)). However, under a modified attributable income principle, if a foreign corporation merely has an agent-type, or a construction-type, permanent establishment in Japan, then it is taxed at the full rates on a net basis upon the total amount of its Japanese source income except certain forms of income (primarily investment income) not attributable to such permanent establishment (JPTL, art. 141 (ii) and (iii)). The latter income will be subject at most to a withholding tax on a gross basis at the statutory rate of 20 percent, in the absence of an applicable treaty. (ITL, art. 179).

If a foreign corporation has no permanent establishment in Japan, then it is subject to taxation at the full rates only upon certain limited forms of income and by withholding upon other prescribed income, primarily investment income (JPTL, art. 141(iv)).

Since foreign corporations are taxed in Japan only upon their Japanese source income, there is no need to extend the application of the foreign tax credit thereto.

The normal tax rates applicable to foreign corporations are generally the same as those for domestic corporations, with the important exception that the reduced rate on income earmarked for dividends is not available to foreign corporations.

C. Tax Treaties

Japan has concluded income tax conventions with approximately thirty countries. These income tax conventions are generally based upon the OECD Model Convention of 1963, with some variations.

II. TAX INCENTIVES RELATIVE TO DEVELOPING COUNTRIES

A. In General

Japan provides a number of incentives in its tax laws to its residents and domestic corporations for investing in or otherwise operating in or with developing countries. As the provisions dealing with residents and corporations are generally similar, the sake of simplicity and brevity, we shall discuss only the provisions which relate to corporations.

Generally speaking, three fundamental devices are employed to provide incentives for foreign related operations: (i) a foreign tax credit (ii) special reserves for foreign investments or operations, and (iii) special deductions for certain prescribed foreign-related income.

Japan has also entered into income tax treaties with a number of developing countries. The treaties serve primarily to avoid double taxation by prescribing uniform source rules to be applied in both Japan and the particular contracting state and by guaranteeing a tax credit for foreign taxes assessed by the other state. In addition, withholding rates on investment income are frequently reduced and sometimes eliminated. Finally, Japan's tax treaties with developing countries frequently contain 'tax-sparing' provisions under which Japan will honor various tax benefits granted in the other contracting state or under the treaty by allowing as a credit against Japanese tax the amount of local tax which would have been assessed in the absence of such special treatment under local law or a reduction of tax under the income tax treaty.

B. Foreign Tax Credit

1. Direct Foreign Tax Credit

Japanese tax law allows its domestic corporations to take, as a yen-for-yen credit against their Japanese tax burden, a foreign tax credit for foreign taxes assessed upon their foreign source income (JPTL, art. 69). This foreign tax credit serves to avoid double taxation and to thus remove a possible disincentive to invest in developing countries.

The foreign taxes subject to the credit must be taxes which are equivalent to the Japanese juridical persons tax and which are assessed under the laws of the foreign country or a political subdivision thereof (JPTL, art. 69(1), JPTL Enf. O., art. 141(1) and (2)).

The creditable foreign taxes, however, are subject to a limitation similar to that found in US law. In short, the amount of foreign taxes which are creditable is limited to the lessor of the following (JPTL, art. 69(1); JPTL Enf. O., art. 142(1)):

(i) the amount of foreign taxes actually paid, or
(ii) the figure resulting from the following formula:

$$\text{total Japanese corporate tax on worldwide taxable income under Japanese tax law} \times \frac{\text{foreign-source taxable income under Japanese tax law}}{\text{world wide taxable income under Japanese tax law}}$$

Foreign source income is income other than domestic source income as determined in accordance with the source rules applicable under Japanese law, unless different rules are provided in applicable tax treaty, in which case the latter rules prevail (JPTL, art. 139, JPTL Enf. O., art. 142(3)).

Foreign source taxable income is to be determined in accordance with the provisions in Japanese tax law (JPTL Enf. O., art. 142(3)). The actual computations, including the treatment of losses and the allocation of deductions between foreign source and domestic source income, are extremely complicated and beyond the scope of this paper.

2. Indirect Foreign Tax Credit

An indirect tax credit is allowed to Japanese corporate shareholders for foreign taxes assessed against the profits of foreign subsidiaries of those shareholders which constitute the basis for the dividends distributed thereby (JPTL, art. 69(4)).

The indirect tax credit is available only with respect to foreign subsidiaries which satisfy a number of conditions. First, the foreign subsidiary must be a foreign juridical person of which 25 percent or more of the total voting shares thereof were owned by the domestic shareholders continuously for at least six months prior to the date upon which the dividends were declared (JPTL, art.

69(4); JPTL Enf. O., art. 146(i)). Second, the foreign subsidiary must be a company the purpose of which is to conduct its business activities by itself (JPTL, art. 69(4); JPTL Enf. O., art. 146(ii)). In other words, it must not be a mere holding company or a paper company. And, third, the foreign subsidiary must not have been established principally for the purpose of reducing taxes (JPTL, art. 69(4); JPTL Enf. O., art. 146(ii)).

The amount of foreign taxes creditable under the indirect credit provisions is determined by the following formula (JPTL, art. 69(4); JPTL Enf. O., art. 147):

$$\text{foreign juridical persons tax amount pertaining to dividends of the foreign subsidiary} \times \frac{\text{amount of dividends received by the parent company}}{\text{amount of taxable income of the subsidiary less the amount of foreign juridical persons tax paid thereon}}$$

The income of the foreign subsidiary for purposes of the indirect credit is the greater of the following: (i) the amount of income constituting the basis for the computation of the amount of dividends (i.e. business accounting income) or (ii) the amount of income computed in accordance with the tax laws of the country of residence of the foreign subsidiary, with prescribed adjustments (JPTL Enf. O., art. 147(2)(iv)).

Japanese law requires that the shareholder, if it elects to take the indirect tax credit, must gross-up its income in the amount of the foreign taxes to be credited (JPTL, art. 28).

The details concerning the computation of the indirect tax credit, including the timing problems, are highly complex and beyond the scope of this paper.

3. Tax Sparing Credit

No tax sparing credits are permitted under Japanese domestic tax law. However, Japan has granted such credits to domestic corporations by means of treaties. Reference is made in this respect to the discussion presented below at H.2.

C. Reserves for Foreign Investments

1. Overseas Investment Loss Reserve

a. In General

Japanese tax law permits the establishment of a number of reserves *(jumbikin)* which may create an incentive to invest abroad in specified regions or for specified purposes. Though often couched in terms which read as if the reserves are intended to be contingent liability reserves to provide for the possible decline in value of the foreign investment, the majority view in Japanese tax and accounting circles is that such reserves are more properly characterized as a mere retention of earnings. In most cases they do not result in an absolute exemption from tax but merely a deferral of tax, as the amounts credited to the reserve account in the year of investment must ordinarily be brought back into income within a specified period of time.

b. Qualified Investments

The investments which are subject to the provisions of the overseas investment loss reserve are limited to those specifically provided in the tax law. These are investments in so-called 'specified corporations' which include (i) specified overseas business corporations; (ii) specified investment corporations; (iii) natural resource development business corporations; (iv) natural resource development investment corporations; (v) natural resource exploration business corporations; (vi) natural resource exploration investment corporations; and (vii) used nuclear fuel re-processing business corporations. The nature of the permissible investments, i.e. equity, debt or both, varies with the category of the recipient corporations, as does the amount which may be credited to the reserve account. The investor must be a domestic corporation.

(1) Specified Overseas Business Corporations

A specified overseas business corporation is defined to be a juridical person (excluding natural resource development business corporations, natural resource development investment corporations, natural resource exploration business corporations, and natural resource exploration investment corporations), which (i) has its head office (i.e. is established) in a developing region, (ii) is engaged in manufacturing, construction, agriculture, forestry, fisheries, marine horticulture, or mining, (iii) operates its business activities solely within the developing region, and (iv) was not established in such developing region principally for tax reasons (TSML, art. 55(3)(i); (*Tax Special Measures Law Enforcement Order* (Cabinet Order No. 43 of 1957, hereinafter, 'TSML Enf. O.'), art. 32-2 (5), (6)). Consequently, for example, foreign corporations engaged in retailing, wholesaling, or service industries are not qualified investments.

'Developing regions' included the following specified territories: (i) within Europe: Iceland, Spain, Portugal, Malta, Greece, Turkey and Cyprus; and (ii) outside Europe: all areas other than Japan (including Okinawa), the United States and affiliated regions, Canada, USSR, Australia, New Zealand, and South Africa (TSML Enf. O., art. 32-2(4)).

In order to take advantage of the resource, the domestic corporation making the investment must hold, itself or in cooperation with other domestic corporations acting as joint venture partners, ten (10) percent or more of the issued shares of the foreign corporation on the last day of the taxable year including the date of the acquisition of the shares in said corporation (TSML, arts. 55(1) and 55(3)(xiv)).

The domestic corporation may make its investment either by acquiring shares or obligations in conjunction with a capital increase, or by purchasing shares from a foreign third party (TSML, art. 55(1)).

In the former case, the investment must consist of so-called 'capital increase shares, etc.', which are defined to include (i) shares of stock in a specified overseas business corporation which was established or which effected a capital increase during the taxable year. including a stock dividend or a transfer of all or a portion of the accumulated profits to its capital account, which shares were acquired by payment by the domestic corporation or in conjunction with the capital increase, and (ii) specified obligations, defined to be loans extended to, or debentures issued by, a specified overseas business corporation with a redemption period of ten years or more in conjunction with the acquisition of shares by the domestic corporation, under circumstances recognized to present difficulties relative to the acquisition of shares (TSML, art. 55(3)(ix) (a) and (c); TSML Enf. O., art. 32-2(13). These circumstances are the following: (i) all or a portion of the shares of the foreign corporation are owned by the Government of Japan or a local public body thereof or by a foreign national or local government: (ii) the foreign entity does not issue shares; (iii) the laws of the local country or the articles of association of the foreign corporation prohibit or restrict the investment by Japanese corporations; or (iv) the procurement of funds by the foreign corporation does not accord with an investment by a Japanese corporation (TSML Enf. O., art. 32-2(14)). Additional requirements are that the obligor must not be a listed company and the obligations must not be secured by property located within Japan or guaranteed by the domestic investor (TSML Enf. O., art. 32-2(13)). An application for a recognition of these facts just be sought and obtained from the Ministry of International Trade and Industry (hereinafter, MITI) (Tax Special Measures Law Enforcement Regulations, (Finance Ministerial Order No. 15 of 1957; hereinafter 'TSML Enf. Reg.'), art. 21-2(5)).

In the purchase situation, the shares (called 'purchased shares, etc.') are those issued by specified overseas business corporations which were owned until the date of transfer by non-resident individuals of foreign corporations the purchase of which constitutes a new foreign investment (TSML, art. 55(3)(x)).

(2) Specified Investment Corporations

A specified investment corporation is defined to be a domestic juridical person which has as its sole purpose the equity investment in, or the extension of long-term financing to, specified overseas business corporations defined in (1) above (or other specified investment corporations as defined herein) and which is recognized by MITI as contributing significantly to the promotion of overseas investment (TSML, art. 53(3)(ii); TSML Enf. O., art. 32-2(7); TSML Enf. Reg., art. 21-2(1)).

The minimum shareholding requirement for investment in a specified investment corporation is only one (1) percent (TSML, art. 55(1)).

The domestic corporation making the investment must do so by the acquisition of capital increase shares, defined for specified investment corporations to include (i) shares issued by specified investment corporations which were established or which effected a capital increase (including by means of a stock dividend or transfer to the capital account of accumulated profits) during the taxable year, which shares were acquired by means of payment by the domestic corporation and (ii) specified obligations defined above (TSML, arts. 55(1) and 55(3)(ix) (b)). It may not make the investment by purchasing such shares from a third party.

(3) Natural Resource Development Business Corporations

A natural resource development business corporation is defined to include (i) juridical persons (either domestic or foreign) the business activity of which currently is limited to the exploration, development, or extraction of natural resources, including petroleum, natural gas, metallic minerals, coal, and timber, in areas outside of Japan; (ii) juridical persons the business activity of which currently is limited to the exploration, development or extraction of petroleum (including liquid natural gas) within Japan; and (iii) juridical persons conducting the activities mentioned in (i) and (ii) above but which are owned by either the Government of Japan or a foreign national government (TSML, art. 55(3)(iv); TSML Enf. O., art. 32-2(8)).

As described above in relation to specified overseas business corporations, a domestic corporation may make its investment in a natural resource development business corporation either by means of acquiring shares or obligations due to a capital increase or by purchasing shares from a foreign third party (TSML, art. 55(1)). The technical requirements regarding the shares and long-term obligations are similar to those concerning the shares, etc. in overseas business corporations. However, in this case, the domestic corporation must receive, in addition, a recognition from MITI to the effect that the investment in the shares or the extension of long-term financing will promote the exploration and development of natural resources and contribute to the stable supply of natural resources for Japan (TSML, art. 55(3)(xii); TSML Enf. O., art. 32-2 (17); TSML Enf. Reg., art. 21-2(8)).

(4) Natural Resource Development Investment Corporations

This is defined to be a juridical person (domestic or foreign the current business activities of which are recognized by MITI to be limited to (i) the provision of financing to natural resource development business corporations discussed above at (3) or (ii) such financing activities as well as natural resource development business activities (TSML, art. 55(3)(v); TSML Enf. O., art. 32-2(9); TSML Enf. Reg., art. 21-2(2)).

The domestic corporation may make the investment only by means of the acquisition of shares or long-term obligations in conjunction witha capital increase and not by purchasing shares from a third party (TSML, art. 55(1)).

(5) Natural Resource Exploration Business Corporations

Natural resource exploration business corporations are defined to include juridical persons which otherwise quality as natural resource development business corporations but whose current business activities are limited to the business of exploring for natural resources, as well as juridical persons engaged in such business activities which are owned by the Government of Japan or by foreign national government (TSML, art. 55(3)(vi)). In particular, this means corporations whose activities are limited to investigating the existence of re- of reserves of natural resources as well as studying the commercial feasibility of the extraction thereof (TSML, art. 32-2(10)).

The domestic corporation may make an investment in a natural resource exploration business corporation either by acquiring shares or long-term obligations due to a capital increase or by purchasing the shares thereof from a non-resident or a foreign corporation (TSML, arts. 55(1) and 55(3)(xiii)).

(6) Natural Resource Exploration Investment Corporations

A natural resource exploration investment corporation is defined to be a juridical person which otherwise qualifies as a natural resource development investment corporation but which has received a recognition from MITI to the effect that it's current business activity is principally the provision of financing for natural resource exploration business corporations or the provision of such financing in addition to the exploration for natural resources (TSML, art. 55(3)(vii); TSML, Enf. O., art. 32-2(11); TSML Enf. Reg., art. 21-2(3)).

In order to take advantage of the reserve, the domestic corporation must make the investment by means of the acquisition of shares or long-term obligations pursuant to a capital increase but not by purchasing shares from non-residents or foreign corporations (TSML, art. 55(3)).

(7) Used Nuclear Fuel Re-Processing Business Corporations

A used nuclear fuel re-processing business corporation is defined to be a foreign juridical person the current business of which is the processing of used nuclear fuel by chemical means in order to separate nuclear materials and other usable materials from nuclear materials which were used as fuel in electricity-generating nuclear furnaces (TSML, art. 55(3)(iii)).

This is a new provision enacted in 1978. The official commentary of the Ministry of Finance states that the reprocessing of nuclear waste involves the situation wherein the Japanese electric power companies must mandate the re-processing to foreign firms (which control the production of the fuel) but must nevertheless provide financing by means of long-term loans for the erection of re-processing plants. This results in the risk for the Japanese firm involved that a huge loss could arise upon the failure to recover the loan proceeds, due to conditions concerning the re-processing, such as the uncertainty involved in re-processing technology (see Kaisai Zeiho no Subete - Showa 53 Nen (The Complete Amended Tax Law - 1978), (Kokuzeicho (National Tax Agency); Tokyo, 1978), p. 141).

The investment must be made in the form of so-called 'used nuclear fuel re-processing business obligations' (TSML, art. 55(1)). A used nuclear fuel re-processing business obligation is defined to be an obligation pertaining to a loan to a used nuclear fuel re-processing business corporation by a domestic juridical person, which satisfies certain conditions to the effect that the acquisition of the obligation contributes to the efficient utilization of used nuclear fuel within Japan (TSML, art. 55(3)(xi)). More concretely, this will be an obligation which a domestic corporation acquires in conjunction with the mandate of the re-processing activities to a used nuclear fuel re-processing business corporation, all or a part of the proceeds of which are to be used for the construction of facilities for such re-processing. (TSML Enf O., art. 32-2(xvi); TSML Enf. Reg., art. 21-2(7)).

c. Qualified Taxpayers

According to the literal provision in the Law, the corporations allowed to take advantage of the overseas investment loss reserve are limited to those domestic juridical persons which file a Blue Return (a special return available only to juridical persons meeting certain bookkeeping and accounting requirements) but which are not specified investment corporations other than special investment corporations or natural resource development investment corporations other than special investment corporations (TSML, art. 55(1)). In other words, qualified investors are limited to (i) domestic juridical persons which are not otherwise qualified as specified investment corporations or as natural resource development investment corporations and (ii) domestic juridical persons which are qualified as specified investment corporations or natural resource development investment corporations but which in addition qualify as so-called 'special investment corporations'.

A 'special investment corporation' is a juridical person otherwise qualifying as a specified investment corporation or a natural resource development investment corporation which makes investments, in either specified overseas investment corporations or natural resource business corporations, respectively, in an amount which exceeds its stated capital (TSML, art. 55(3)(viii)).

The purpose of this provision becomes apparent upon analysis of the relationship between the various qualified investments. Fundamentally, specified investment corporations and natural resource development investment corporations serve as vehicles through which to invest in specified overseas business corporations or natural resource development business corporations. As a matter of policy, however, in order to avoid the mutiple accumulation of overseas investment loss reserves with respect to be same investment, e.g. where the first-tier domestic corporation (the primary investor) makes its investment through a second-tier domestic corporation (either a specified investment corporation or a natural resource development investment corporation), the overseas investment loss reserve should not be granted to the latter corporations.

However, occasionally such specified investment corporations or natural resource development investment corporations will receive, in addition to the amounts invested as stated capital by the primary invester, loan funds from the Overseas Economic Cooperation Fund or the Export-Import Bank of Japan and subsequently direct these funds as well to the qualified investments. In this case, the establishment of the overseas investment loss reserve by the specified investment corporation or the natural resource development investment corporation, will be allowed, subject to the restriction that the acquisition cost of the investment for purposes of the reserve in this case is limited to the amount by which the total investment exceeds the stated capital of the investor (i.e., the amount of the other funds received which are invested).

d. Technical Aspects

The amount which may be deducted as an expense and credited in a particular year to the overseas investment loss reserve account is defined to be any amount up to a limit comprised of a specified percentage of the acquisition cost (or value) of shares received or the principal amount of obligations, as the case may be (TSML, art. 55(1). The appropriate amount must be credited to the reserve in the taxable year during which the investment is made.

Investment	*Percentage Deductible*
1. Specified Overseas Business Corporations	15
2. Specified Investment Corporations	15
3. Natural Resource Development Business Corporations	40
4. Natural Resource Development Investment Corporations	40
5. Natural Resource Exploration Business Corporations	100
6. Natural Resource Exploration Investment Corporations	100
7. Used Nuclear Fuel Re-Processing Business Corporations	40

Generally speaking, the total amount credited to the reserve may remain in the reserve account free of taxation up to a maximum of five years but beginning with the sixth year must be taken back into income at least in the amount of twenty (20) percent thereof per annum during the subsequent five-year period (TSML, art. 55(4)). In addition, the law provides that certain contingencies will result in the requirement to take back into income all or a portion of the amount credited to the reserve, including such situations as the disposition of the shares or obligations involved, failure to hold the requisite percentage of shares in the foreign corporation, change in status or dissolution of the foreign corporation, or a reduction in the book value of the shares or obligations involved (TSML, art. 55(5)). Finally, the domestic corporation may freely reverse the reserve in any amount and at any time, provided it satisfies the maximum five-year requirements outlined above (TSML, art. 55(5)(viii)).

2. Overseas Large-scale Construction Loss Reserve

In 1976, an addition was made to the overseas investment loss reserve whereby a domestic corporation engaged in certain large-scale construction projects overseas would be allowed to credit to a reserve a prescribed percentage of the expenditures made for the project.

a. *Qualified Taxpayers*

In order to take advantage of this provision, the taxpayer must satisfy the following conditions: (i) it must be a domestic juridical person qualified to file a Blue Return; (ii) it must have concluded a so-called 'specified overseas construction contract' during the period from April 1, 1976 until March 31, 1980; and (iii) it employ the 'percentage of completion' method of accounting in accordance with Japanese tax accounting rules continuously from the date of commencement of the construction project, in connection with the revenues from the long-term construction conducted pursuant to that specified overseas construction contract (TSML, art. 55(2)).

b. *Qualified Contracts*

A 'specified overseas construction contract' is one for which recognition has been applied and received from MITI with respect to the fact that it satisfies all of the following conditions: (i) the construction has been undertaken pursuant to a business plan which constitutes the subject of economic cooperation in accordance with an international agreement between the Government of Japan and a foreign country (limited to those countries located within the prescribed developing regions); (ii) the amount of the construction contract is in excess of one hundred billion yen; (iii) the construction period is in excess of three years; (iv) no other Japanese corporation has undertaken a similar project, on a similar scale, in that foreign country; (v) the other party to the contract (a) is a foreign government or other such juridical person, (b) is not a specified corporation for which an overesas investment loss reserve has been set up and (c) is not a juridical person which is in a family relationship with the domestic juridical person which concluded the contract; and (vi) the contract was concluded in a competitive bidding situation (TSML, art. 55(2) and (3) (xv); TSML Enf. O., art. 32-2(22)).

c. *Technical Aspects*

The domestic party to the contract may take as a current expense and credit to the reserve an amount equivalent to up to seven (7) percent of the total expenditures made for the cost of materials, labor expenses and other expenses during the taxable year, for the construction project (TSML, art. 55(2); TSML Enf. O., art. 32-2(3)).

As with the ordinary overseas investment loss reserve, the total amount credited to the reserve in a particular year may remain in the reserve account free of taxation up to a maximum five years but beginning with the sixth year must be taken back into income at least in the amount of twenty (20) percent thereof per annum over the subsequent five-year period (TSML, art. 55(4)). In addition, the domestic corporation may freely reverse the reserve in any amount and at any time, provided it satisfies the maximum five-year requirements (TSML, art. 55(5)(viii)). However, the total amount credited must be taken back into income on the date of the completion of the project or on the date upon which the contract fails to remain qualified as a specified overseas construction contract (TSML, art. 55(5)). Thus, even though the law would require only one-fifth of the amount credited to the reserve to be added back into taxable income annually beginning with the sixth year, it is generally believed that in the usual case the project would be completed within three to five years from the commencement thereof and, consequently, that the reserve will be reversed in toto at that time.

3. Incentive Effects

It is difficult to estimate the actual extent to which the overseas investment loss reserve or the overseas large-scale construction loss reserve encourage investment in developing countries.

The Ministry of Finance has yet to adopt a policy under which it would prepare an annual comprehensive tax expenditure budget similar to that prepared by the US Treasury. However, the MOF has published an abbreviated list which represents an attempt to identify revenue losses incurred due to various incentive measures.

According to the latest figures available, the revenue losses incurred due to the overseas investment loss reserve (including the overseas large-scale construction loss reserve) were 26 billion yen in 1975 and 20 billion yen in 1976 (Kaisei Zeiho no Subete - 51 Nendo Han (The Completed Amended Tax Law - 1976) (Okura Zeimu Kyokai: Tokyo, 1976) p. 11).

However, these total figures are not broken down into revenues losses incurred due to particular types of investments, such as investments in overseas business corporations or in natural resource development activities. Consequently, it is impossible to estimate benefits derive with respect to the different kinds of investments.

Also, of course, the revenue loss figures are somewhat misleading in that they do not take into account the fact that these revenues are not lost but merely deferred until the amounts credited to the reserves are brought back into income. At most, these figures seem to represent the total amount of interest-free loans made by the Government of Japan to the investing corporations for the period during which the amounts remain in the reserve tax-free.

It is also essential to take into account the degree to which the availability of the benefits are restricted by the requirement to acquire a 'recognition' from the Ministry of International Trade and Industry (MITI) to the effect that a particular investment satisfies the requirements of the reserve or 'will contribute' to the various economic objectives outlined in the various provisions. It is not clear how strictly MITI scrutinizes the subject investments.

In addition, the overseas large-scale construction loss reserve is drafted so as to reach only a limited range of construction activities. An official commentary published at the time of the enactment of this provision states that the projects likely to satisfy the requirements are such projects as 'the fertilizer plant and the petro-chemical plant in Iraq, the railroad construction plant in Iran, and the pipeline, etc. in Saudi Arabia' (Kaisei Zeiho no Subete - 51 Nendo Han (The Complete Amended Tax Laws - 1976), (Okura Zaimu Kyokai: Tokyo, 1976), p. 98).

Furthermore, it might be fair to say that, with or without tax incentives to engage in natural resource development or even in general business activities overseas, Japanese corporations would probably make such investments due to the serious shortage of natural resources in Japan as well as the increasing economic need to engage in direct investment abroad, for such reasons as congestion, high labor costs, and environmental controls at home.

As a final note, it should be pointed out that the benefits available for general overseas business investments under overseas investment loss reserve have been gradually reduced during recent years and it is believed that this trend is likely to continue.

D. Special Exemption for Overseas Technical, etc. Transaction Income

1. In General

The system of special exemptions for income derived from overseas, technical, etc. transactions was originally established in 1964. Prior to that time, Japan had maintained a wide-ranging system of special exemptions for export transactions but this system was substantially cut back when it was claimed to be in violation of GATT prohibitions on export subsidies. It was limited to extend only to technical and service transactions, such as the assignment (transfer) of industrial property rights and the provision of shipping services, etc. Though the scope of the provision was increased for a time, since 1971 the benefits have been reduced periodically and in 1972 were limited solely to income from the transfer or provision of industrial property rights and copyrights, and the provision of certain technical services. In 1976 and 1978, the exemptions were further reduced.

2. Scope of Overseas Technical, Etc. Transactions

Overseas technical, etc. transactions are defined to include the following (TSML, art. 58(2)):

(i) the assignments (transfer) or provision of industrial property rights, other rights concerning technology and production methods by means of special technology (i.e. know-how), which were acquired due to the results of the company's own research, where the consideration therefore is received by means of a so-called outward method of payment (defined below).

(ii) the assignment or provision of industrial property rights, etc., which were acquired based upon the results of the company's own research, where the consideration therefore was received by means of a method other than an outward method of payment, to a person who thereafter assigns or provides such industrial property rights, etc. to another and receives the consideration therefore by means of an outward method of payment;

(iii) the assignment or provision of copyrights (excluding exhibition rights for motion pictures) carried out by taking an outward method of payment as consideration (or, when the transaction is conducted through a third party, whereby that third party receives an outward method of payment as consideration); and

(iv) the provision of services involving research, planning, drafting, consulting, designing, supervising, or inspecting, which requires professional knowledge concerning chemical technology, in connection with the construction or manufacturing of production facilities or other things corresponding thereto, the provision of technical guidance concerning the agriculture or fishing industries, and the provision of services in connection with surveying, the consideration for which is received by means of an outward method of payment (or, when transaction is conducted through a third party, whereby that third party receives an outward method of payment as consideration).

It is readily apparent that the system is structured only to benefit those transactions which involve payment by means of a so-called 'outward method of payment.' An outward method of payment (defined in the *Foreign Exchange Control Law)* refers to methods of payment (e.g., bank certificates, government script, checks, exchange notes, or letters of credit) which are denominated in foreign currency or which may be used as a method of payment in a foreign country regardless of whether it is denominated in a foreign currency or other unit of currency (TSML, arts. 20(2)(i) and 58(2)(i); *Foreign Exchange and Foreign Trade Control Law* (Law No. 228 of 1949), art. 6(1)(viii)).

Consequently, the benefits of the system are directed only to income from transactions which generate foreign exchange for Japan.

3. Computation of Exempt Amount

The amount which may be deducted from the revenues received from qualified transactions, and which consequently is exempt from tax in Japan, is the lesser of (i) fifty (50) percent of the income of the domestic corporation, computed based upon the ordinary rules with prescribed adjustments, or (ii) the sum of thirty-five (35) percent of the gross revenues obtained from the assignment or provision of industrial property rights, etc. and twenty (20) percent of the gross revenues obtained from the assignment of copyrights or the provision of services (TSML, art. 58(1); TSML Enf. O., art. 34(1)). One-half of the ordinary income (adjusted) of the corporation thus constitutes the limitation upon the exemption.

4. Incentive Effects

The most recent figures available state that indicate that the revenues losses incurred due to the special deduction for income from overseas technical, etc. transactions amounted to 12 billion yen for 1975 but only 8 billion for 1976 (Kaisei Zeiho no Subete - 51 Nendo (The Complete Amended Tax Law - 1976) (Okura Zaimu Kyokai; Tokyo, 1976), p. 11).

It is noteworthy that this provision is designed to benefit only transactions which generate foreign exchange for Japan. Whether this is the primary reason for the provision is unclear. If it is, however, then it may be subject to reconsideration as Japan's foreign exchange surplus continues to grow.

E. Special Treatment for Overseas Mineral Exploration Activities

1. Exploration Reserve

As a number of other countries, Japan has employed the income tax system to provide benefits to companies engaged in mineral exploration activities both within and without Japan. Though the percentage depletion method per se has been rejected in Japan as an unfair system resulting an outright exemption from tax, Japan has enacted a provision whereby a corporation engaged in mining may establish an 'exploration reserve' ostensibly in order to prepare for expenditures made for new mineral deposit exploration expenses either within or without Japan (TSML, art. 58-2(1)). The corporation may take as a current deduction and credit into the reserve an amount not in excess of the lesser of either (i) thirteen (13) percent of the revenues derived from the sale of minerals extracted thereby or (ii) fifty (50) percent of the extraction income attributable to such sales (TSML, art. 58-2(1)). The amounts credited to the reserve must be reversed back into income at least three years later (TSML, art. 58-2(4)). Consequently, the reserve system alone does not result in an exemption but only deferral of tax.

2. Special Deduction for New Mineral Deposit Exploration Expenses

However, an outright exemption is ultimately obtained due to a special deduction for 'new mineral deposit exploration expenses'. In accordance with this special provision, the lesser of (i) the sum of new mineral deposit exploration expenses disbursed and the depreciation of exploration machinery and equipment taken during the taxable year, (ii) the amount in the exploration reserve which is reversed and taken into income during the taxable year, or (iii) the amount of ordinary income for the taxable year, may be deducted, over and above the amounts actually shown and deducted as expenses or depreciation (TSML, art. 58-3(1)). This can result in a 'double deduction' for the actual expenses incurred. The 'new mineral deposit exploration expenses' are defined to include expenses required for land quality investigations ar drilling etc. for exploratory purposes (TSML, art. 58-2 (3); TSML Enf. O., art. 34-2 (8) and (4)).

3. Overseas Exploration Reserve

In 1975, an additional provision was enacted to allow treatment similar to that under the exploration reserve where the domestic corporation doesn't extract the minerals itself but purchases them from a third party. Under this provision, a so-called 'domestic mining corporation' may establish an 'overseas exploration reserve' in order to provide for expenditures for new overseas mineral deposit exploration expenses. This reserve is currently in effect from April 1, 1975 until March 31, 1980. A 'domestic mining corporation' is defined to be a domestic juridical person (or a subsidiary thereof in which it holds at least 95 percent of the issued shares) which owns mines in Japan and which (together with its subsidiary) is recognized by MITI as conducting principally a mining business within Japan (TSML, art. 58-2(2); TSML Enf. O., art. 34-2(4); TSML Enf. O. Reg., art. 21-8(2)). This narrow definition serves to exclude such entities as petroleum refining companies and steel companies which may purchase substantial quantities of minerals from abroad but do not conduct local mining activities.

The domestic mining corporation is permitted to credit to the reserve, and take as a current deduction, an amount not in excess of fifty (50) percent of the 'overseas extraction income' attributable to the revenue derived from the sale of minerals (including the major metallic and non-metallic minerals) acquired from an 'overseas independent development corporation'. An 'overseas independent development corporation' is defined to be a foreign juridical person which has received a recognition from MITI to the effect that the following conditions have been satisfied: (i) the domestic mining corporation, and other domestic corporations which are joint venture partners thereof, have provided equity investment or long-term loans equal to or greater than fifty (50) percent of the capital thereof; (ii) the overseas independent development corporation owns an overseas mine which it developed by means of the funds received pursuant to such equity investment or long-term loans; and (iii) fifty (50) percent or more of the minerals extracted from the overseas mine were taken by Japanese corporations (TSML Enf. O., art. 34-2(5); TSML Enf. Reg., art. 21-8(3)).

The 'overseas extraction income' is the sum of the amounts of income derived based upon the following revenues less the sum of the amounts of losses related thereto: (i) revenues derived from the sale of raw minerals; (ii) revenues derived from the sale of refined minerals; and (iii) revenues derived from the sale of products manufactured from the minerals, which are attributable to the refined ore (TSML Enf. O., art. 34-2(6)).

The amounts credited to the reserve must be returned to income at the latest three years thereafter, provided, however, that the entire amount must be reversed immediately of the domestic corporation loses its qualifications as a domestic mining corporation (TSML, art. 58-2(3)-8)).

4. Special Deduction for Overseas New Mineral Deposit Exploration Expenses

In conjunction with the enactment of the overseas exploration reserve, a provision was established under which a special deduction for overseas new mineral deposit exploration expenses would be allowed for corporations maintaining an overseas exploration reserve (TSML, art. 58-3(2)). The computation of the special deduction in this case is conceptually similar to that discribed above concerning new mineral deposit exploration expenses but it is significantly more complicated. A detailed discussion of this computation is beyond the scope of this paper.

5. Incentive Effects

As with the overseas investment loss reserve discussed above, it is difficult to estimate the incentive effect provided by these various measures to benefit overseas mineral exploration activities.

The latest figures available state that the revenue losses incurred due to the special deduction for 'new mineral exploration expenses, etc.', presumably (but not certainly) including the explorations reserve, special deduction for new mineral deposit exploration expenses, overseas exploration reserve, and special deduction for overseas new mineral deposit exploration expenses, amounted to 2 billion yen for both 1975 and 1976 (Kaisei Zeiho no Subete - 51 Nendo (The Complete Amended Tax Laws - 1976), (Okura Zaimu Kyokai; Tokyo, 1976), p. 11).

The number of taxpayers qualified to take advantage of the overseas exploration reserve is apparently limited. An official commentary published at the time of the enactment of the reserve states that there were at that time probably about seven Japanese companies which could qualify as 'domestic mining corporations', as well as seven foreign corporations which could qualify as 'overseas independent development corporations'. (Kaisei Zeiho no Subete - 50 Nendo) (The Complete Amended Tax Laws - 1975), (Okura Zaimu Kyokai: Tokyo, 1975), p. 134).

F. Small and Medium Enterprise, etc. Overseas Market Development Reserve

1. In General

The small and medium enterprise market development reserve is a reserve which a corporation may establish, ostensibly in order to 'prepare for expenses required in the development of overseas markets' under which an amount equivalent to a prescribed percentage of the revenues from qualified transactions during a prescribed 'standard year' may be deducted currently and credited to the reserve account and subsequently brought back into income in the amount of at least twenty (20) percent of the amount credited into the reserve in a particular year during each of the succeeding five years (TSML, art. 54(1)). This reserve (initially called the 'overseas market development reserve') was established in 1964 upon place of various special export-related deductions felt to be in violation of GATT provisions. The benefits have been steadily reduced, however, with the provision now applicable only for corporations with a stated capital of no more than one billion yen.

2. Qualified Transactions

The following are the principal qualified transactions, the revenues of which form the basis for the amounts included in the reserve account but excluding transactions falling within the scope of the overseas technical transaction income special deduction (TSML, art. 54(2));

(i) exports of goods purchased from another, including the assignment or provision of industrial property rights, other rights concerning technology, or production methods by means of special technology, and the use rights related thereto acquired from another person, which were assigned or provided (to another) taking an outward method of payment as consideration;
(ii) exports of goods (except for primary products) acquired due to the company's own production, extraction or harvesting activities;
(iii) sales of products listed in (ii) to an exporter (including sales to a middleman who in turn sells to an exporter);
(iv) the processing of goods to be exported by an exporter who had mandated such processing to the company;
(v) various kinds of processing, for export purposes, the mandate of which was received from a textile manufacturer; and
(vi) the large-scale repair of ships (i.e. alteration in size or type of vessel), the consideration for which was comprised of an outward method of payment.

3. Technical Aspects

The amount which may be taken as a current deduction and credited into the reserve in a particular year is total of the following amounts, categorized by type of transaction, which are attributable to revenues generated in the prescribed standard year from the respective transactions (TSML, art. 54(1)):

Transaction	*Percentage*
(i) Exports of goods purchased from another:	
(a) corporations with capital of not more than 100 million yen –	.017
(b) corporations with capital of more than 100 million yen but not more than one billion yen –	.0085
(ii) All other qualified exports:	
(a) corporations which capital of not more than 100 million yen –	.023
(b) corporations with capital of more than 100 million yen but not more than one billion yen –	.0115

The prescribed 'standard year' is the preceding business year where the business year is one year in length, or the business year prior to the preceding business year where the business year is less than one year (TSML, art. 54(1)).

The amounts entered into the reserve in a particular business year must be taken back into income at least in the amount of twenty (20) percent thereof per year during the succeeding five years (TSML, art. 54(6)). On the other hand, the corporation may freely reserve the amounts so credited at any time and in any amount provided that the above-mentioned requirement is satisfied (TSML, art. 54(7)).

G. End of Deferral for Haven Operations

1. In General

On March 31, 1978, the National Diet of Japan promulgated the *Law to Amend Portions of the Tax Special Measures Law* (Law No. 11 of 1978) to include in the *Tax Special Measures Law* (Law No. 26 of 1957) provisions intended to end deferral of taxation of the profits of foreign (i.e. non-Japanese) subsidiaries which are considered to be essentially 'tax haven' operations. The new provisions are similar to the rules found in Subpart F of the US Internal Revenue Code as well as certain provisions of the Foreign Tax Law *(Aussensteuergesetz)* in Germany.

Basically, the anti-tax haven legislation provides that Japanese income tax shall be imposed on a current basis upon the pro rata share of the undistributed income of so-called 'specified foreign subsidiaries' attributable to Japanese resident or corporate shareholders owning, directly or indirectly, 10 percent or more of the total issued shares of the said foreign subsidiary (TSML, art. 66-6(1)).

2. Specified Foreign Subsidiaries

A specified foreign subsidiary is defined to be (a) a foreign affiliated company (i.e., a foreign corporation or other legal entity more than fifty percent of the issued shares of which are owned, directly or indirectly, by Japanese residents or corporations), (b) which has a Japanese resident or corporate shareholder who either (i) owns, directly or indirectly, ten percent or more of the total shares issued by such foreign subsidiary or (ii) belongs to a single family shareholding group which owns, directly or indirectly, ten percent of the shares issued by such foreign subsidiary, and (c) which is incorporated in a low tax country prescribed by Cabinet Order as one which imposes a tax which is low when compared with Japanese tax (TSML, art. 66-6(1)).

3. Low Tax Countries

According to the related Cabinet Order, a low tax country shall be a country which assesses no tax or significantly low tax upon either (i) worldwide income, (ii) offshore income or (iii) income from certain kinds of business activities (TSML Enf. O., art. 39-13(1). No additional details are provided by the Law or the Cabinet Order. The determination of low tax countries is further delegated to the Minister of Finance for disposition on a case-by-case basis.

The Minister of Finance issued a notification which lists the countries designated as low tax countries.[1] This list is as follows:

Category I (worldwide income)

1. Andorra
2. Bahamas
3. Bahrain
4. Bermuda
5. Channel Is. (UK)
6. Virgin Is. (UK)
7. Cayman Is.
8. Djibouti
9. Hong Kong
10. Isle of Man
11. Liechtenstein
12. Macao
13. Nauru
14. New Hebrides
15. Turks and Caicos

Category II (offshore income)

Panama

Category III (income from specified business activities):

	Country or Region	*Business Activity*
1.	Antigua	Business activities of an international business company provided in the tax laws Antigua.
2.	Barbados	Business activities of an international business company provided in the tax laws of Barbados.
3.	Granada	Business activities of an international business company provided in the tax laws of Granada.
4.	Gibraltar	Business activities of an international business company provided in the tax laws of Gibraltar.
5.	Jamaica	Business activities of an international business company provided in the tax laws of Jamaica.
6.	Liberia	Business activities of a non-resident Liberian entity provided in the tax laws of Liberia.
7.	Luxembourg	Business activities of a holding company provided in the tax laws of Luxembourg.
8.	Montserrat	Business activities of an offshore company provided in the tax laws of Montserrat.

1. Notification to Designate Countries and Regions in which the Tax Burden Assessed Upon the Global Income or Specified Income of Juridical Persons is Significantly Law in comparison with the Tax Burden Assessed Upon the Income of Juridical Persons in Japan as Provided in Tax Special Measures Law Article 40-4(1) and Article 66-6(1) and Business Activities Prescribed in the Related Order Article 25-8(1) (iii) and Article 39-13(1) (iii). (Finance Ministry Notification No. 38, March 31, 1978).

Country or Region	*Business Activity*
9. Netherlands Antilles	Business activities of an investment company provided in the tax laws of the Netherlands Antilles.
10. Netherlands Antilles	Business activities of a patent holding company provided in the tax laws of the Netherlands Antilles.
11. Saint Vincent	Business activities of an international business company provided in the tax laws of Saint Vincent.
12. Saint Vincent	Business activities of an international company provided in the tax laws of Saint Vincent.
13. Switzerland	Business activities of a holding company provided in the tax laws of Switzerland.
14. Switzerland	Business activities of a domiciliary company provided in the tax laws of Switzerland.
15. Liberia	Business activities involving the operation, leasing or purchase-and-sale of ships or aircraft.

No indication is given in the notification as to the criteria employed for determining what constitutes a low tax country. However, an official interpretation of the legislation prepared by the Ministry of Finance states that such a country is interpreted to be one which imposes a corporate income tax at an actual rate of less than one-half of Japan's approximate actual rate of 50 percent, or an actual rate of less than 25 percent. (Kaisei Zeiho no Subete - 53 Nendo (The Complete Amended Tax Law - 1978), (Kokuzeicho (National Tax Agency): Tokyo, 1978), p. 159).

4. Exempted Specified Foreign Subsidiaries

An exemption from this current taxation will be allowed if the specified foreign subsidiary possesses certain attributes. In short, (a) it must not be a mere holding company; (b) it must have a physical facility in its country of residence necessary for its business activities; (c) management and control must be conducted locally; (d) it must engage in its principal business activities principally with non-related parties or in its country of residence, depending upon its particular business activity; and (e) it must not have received five percent or more of its gross income in the form of dividends from other specified foreign subsidiaries (TSML, art. 66-6(3)).

5. Technical Aspects

The mechanics of imposing the tax are similar to those found under US law. The foreign subsidiary first determines its amount of 'undisposed income' according to either Japanese tax law or local tax law with adjustments (TSML, art. 66-6(2)(ii); TSML, Enf. O., art. 39-14(1)). Corporate taxes and dividends distributed are then deducted from this amount to determine the 'subject undistributed amount' (TSML, Enf. O., art. 39-15(1)). The 'taxable undistributed amount', which is to be aggregated with the gross income of the Japanese shareholder, is the shareholder's pro rata share of the subject undistributed amount (TSML, Enf. O., art. 39-15(2)). The taxpayer's income is grossed up in the amount of the local foreign income tax paid thereon (TSML, art. 66-7(2)). Japanese tax is assessed and an indirect foreign tax credit is allowed for the local income tax paid (TSML, art. 66-7(1)).

6. Disincentive Effects

The anti-tax haven provisions are narrowly drawn to reach operations conducted solely in prescribed low tax countries. A survey of the list of low tax countries currently prescribed reveals that it includes only well-known (and a few not-so-well-known) tax havens rather than any developing countries which would likely be the object of any substantial direct investment by Japanese corporations. Consequently, one can conclude that the anti-tax legislation will have no (or at most, a minimal) direct effect upon Japanese investment in those developing countries.

In addition, it is essential to note that, rather than defining particular kinds of income (e.g., foreign base company sales income or foreign base company services income), which are to be regarded as 'tainted', Japan has opted to define particular kinds of companies as 'tainted', i.e. those incorporated in a low tax country and which have no economic substance and appear to be operated primarily for tax avoidance motives. The result is that investment even in a low tax country will not be impaired provided it represents a substantial business operation.

H. Tax Treaties With Developing Countries

1. In General

As of November 1, 1978, Japan had concluded income tax treaties with the following countries which are considered under Japanese tax law to be 'developing regions': India, United Arab Republic, Korea, Zambia, Singapore, Sri Lanka, Brazil, Malaysia, Spain, Pakistan, Thailand.

The benefits provided in the treaties to encourage Japanese investment in the developing countries are composed principally of tax-sparing credits and the reduction or elimination of the withholding taxes on investment income received from a developing country and tax-sparing credits.

2. Tax-Sparing Credits

The most important benefits provided by many of the tax treaties Japan has concluded with developing countries are the so-called 'tax sparing credits'. Generally speaking, a tax sparing credit is a foreign tax credit which Japan is obliged to allow for local taxes which were reduced of exempt from tax (either under the treaty or local law) and therefore not actually paid. The result is that the local government in a developing country is allowed to encourage investment therein by granting various kinds of tax reductions or exemptions or tax holidays, etc., which will be recognized by Japan. In the absence of such a tax-sparing credit, of course, the Japanese direct foreign tax credit and the indirect credit would allow a credit against Japanese tax of only the taxes actually paid. This would result merely in a transfer of the tax benefit from the local government to the Japanese treasury and no overall benefit for the Japanese investor.

The tax sparing credits provided to Japanese residents under Japan's tax treaties with developing countries as of November 1, 1978 are indicated below.

(1) Thailand Treaty

The following taxes are deemed paid (Treaty, art. 14(2)(b)):

a. Taxes exempted or reduced under the treaty:
   (i) Withholding taxes reduced with regard to dividends paid by enterprises engaging in manufacturing (Treaty, art. 6(2)).
   (ii) Withholding taxes exempted with regard to government bonds (Treaty, art. 7(3)).
b. Taxes exempted or reduced under the *Promotion of Industrial Investment Act* of Thailand.

(2) Korean Treaty

The following taxes are deemed paid (Treaty, art. 18(3)):

a. Taxes reduced under the Treaty:
   (i) Withholding taxes reduced with regard to dividends (Treaty, art. 9(1)).
   (ii) Withholding taxes reduced with regard to interest (Treaty, art. 10(1)).
b. Taxes reduced or exempted in accordance with special incentive measures designed to promote economic development in Korea as agreed to by the Government of Korea and Japan.

(3) Malaysia Treaty

The following taxes are deemed paid (Treaty, art. 18(4)):

a. Taxes reduced under the Treaty:
   (i) Withholding taxes reduced with regard to interest on loans to industrial enterprises (Treaty, art. 9(3)).
   (ii) Taxes reduced with regard to gains from the alienation of intangible property (Treaty, art. 10(3)).
b. Taxes exempted in accordance with special incentive measures designed to promote economic development in Malaysia as agreed to by the Governments of Malaysia and Japan.

(4) Pakistan Treaty

The following taxes are deemed paid (Treaty, art. 14(3)):

a. Taxes exempted under the Treaty:
   (i) Witholding taxes with regard to interest on government bonds (Treaty, art. VIIA(3)(a)).

(ii) Withholding taxes with regard to interest on loans to Pakistan enterprises engaged in specified industrial undertakings (Treaty, art. VIIA (3)(b)).

b. Taxes exempted under local law: None.

(5) India Treaty

The following taxes are deemed paid (Treaty, art. XI(3)(b)):

a. Taxes reduced under the Treaty: None.

b. Taxes reduced or relieved in accordance with special incentive measures designed to promote economic development in India as agreed to by the Governments of India and Japan.

(6) Singapore Treaty

The following taxes are deemed paid (Treaty, art. 21(3) and (4)):

a. Taxes reduced or exempted under the Treaty:
   - (i) Withholding taxes exempted with regard to interest on debentures issued by, or loans made to, an enterprise of Singapore engaged in specified industrial undertakings (Treaty, art. 11(5) and (6)).
   - (ii) Withholding taxes exempted with respect to royalties paid by the Government, a local authority or a resident of Singapore (Treaty, art. 12(1)).
   - (iii) Taxes exempted with respect to gains on the alienation of intangible property (Treaty, art. 12(5)).

b. Taxes exempted in accordance with special incentive measures designed to promote economic development in Singapore as agreed to by the Governments of Singapore and Japan.

(7) Brazil Treaty

The following taxes are deemed paid (Treaty, art. 22(b)(i) and (ii)):

a. Taxes reduced or exempted under the Treaty:
   For purposes of the foreign tax credit, Brazilian withholding taxes shall be deemed to be the following, regardless of the amount actually paid:
   - (i) 25 percent in the case of dividends or dispositions of profits by a Brazilian permanent establishment. The Treaty imposes a limitation of 12.5 percent on the actual taxes (Treaty, art. 9(2)).
   - (ii) 25 percent in the case of royalties paid by the Government, a local authority or a resident of Brazil, for the use of intangible property other than trademarks or copyrights of films or tapes. The Treaty imposes a limitation of 12.5 percent on the actual taxes (Treaty, art. 11(2)(c)).
   - (iii) 25 percent in the case of royalties paid by the Government, a local authority, or a resident of Brazil, for the use of copyrights of films or tapes. The Treaty imposes a limitation of 15 percent on the actual taxes (Treaty, art. 11(2)(b)).
   - (iv) 20 percent in the case of interest paid by the Government, a local

authority or a resident of Brazil. The Treaty imposes a limitation of 12.5 percent on the actual taxes (Treaty, art. 10(2)).

b. Taxes exempted or reduced in accordance with special incentive measures designed to promote economic development in Brazil as agreed to by the Governments of Brazil and Japan.

(8) Zambia Treaty

The following taxes are deemed paid (Treaty, art. 22(2)(c)):

a. Taxes reduced or relieved under the Treaty:
   (i) Withholding taxes reduced with respect to interest paid by the Government, a local authority, or a resident of Zambia (Treaty, art. 10(2)).
   (ii) Withholding taxes reduced with respect to royalties paid by the Government, a local authority, or a resident of Zambia (Treaty, art. 11(2)).

b. Taxes reduced or relieved in accordance with special incentive measures to promote economic development in Zambia as agreed to by the Governments of Zambia and Japan.

(9) Spain Treaty

The following taxes are deemed paid (Treaty, art. 23(4)):

a. Taxes reduced or relieved under the Treaty: None.

b. Taxes reduced or exempted in the case of dividends, interest, or royalties, in accordance with special incentive measures designed to promote economic development in Spain as agreed to by the Governments of Spain and Japan.

(10) Sri Lanka (Ceylon) Treaty

a. Taxes relieved under the Treaty:
   (i) There shall be deemed not to have been refunded in respect of dividends to which provisions of paragraph (3) of Article VI of the Treaty apply, the amount of Ceylon tax refunded under the said provisions.
   (ii) In addition to the reduced amount of Ceylon tax payable on royalties under provisions of paragraph (2) of Article VIII of the Treaty (i.e., a 50 percent reduction of tax under Ceylon domestic law), there shall be deemed to have been paid by a resident of Japan in respect of such royalties 25 percent of the amount of Ceylon tax that would be payable if the said provisions did not apply.

b. These shall be deemed to have been paid by a company resident in Japan in respect of dividends received by that company from a company resident in Ceylon, as is referred to in sub-section (1) of section 6 of the Ceylon Inland Revenue Act and not less than 10 percent of the shares of which are held by one or more residents of Japan, the amount of Ceylon tax that would be payable if the provisions sub-section (3) of section 6 of the said Act did not apply.

Netherlands

A. Hartman *

1. INTRODUCTION

Dutch tax acts do not contain special provisions to stimulate investments by Dutch residents (individuals or corporations) in developing countries. On the other hand the Dutch tax system cannot be said to prevent or to make it difficult for Dutch residents to do so.

Where no special benefits are granted it has to be studied how the Dutch tax system works out on investing in developing countries.

Thus, a description has to be given of the methods of avoiding double taxation in respect of income arising from investments in developing countries.

A distinction can be made between the treatment of foreign income arising from developing countries with which the Netherlands has a tax treaty and with which the Netherlands does not have a tax treaty.

2. DEFINITION OF A DEVELOPING COUNTRY

With reference to the above it is not surprising that Dutch tax acts do not provide for a general definition of a 'developing country'.

However a specific list of developing countries was published in May 1970 for purposes of the unilateral measures for avoiding double taxation. (It is worth noticing that this list has been drawn up by the Minister of Finance in agreement with the Minister dealing with developing country matters as part of tax legislation.) Appendix I shows the list of 'developing countries'.

3. FISCAL TREATMENT OF FOREIGN INCOME ARISING FROM DEVELOPING COUNTRIES WITH WHICH THE NETHERLANDS DOES HAVE A TAX TREATY

The Netherlands has a tax treaty with the following developing countries:

1. Singapore: February, 1971
2. Indonesia: March 5, 1973
3. Israel: July 2, 1973
4. Thailand: September 11, 1975
5. Surinam: November 25, 1975
6. Malta: May 18, 1977
7. Morocco: August 12, 1977
8. Zambia: December 19, 1977.

* Loyens and Volkmaars.

Apart from Surinam all abovementioned countries are found in the published list (see under 2).

All abovementioned treaties – apart from Thailand and Morocco – provide for 'tax-sparing clauses'.

The limited number of tax treaties with developing countries makes it possible to discuss each treaty more extensively.

3.1. Singapore

This is the eldest treaty between the Netherlands and a developing country.

This treaty generally follows the OECD model convention; however the treaty differs in respect of shipping and airtransport income, and in respect of the methods for eliminating double taxation.

Shipping and airtransport income

The basic philosophy of taxing this type of income in the country of the actual management of the company has not been implemented.

Article 8 provides that such profits may be taxed in the other state, but only in so far as such profits are derived from that other state. This article further provides that the applicable tax rate shall be 50 percent of the normal rate, and that such profits will not exceed 5 percent of certain sums receivable in respect of the transportation. The Netherlands will allow a tax credit for the tax paid in Singapore with the restriction that this credit will never exceed the outcome of the following formula:

$$\frac{\text{Singapore source income}}{\text{Worldwide income}} \times \text{Dutch tax on worldwide income} = \text{maximum credit}$$

Dividends

Apart from its income tax of 40% Singapore will not levy any withholding tax on dividends.

The Netherlands will give the reduction of Dutch taxes according to the following formula:

$$\frac{\text{Singapore dividends}}{\text{Worldwide income}} \times \text{Dutch tax on worldwide income} = \text{reduction}$$

Interest

Singapore reduces its income tax on interest payments to 10 percent. The Netherlands grants a tax credit – by way of tax sparing credit – which equals the amount of tax which Singapore has actually levied thereon increased by twice the difference between this amount and 10 percent of the amount of the interest.

Royalties

Singapore reduces its income tax on certain type of royalties (not literary/artistic/films etc.) to nil percent. The Netherlands grants a tax credit of 20 percent of the amount of the royalty, so that this credit can be qualified as a tax sparing credit.

The amount of tax-sparing credit which the Netherlands grants in respect of royalties and interest is limited as follows:

The credit will not exceed the lower of:

1. 50 percent of the amount of tax which Singapore would have levied without the existence of the treaty, and without its special incentives;
2. the outcome of the following formula:

$$\frac{\text{Singapore interest and/or royalties}}{\text{Worldwide income}} \times \text{Dutch tax on worldwide income}$$

As in all treaties between the Netherlands and developing countries providing for tax-sparing clauses, the Protocol of this treaty provides for a consultation after ten years between the two compentent authorities in respect of the opportunity to amend the tax-sparing clauses.

3.2. Indonesia

Dividends

Indonesia may levy 20 percent withholding tax on dividends. It will reduce the 20 percent to 10 percent if the dividends are paid to a resident of the Netherlands and in the Netherlands the dividends do not attrack taxation. If this is the case the Netherlands does not grant a credit for the 10% Indonesian tax. In the case where Indonesia levies 20% the Netherlands grants a credit of 20%. Should Indonesia offer an investment incentive by lowering its withholding tax the Netherlands will still allow a credit of 20 percent – a tax-sparing credit.

Interest

In general Indonesia will levy 20 percent withholding tax on interest.

Based upon article 10 (3) of the treaty the Indonesian withholding tax will be reduced to 10 percent if the payer of the interest is a bank or a financial institution, or an enterprise engaged in certain specific fields of business. The Netherlands grants a credit for the Indonesian withholding tax (20% resp. 10%). In the case that Indonesia withholds less than 10 percent by way of an incentive, the Netherlands will grant a tax-sparing credit which equals the amount of tax which Indonesia actually has levied thereon increased by twice the difference between this amount and 10 percent of this amount. (The same clause as used in the treaty between the Netherlands and Singapore (see 3.1. above).)

Royalties

Indonesia may levy 20 percent withholding tax on royalty payments. However on certain royalties (– essential for the developing of the country –) the withholding tax is further reduced to either 10 or 5 percent.

The Netherlands will allow the following credits:

- if Indonesia has levied 20%: a full credit of 20 percent;
- if Indonesia may levy 10%: a full credit of 10 percent whether or not Indonesia has levied, a tax-sparing credit;
- if Indonesia has levied 5%: a tax-sparing credit of 15 percent;
- if Indonesia by way of incentive reduces this 5%, then the Netherlands will grant a credit of 15% plus 1% for each percent that Indonesia levies less then 5% (e.g. if Indonesia does not levy a withholding tax: then the credit will be $15 + (5 - 0) = 20$).

It has to be noted that the credits and/or tax-sparing credits described above are so limited that the Netherlands will never allow a credit which exceeds the Dutch tax payable on such income.

3.3. Israel

Dividends

Israel may levy 15 percent on dividends. The Netherlands – in situations where the dividends received are not tax exempt – will grant a credit of 15 percent. If Israel as an incentive levies less than 15 percent, the Netherlands will grant a tax-sparing credit of 15 percent on gross dividends.

Interest

Israel may levy 15 percent, respectively 10 percent on interest. The Netherlands will grant a credit of 15, 10 percent. If Israel levies less than 15 percent (interest to non-banks and or financial institutions) the Netherlands grants a tax-sparing credit of 15 percent of the gross amount of the interest. In the case that Israel reduces the 10 percent rate by way of an incentive, then the Netherlands will grant a credit equal to the amount of tax which Israel has actually levied thereon increased by twice the difference between this amount and 10 percent, *provided* that the credit shall not exceed 15 percent of the amount of such interest.

Royalties

Israel may levy a withholding tax of 10 percent on film/radio/TV royalties and 5 percent on all other royalties.

The Netherlands allows a credit for this withholding tax. If Israel by way of incentive reduces these rates, then the Netherlands will in all cases grant a credit of 10 percent of the amount of the royalties.

Also under this treaty all ordinary and/or tax-sparing credits are limited to the amount of Dutch tax payable on such income.

3.4. Thailand

In the Dutch government's note on this treaty it is stated: 'However, it is remarkable, that the provisions in those ('other treaties with Thailand') agreements – even if they have been recently concluded – are mostly focused on the avoidance of double taxation as such. Provisions which would make it more interesting for residents of industrialized countries to invest in Thailand, hardly appear. The fact that Thailand's position as developing country has been taken into consideration is seen in that to a greater extent withholding taxes have been agreed upon.'

No special tax-sparing clauses are included in this tax treaty.

3.5. Surinam

Before Surinam became independent (November 25, 1975), the avoidance of double taxation between the two countries was governed by the so-called Tax Arrangement for the Kingdom (Belastingregeling voor het Koninkrijk), an act passed in October 28, 1964. The same act is still applicable in the relationship between the two remaining parts of the Kingdom of the Netherlands: The Netherlands Antilles and the Netherlands.

This tax treaty with Surinam follows in principle the OECD-pattern. Seen the developing status of Surinam some special provisions have been included in respect of dividends, interest and royalties.

Dividends

Surinam will withhold 7½ percent withholding tax if a Dutch company holds more than 25 percent of the capital of the paying corporation, *and* if those dividends are tax exempt in the Netherlands. In case the received dividends are tax exempt in the Netherlands *and* the shareholding is less than 25 percent, then Surinam will withhold 15 percent. In all other cases Surinam is entitled to withhold 20 percent.

In the latter case the Netherlands will grant an ordinary credit, but if Surinam levies less than 20 percent by way of an incentive, then the Netherlands nevertheless will allow 20 percent as a credit, a clear tax-sparing credit.

Interest

Surinam may levy a 5 percent withholding tax in case of interest paid to a bank or a similar institution; in all other cases the rate will be 10 percent. The Netherlands will allow a credit and/or a tax-sparing credit.

The tax-sparing credit in the case of interest on which Surinam could withhold 10 percent equals the amount of tax which Surinam actually has levied thereon increased by twice the difference between this amount and 10 percent.

The tax-sparing credit in the case of interest on which Surinam could withhold 5 percent amounts to 15 percent plus 1 percent for each percent that Surinam levies less than 5 percent (see Singapore in respect of royalties).

Royalties

Surinam may levy 10 percent in respect of films and tapes etc., and 5 percent on all other royalties. The Netherlands generally will grant a normal credit for the Surinam withholding tax of 10 percent. If the 5 percent rate is not reduced by Surinam, the Netherlands will allow a credit of 15 percent of the gross amount. In cases where the 5 percent is further reduced as an incentive the Netherlands grants a tax-sparing credit as discussed above for certain interest from Surinam.

It should be noted that at present Surinam does not levy any withholding tax at all on interest and royalties; therefore the tax-sparing provisions are not yet applicable.

Also under this treaty all ordinary and/or tax-sparing credits are limited to the amount of Dutch tax payable on such income.

3.6. Malta

Only in respect of interest and royalties does the treaty provide for a tax-sparing credit.

Interest

Interest paid to certain stated (government) financial institutions are not subject to withholding tax. In all other cases Malta may levy a 10 percent withholding tax.

The Netherlands will allow a tax-sparing credit of 10 percent.

Royalties

Malta may levy a 10 percent withholding tax. If Malta grants by way of incentive a reduction, then the Netherlands will still allow a tax-sparing credit of 10 percent. (Royalties for films/TV etc. are excluded.)

Also under this treaty all ordinary and/or tax-sparing credits are limited to the amount of Dutch tax payable on such income.

3.7. Morocco

This treaty is not yet ratified (August 1978). Although Morocco is a developing country, the treaty does not contain any tax-sparing clauses. In general it follows the OECD-draft convention of 1963.

3.8. Zambia

Dividends

Zambia may levy 15 percent withholding tax on dividends. In the case that the receiving company holds at least 25 percent of the capital of the paying company this 15 percent is reduced to 5 percent. The Netherlands grant a credit for such withholding tax, unless the dividends qualify for the participation exemption (see Par. 4.5 and 5).

Interest

Zambia may levy 10 percent withholding tax on interest. Only in the case that the interest is paid to the Dutch Government or another public entity such interest will be exempt of withholding tax. The Netherlands grant a credit for such withholding tax.

Royalties

Zambia may levy 10 percent withholding tax on royalties. The Netherlands grant a credit for such withholding tax.

The treaty contains a tax sparing clause in respect of dividends: The Netherlands will allow a credit of (presently) 20 percent if Zambia by way of incentive reduces its withholding tax on dividends.

4. FISCAL TREATMENT OF FOREIGN INCOME ARISING FROM DEVELOPING COUNTRIES WITH WHICH THE NETHERLANDS HAS NO TAX TREATY

In the absence of a tax treaty the avoiding of double taxation is provided for by Royal Decree (1965) and amended in 1970 and again in 1976.

4.1. The basic principle of the Dutch system of avoiding double taxation is 'exemption with progression', so that the foreign incofe itself is not taxed but only the domestic income is taxed at the same rate as was the foreign income in fact domestic income. This basic system is also adopted in various tax treaties concluded by the Netherlands.

4.2. Under the unilateral rules only certain categories of income can qualify for the exemption. Those categories are:

- income of a foreign enterprise, exercised in a foreign permanent establishment;
- income from real estate located abroad belonging to a foreign enterprise; and, the following categories (in sofar they cannot be considered as income of a foreign enterprise);
- income from personal labour activities, performed outside the Netherlands;
- income from real estate located abroad;
- income from debts insured by mortgage on real estate located abroad;
- income from profitsharing in a foreign enterprise, neither as a shareholder and nor as an employee;
- some periodic payments from foreign public entities.

4.3. A very important provision for the exemption is that the above-mentioned income must be subject to an income tax levied by another state. This additional requirement does not come into the scope of most of the tax treaties concluded by the Netherlands.[1]

The question remains that if a foreign developing country grants a tax holiday as an incentive, is the above requirement still met?

Because the answer mainly depends from the specific tax system of the foreign country a general answer to this question cannot be given.

4.4. Apart from the special provisions in respect of dividends, interest and royalties flowing from developing countries (see below par. 4.5) the unilateral measures do not contain provisions specially made to encourage foreign investments. However, the system as such does not in general create obstacles for investment in (developing) foreign countries. A brief outline may clarify this statement:

I. An individual resident (married with 2 children) has a worldwide taxable income of Dfl. 100.000; Dfl. 10.000 of it qualifies as foreign income, which has been subject to a foreign income tax.

Then the tax on Dfl. 100.000 would be Dfl. 41.398 = 41,389% (1978 in-

1. E.g. the US-Dutch tax treaty refers to this Dutch unilateral method.

come tax rates). Based upon the Decree of 1965 the following deduction on this tax would be applied:

$$\frac{10.000}{100.000} \times 41.398 = 4.139,80.$$

As a result Dfl. 37.258,20 would be payable in the Netherlands. (41,398% of Dfl. 90.000). Apart from the impact on the rate of progression applicable on the non-foreign income, this method is neutral in respect of the amount of tax paid on the foreign income. If a developing country should levy only a minor tax rate on certain business profits, then the Dutch system does not withdraw these advantages.

II. Due to the fact that the Dutch corporate income tax rate is proportional above a taxable profit of Dfl. 50.000, presently 48 percent, this system works out as a complete exemption for taxable profits above that amount.

Company X: worldwide taxable income:	Dfl. 1.000.000
Dutch corporate income tax: 48%:	Dfl. 480.000
Foreign branch income:	Dfl. 100.000

Company X will receive a deduction of its tax liability of:

$$\frac{100.000}{1.000.000} \times 480.000 = \text{Dfl. } 48.000.$$

In fact Dfl. 900.000 is taxed at 48 percent. In this situation an incentive granted by the foreign country is not effected at all by the Dutch tax system.

The Royal Decree (1965) provides for relief of double taxation in general. This probably implies that profits and losses from various foreign sources have to be compensated with each other, before applying the abovementioned exemption computation. Recapture rules – which can work out to be very complicated – are included in those unilateral measures.

4.5. Dividends, interest and royalties. It should be noted that dividends, interest and royalties in principle are subject to income and/or corporate income tax. Under most tax treaties which the Netherlands has concluded the Netherlands grant a credit for the foreign withholding tax, with the limitation that this credit will never exceed the Dutch tax payable on such income. It should be noted that in the case that the dividends are not taxed in the Netherlands by virtue of the participation exemption the Netherlands does neither give a credit for foreign dividend withholding tax, nor a deduction. This also applies if tax treaties are involved. The Decree of 1965 contains special provisions in connection with dividends, interest and royalties from developing countries. (Article 3a, 3b and 3c of the Royal Decree 1965.) In other cases – apart from the special treatment of certain qualifying dividends, to be discussed later under 'Dutch Participation Exemption' – any foreign tax is only deductible as expense from the taxable income. The articles 3a and 3b provide for a normal tax credit, within certain limits, and the possibility of a carry-over of foreign taxes during 6 years, in so far such taxes did not result in a deduction of Dutch taxes. Article 3c creates the possibility for the tax-payer to elect on an annual basis for the treatment on the basis of article 3a and 3d.

The credit granted on the base of article 3a and 3b is limited as follows: the credit is the lesser of the following amounts:

(i) the amount actually levied in that year by developing countries, increased by such levied tax in the prior 6 years, which has not already given raise to a deduction;

(ii) the outcome of the following formula:

$$\frac{A}{B} \times C = D.$$

A = net-dividends/royalties/interest from developing countries
B = income less certain prior losses
C = Dutch tax on taxable income (including foreign income)
D = reduction.

5. LOCAL CORPORATE-SHAREHOLDER TAX REGIME

Dividends received by a resident corporate income tax payer are tax exempt in the following situation (art. 13 Corporate Income Tax Act 1969):

- if the company holds at least 5 percent of the nominal paid up capital of the distributing company;
- if the shares are held from the beginning of the companies' financial year.

These are the only two requirements to be met in case of dividends from a domestic company; however, in respect of dividends from a foreign subsidiary two additional requirements have to be met:

- the subsidiary itself must be subject to a foreign income tax;
- the shareholding in this subsidiary must not be of a portfolio nature.

Under this so-called participation exemption ('deelnemingsvrijstelling') realized and unrealized capital gains are also exempted from tax.

6. TAXATION OF DIVIDENDS OF A RESIDENT CORPORATION

The applicable system of taxation for the shareholder is the so-called classic system. As a result of that the shareholder of a Dutch corporation cannot credit any underlying corporate income tax against his personal income tax liability. Due to this system it is not relevant whether the dividends are partly from profits of a branch or subsidiary of the Dutch corporation. Consequently it is not important if such branches or subsidiaries are located in developed or in developing countries.

6.1. Resident Shareholders

Under par. 5 above the participation exemption is discussed, so that this paragraph will focus on individual shareholders of a Dutch corporation. Dividends are subject to individual income tax at progressive rates, without any credit facility. In general capital gains are not taxed, unless the shareholder holds a substantial interest in the sharecapital of the company.

A substantial interest exists if the shareholder alone (or together with his spouse) holds at least 7 percent of the nominal paid-up capital and together with a certain group of relatives at least one-third of the nominal paid-up capital. If a substantial interest exists then capital gains are taxed at a special rate of 20 percent.

6.2. Non-resident Shareholders

Individuals

The Netherlands levies a dividend withholding tax of 25 percent on dividends, unless reduced by tax treaties. This dividend withholding tax is a provisional levy of the Dutch personal income tax in the case that the recipient holds a substantial interest as described under 6.1. Then, the recipient is subject to income tax at the normal rates. In all tax treaties the dividend-article limits this tax liability to dividend withholding tax of 25 percent or less. Only non-resident individuals having a substantial interest are liable to twenty percent income tax on capital gains. Under most treaties this is only applicable for non-residents which have been residents of the Netherlands, and sell their shares within five years after their emigration.

Corporations

The Netherlands levies a dividend withholding tax of 25 percent of dividends, unless reduced by tax treaties. Only in the case that a foreign entity, which does not have an enterprise has a substantial interest (see above 6.1), dividends and/or capital gains are subject to corporate income tax at normal rates (e.g. foreign trusts).

APPENDIX I

Afghanistan, Algeria, Argentina, Barbados, Burma, Burundi, Bolivia, Botswana, Upper-Volta, Brazil, Central African Republic, Ceylon, Chile, China, Colombia, Costa Rica, Cuba, Cyprus, Dahomey, Democratic Republic Congo, Dominica, Ecuador, El Salvador, Ethiopia, The Philippines, Gabon, Gambia, Ghana, Guatemala, Guinea, Guyana, Haïti, Honduras, India, Indonesia, Iraq, Israel, Ivory-Coast, Jamaica, Yemen, Jordania, Cambodja, Cameroons, Kenya, Kuwait, Korea, Laos, Lesotho, Libanon, Liberia, Libya, Madagascar, Malawi, The Maldives, Malaisia, Mali, Malta, Morocco, Mauritania, Mexico, Mongolian People's Republic, Muscat and Oman, Nepal, Nicaragua, Niger, Nigeria, Uganda, Pakistan, Panama, Paraguay, Peru, Ruanda, Trinidad and Tobago, Saudi Arabia, Senegal, Sierra Leone, Singapore, Sudan, Somaliland, Swaziland, Syria, Thailand, Togo, Chad, Tunisin, Turkey, Uruguay, Venezuela, United Arabian Republic, United Republic Tanzania, Vietnam, People's Republic Congo, Western Samoa, Zambia, Southern Yemen and Yugoslavia.

Sweden

Sten Sandell *
Torbjörn Sköld *

1. INTRODUCTION

The establishment of wholly-owned subsidiaries has for a long time dominated Swedish industrial investments in developing countries. However, this trend has slowly changed during recent years to a tendency to create joint ventures in these countries to meet their demands for domestic influence – notably in India, Latin-America and in some African countries. Most of the Swedish industrial investments in these and other foreign countries are linked to and supportive of the export activities of the companies.

In 1969 the Swedish Parliament enacted an investment guarantee system but restricted the use of the system to certain so-called 'program countries', consisting of 13 developing countries.

The system seems to have failed because Swedish industry has shown only slight interest in investing in the program countries: up to now, only two applications for investment guarantees have been made, both of which were rejected for formal reasons. In 1973 Swedish enacted a system of export aid to support the Swedish export industry. Under that system Swedish taxpayers are entitled to reduce their taxable income by certain specified limited costs to support their export financing. But this system also seems to have had little practical effect on the Swedish industry's willingness and interest in adopting plans for investment in the developing countries. It is likely that proposals for further export stimulating measures will be put in the near future, but it seems unlikely that these will have as their primary aim any inducements to invest in the developing countries.

One way to support foreign trade activities with the developing countries is to allow exemption from duty for certain products with origin in some countries. This method has been adopted by Sweden, which allows duty free importing of certain goods with origin in 72 developing countries.

2. TAX TREATIES

As foreign trade is of great importance for the Swedish economy, Sweden's network of tax treaties is one of the widest in the world. A long row of tax treaties has been signed with the developing nations of Asia, Africa and Latin-America. India's treaty 1959 with Sweden, for example, was the first to come into force between India and any European country.

At the present time general tax treaties are in force with 17 developing countries and negotiations are underway with 4 more.

* Attorneys at Law, Malmö and Paris.

Sweden's tax treaties in the past generally were based on the tax exemption method. These older treaties allocate items of income for tax purposes to one of the treaty countries and exempt them from tax in the other. In 1965 Sweden changed its treaty method of avoiding double taxation and adopted the tax credit method of relief from double taxation.

Like many other developed countries Sweden has adopted the system of 'matching' credit, thus including 'tax sparing' provisions in many of its treaties with developing countries. Under these treaty provisions Sweden gives its taxpayers credit not only for tax paid to those countries but also for taxes waived or 'spared' by those countries under their respective tax incentive laws. Such clauses may be found in nine treaties.

3. FOREIGN TAX CREDIT

From January 1, 1967, Sweden enacted a general foreign tax credit to take care of any gaps that might exist in its tax treaty network. The foreign tax credit relates only to taxes paid to countries with which Sweden does not have tax treaties ('non-treaty credit'). The act was designed to encourage Swedish companies to participate in the expansion of industry and trade in those developing countries with which Sweden had no tax treaties and with which it was often difficult to conclude treaties. The 'non-treaty credit' has no 'tax sparing provision'; the credit extends only to taxes actually paid out. Moreover, the 'non-treaty credit' is limited to taxes paid by the Swedish taxpayer itself. It provides no 'indirect credit' for any corporation income tax paid by a Swedish taxpayer's foreign subsidiary.

Foreign tax credit may be claimed only against the Swedish national income tax and may not exceed the amount of that tax which is attributable to the foreign income. Consequently, only foreign taxes comparable to the Swedish national income tax qualify for credit.

4. TAXATION OF INVESTMENTS IN DEVELOPING COUNTRIES

As aforesaid the special act concerning tax deductions for certain export financing costs and the 'non-Treaty credit' are applicable to activities regarding all countries.

Except for the 'tax sparing' provisions the Swedish tax system, contrary to the tax systems of many developed countries, does not contain any special provisions favoring investments in developing countries. In many ways the Swedish tax system instead makes it more attractive to invest in Sweden than abroad. Thus, the Swedish tax system allows, for example, contributions within a group of Swedish companies but not from a Swedish parent company to a subsidiary abroad. Sweden has instead created a broad scheme of aid to developing countries through government decisions in which scheme the Swedish industry takes part only to a small extent.

Switzerland

Dr. Robert Briner *

1. SWISS TAX SYSTEM

Switzerland is a Confederation of 26 cantons. Taxes are therefore levied on three different levels, namely on the federal level, the cantonal level and the municipal level. Unlike the systems prevailing in other federally organized countries cantonal taxation is still more important than federal taxation.

Federal Taxation

1.1. The Swiss Confederation levies a uniform income tax (Federal Defence Tax Act of December 9, 1940) (SR 642.11) on all persons who reside in Switzerland or who have a lucrative activity within Switzerland as well as on all legal entities who have their registered office in Switzerland. In the following we shall only deal with the taxation of legal entities.

All legal entities having their registered office in Switzerland are subject to the federal income tax at a graduated rate based on the relationship between the taxable income and the paid-in capital and surplus. The minimum rate is 3.63 per cent as long as the yield on the paid-in capital and surplus does not exceed 4 per cent. The maximum rate of 9.8 per cent is imposed on the total income if the yield amounts to more than approximately 23 per cent. Rates as in effect on January 1, 1979. The Swiss people will decide in a referendum on May 20, 1979 if these rates are to be increased to 3.5 per cent as long as the yield on the paid-in capital does not exceed 4 per cent. The maximum rate of 11.5 per cent is imposed on the total income if the yield amounts to more than approximately 23 per cent.

Furthermore an annual tax of 0.0825 per cent is levied on the paid-in capital and surplus. The new rate would amount to 0.08 per cent if the change of the law is approved in the referendum of May 20, 1979.

Companies which have their registered office outside Switzerland are subject to the Swiss federal income tax if they have a permanent establishment in Switzerland or own real estate in this country. The tax is levied on the income generated by the permanent establishment or the Swiss real estate. Furthermore federal capital tax is levied on the Swiss assets.

Cantonal and Municipal Taxation

1.2. Each canton levies its own tax on legal entities which have their registered office in the canton or a permanent establishment or real estate within the canton. The rates vary from canton to canton as does the taxation system

* Lenz, Schluep, Briner & De Coulon, Geneva.

(rates of depreciation, deductibility of taxes paid, one or two year assessment base, tax loss carry forward period, etc.).

Normally, the municipal taxes are levied as a percentage of the cantonal tax rate and vary from municipality to municipality. Furthermore the cantonal and municipal tax rates are modified frequently as they are normally fixed only for a limited period of one to three years.

Taking into account that, with respect to the federal income tax, taxes paid constitute operating expenses which can be deducted for the purpose of computing the taxable net income and as many cantons follow the same principle, the overall federal, cantonal and municipal maximum taxes rates which are approximately between 35 and 45 per cent are in effect reduced to a maximum of approximately 26 to 37 per cent on pretax income.

Furthermore a capital tax is levied in all cantons, the overall rates including the federal taxes, are between 0.4 and 1 per cent.

Federal Withholding Tax

1.3. All distributions of profits made by a Swiss corporation to its shareholders are subject to a federal withholding tax of 35 per cent (Federal Anticipatory Tax Act of October 13, 1965) (SR 642.21). The tax payer resident in Switzerland gets a refund or a tax credit against his income taxes for the full amount.

Shareholders with residence outside Switzerland can only claim a reduction or possibly a full waiver of this tax if a convention for the avoidance of double taxation between their country of residence and Switzerland so provides.

All constructive dividends made by a Swiss company to its shareholders or to a person related to the shareholder, i.e. all advantages of a pecuniary nature made to such a person which are not justified under the rule of dealing at arm's length between the Swiss corporation and its shareholders, are treated in the same way as dividends.

International Taxation

1.4. Individuals residing and corporations incorporated in Switzerland have to include in their taxable base their worldwide income and their worldwide fortune (net assets). Special rules for relief apply if the Swiss taxpayer has a permanent establishment abroad or in the case of Swiss corporations which receive dividend income.

Under Swiss internal tax law no relief whatsoever is granted for foreign taxes levied on the income or the assets of the Swiss tax payer. The taxes paid abroad are, however, allowed as a deduction. According to certain conventions for the avoidance of double taxation concluded by Switzerland a tax credit for foreign taxes is granted in specific cases (see below 4).

Outlook

1.5. The Swiss people approved a constitutional amendment on June 12,

1977 according to which cantonal taxes will in the future be harmonized. This will mean that the basic principles applied to taxation will eventually be uniform throughout Switzerland (probably not before the mid-eighties) but the cantons will remain free to set their tax rates.

2. TAX INCENTIVES

2.1. Federal Defence Tax

2.1.1. Holding Companies

For Swiss corporations which participate in other companies (domestic or foreign) to the extent of at least 20 per cent of the fixed capital or capital stock of such a subsidiary, the Swiss federal income tax computed on the total income of the entity receiving the dividends will be reduced in the proportion that the total qualified dividend income has to the company's gross income from all sources. Therefore, if all income consists of such dividend income, a Swiss holding company pays no federal income tax. The same deduction is available to Swiss holding companies if the investment in the subsidiary company amounts to at least Sw.Fr. 2,000,000 although it does not reach the 20 per cent level (Article 59 Federal Defence Tax Act).

2.1.2. Permanent Establishments and Real estate abroad

A similar deduction of the Swiss federal defence tax is available to Swiss corporations which have real estate or permanent establishments abroad (Article 55 Federal Defence Tax Act). In such cases the Swiss tax will also be first computed into account the income of the foreign permanent establishment or from the foreign real estate but the tax will then be reduced in the same proportion as the foreign income bears to the overall income of the Swiss corporation. In the case of permanent establishments it is normal to make a first allocation of 10 to 30 per cent of the income of the permanent establishment to the head office and which is fully subject to normal Swiss taxes, to take into account the role of the head office. The above mentioned reduction rule is then applied to the remaining balance.

2.2. Cantonal Taxes

Most cantons have rules similar to the ones mentioned for the federal income tax regarding income from subsidiaries and the taxation of foreign permanent establishments. Regarding holding income most cantons go further and fully exempt foreign dividend income.

Furthermore most cantons (the notable exception being Zurich) provide for special taxation of so called domiciliary companies. These are normally companies which do not have a commercial activity in Switzerland. In some cantons they may not have an office whereas in other cantons this is possible. Taxation of such domiciliary companies therefore varies greatly from canton to canton. In certain cases all foreign source income is fully exempted. In other cases the ordinary cantonal tax rates are reduced by a factor of 5 or even 10, or a relatively low flat rate for all foreign source commercial income is applied. The overall cantonal tax rates for domiciliary companies therefore vary between 0 and approximately 10 per cent. Normally these domiciliary companies have to be predominantly foreign owned but in some cantons it is possible to have Swiss shareholders. Generally the income must stem from non-Swiss sources.

3. OTHER TAX INCENTIVES FOR INVESTMENT IN SWITZERLAND

A number of cantons are willing to grant for cantonal tax purposes special privileges which can go to a full tax holiday for a period which may extend up to 10 years if a new company is formed and new facilities are created within the canton which help its industrialization and create new qualified jobs.

4. INTERNATIONAL TAX INCENTIVES

Switzerland does not have any unilateral fiscal incentives for investments abroad, including investments in developing countries, other than the holding privileges and the non-taxability of income from permanent establishments mentioned above under 2.1. Obviously the cantonal tax privileges for domiciliary companies and for holding companies are often used as they permit the flow of foreign dividends or of financial income to a Swiss company at an advantageous cantonal tax rate. These privileges, however, are available for all such foreign income and no distinction is made between developing and developed countries.

Within the framework of the double taxation conventions concluded by Switzerland a certain relief is granted, especially in the field of interest income and royalties. In view of the fact that under the Swiss tax system dividend income is generally privileged, normally no special rules had to be set up for such income.

Under the old conventions the respective withholding taxes on dividends, interest payments and royalties are either fully waived or greatly reduced and the country receiving the income can tax it fully. This is the case regarding the conventions with Denmark (SR 0.672.931.41) (although a new convention was signed in 1973, it follows the old principle, whereby only the country of residence of the recipient of dividend, interest and royalty income can tax such income), Finland (SR 0.672.934.51), Hungary (SR 0.672.941.81), Norway (SR 0.672.959.81) and the United States of America (SR 0.672.933.61). Since 1965 and under the influence of the model convention of the OECD, Switzerland has agreed to grant a credit for the foreign remaining withholding tax on dividends, interest payments and royalties. Under this system the foreign state usually reduces its statutory withholding tax rate by a certain percentage and Switzerland grants a credit against its own taxes for the amount which remains taxable in the foreign state. Such conventions have been concluded with Austria (SR 0.672.916.31), Canada (AS 1977 1525), the Federal Republic of Germany (SR 0.672.913.62), France (SR 0.672.934.91), Great Britain (RO 1978, p. 1465), Ireland (SR 0.672.944.11), Japan (SR 0.672.946.31), Netherlands (SR 0.672.963.61), South Africa (SR 0.672.911.81) and Sweden (SR 0.672.971.41). Conventions have also been concluded with Italy in 1976 and with Belgium in 1978 but have not yet been ratified.

In its double taxation conventions with developing countries Switzerland has gone a step further. Under the old system which did not yet provide for a tax credit, the convention with Pakistan (SR 0.672.962.31) of December 30, 1959/ June 15, 1962 put a maximum limit of 10 per cent on the rate of tax Switzerland can levy on the interest of an authorized credit made by a Swiss corporation to a person residing in Pakistan. Furthermore Pakistan agreed not to levy any withholding tax on such interest payments.

The newer tax treaties with developing countries provide for a 'matching credit' or 'tax sparing'. According to this method Switzerland still grants its tax credit for the foreign withholding tax which under the convention could be levied by the foreign country but which is not levied in order to attract foreign investment. In other words Switzerland grants a credit, i.e. a reduction of Swiss income taxes, for a foreign tax which is not levied. On the other hand, the developing state forgoes the possibility of collecting this withholding tax in order to attract foreign capital at an advantageous rate of taxation, both in the developing country and in Switzerland.

Such matching credits have been agreed upon in the conventions for the avoidance of double taxation with following countries:

Malaysia (December 30, 1974, SR 0.672.952.71)

Interest and royalty payments on authorized loans and licensing agreements are not subject to any withholding taxes in Malaysia and Switzerland grants a matching credit of 10 per cent. In view of the fact that Malaysia does not currently levy a withholding tax on dividends Switzerland also grants a 10 per cent tax credit on the net amount of the dividends for so long as the tax system in Malaysia does not change.

Portugal (September 26, 1974, SR 0.672.965.41)

A matching credit of 10 per cent is granted on interest payments; under internal Portuguese law no withholding tax is levied in order to attract foreign capital.

Singapore (November 25, 1975, SR 0.672.968.91)

A matching credit of 10 per cent is granted on interest income and royalties.

Spain (April 26, 1966, SR 0.672.933.21)

A matching credit of 10 per cent is granted on interest on certain qualified loans which are exempt in Spain from withholding tax.

Trinidad and Tobago (February 1, 1973, SR 0.672.975.41)

A 10 per cent matching credit is granted on interest income on authorized investments. Similar provisions have been included in a double taxation convention negotiated between South Corea and Switzerland. It is expected that this convention will be ratified within the year.

CONCLUSION

According to the official Swiss viewpoint fiscal policy should basically not be used as a tool to help developing countries.

There exist two exceptions from this rule:

- the federal and cantonal holding privileges for income from subsidiaries and the cantonal privileges for domiciliary companies. These privileges apply to income from all foreign sources and are not aimed particularly to encourage investments in developing countries
- the only direct fiscal incentive for investment in developing countries are the matching credits for foreign withholding taxes, mainly in the field of interest payments, and in certain cases also with respect to dividend and royalty payments. These are only available in case of investments in a limited number of developing countries with which Switzerland has concluded conventions for the avoidance of double taxation.

Other than the cantonal tax holidays for new investments, there are no fiscal measures which can be considered as important disincentives to foreign investments through inducing investment at home.

According to Swiss policy, aid to developing countries is either made through financial aid, be it multilateral or bilateral, or by encouraging Swiss investments by granting federal insurance coverage against risks in the case of investments in developing countries, or by concluding bilateral treaties regarding the treatment of Swiss investments in the host country.

United Kingdom

Peter M. B. Rowland *

For upwards of a century private enterprises in the United Kingdom were wont to invest capital and reinvested profits on a large scale in foreign countries, mainly those now called 'developing' countries.

Already by 1964, however, when the Labour administration withdrew the tacit Governmental approval for such investment which had formerly existed, the source was tending to dry up as a result of currency problems, high taxation and low productivity; in addition, the attitude of some of the debtor nations had tended to sap previous enthusiasm. In recent years, therefore, the main emphasis has not surprisingly been on investment at home.

EXCHANGE CONTROL

Although this brief inquiry is directed to matters of taxation, it would be misleading to omit a reference to exchange control since this has had a considerable effect in reducing the outflow of investment funds from the United Kingdom, especially since June 1972. Previously there had been no exchange control bar on investment in the old 'Scheduled Territories' which corresponded roughly to the whole of the British Commonwealth with the exception of Canada.

In the case of a direct investment – portfolio investment is treated quite differently – the Bank of England will grant or withhold permission depending upon the estimated effect on the balance of payments. Generally applications for direct investment made by companies are authorized unless a net disadvantage to UK foreign exchange reserves is expected. The reserves would, of course, suffer if an investment was likely to be a bad one and might result in a loss. Consequently, the Bank, by way of safeguard, only considers applications from those with adequate expertise in the field in question.

Further, foreign currency may only be purchased at the current market rate in the official exchange market if the 'super criterion' is satisfied. This is that the investment will directly promote export of UK goods and services and is likely to produce benefits to the balance of payments equal to or exceeding the amount invested within 18 months and continuing thereafter. Otherwise the investment must be made with foreign currency purchased from a limited pool at a premium over the official rate which fluctuates with supply and demand but is usually very high. Moreover, upon repatriation of the funds only three-quarters goes into the pool; one-quarter of the then current premium is, therefore, lost. This is a powerful disincentive to investing abroad.

* Rowland, Debono, Limited, London.

FISCAL RESTRICTIONS ON INVESTING ABROAD

In addition to the need for Bank of England consent in order to invest outside the present sterling area – which comprises the United Kingdom, Ireland, the Channel Islands, Isle of Man and Gibraltar – there is the quite distinct requirement that permission from the Treasury must be obtained to take any action which directly or indirectly has the effect of transferring the whole or part of a company's trade abroad. This obligation, being concerned entirely with preventing avoidance of UK taxation, applies even though the transfer is within the sterling area, for example, to Jersey, and its administration has been delegated by the Treasury to the Inland Revenue. In practice, tax and commercial considerations are balanced against each other. Thus, consent would normally be given to the transfer of part of a company's manufacturing operations to a foreign subsidiary notwithstanding the loss of tax to the UK Revenue provided that there was a clear financial benefit from doing so, by reason, for example, of the availability of cheap labour or materials and/or nearness to foreign markets. In practice, this sometimes makes it easier for part of a trade to be transferred to a developing country but if so it is fortuitous; the Revenue is concerned only with the considerations already mentioned and not with favoring one group of countries over another.

INDIRECT DISINCENTIVES TO INVESTING ABROAD

Turning from these direct impediments to the outflow of capital abroad to those which are indirect, one finds they are now very important, particularly the system of capital allowances on plant and machinery and the generous grants and other tax incentives which are available where particular types of investments are made in the United Kingdom.

The capital allowance provisions are very complicated but the main features may be summarized as follows.[1]

Industrial buildings and structures (which exclude offices): The initial allowance of expenditure was increased as from 12th November 1972 to 52 percent. The annual writing-down allowance is 4 percent.

Plant and machinery: There is an immediate write-off of expenditure on almost all kinds of plant and machinery incurred after 21st March 1972. Exceptions are expensive motor cars, where the write-off is limited, and ships, where the write-off can be taken at any time. N.B. Deferral is sometimes beneficial; any balance of expenditure not written off – mainly that incurred before the date mentioned – is depreciated at an annual rate of 25 percent on the reducing balance.

Mines: There is an initial allowance of 40 percent – 100 percent if in Northern Ireland or a 'development area' – and a writing-down allowance of 5 percent (or a percentage based on output, if greater).

Dredging: There is an initial allowance of 15 percent and an annual allowance of 4 percent.

1. For foot-notes 1 to 3, see page 165.

Agricultural and forestry buildings and works: There is an initial allowance of 20 percent, followed by a write-off over 10 years is permitted.

Scientific research: A 100 percent write-off in the first year is allowed.

Because of these generous allowances it has been necessary to introduce a system of cash grants to encourage special types of expenditure. This was also felt to be often desirable because a capital allowance is only effective in reducing or eliminating tax and no tax is leviable until profits are earned, which may be long afterwards.

The entitlement to a grant may arise under any one of a number of statutory provisions which, taken together, cover a fairly wide area. Their general nature may, however, be gathered from the fact that they arise under the Industrial Development Act and Orders made under it, and that there are grants for expenditure on fishing vessels, grants made under the Agriculture Act 1967, grants under similar enactments applying to Northern Ireland and grants under certain Transport Acts.

They are only made when the capital expenditure is incurred by a person carrying on a business and they reduce the cost of the asset for the purpose of calculating capital allowances. This also applies in the case of subsidies and contributions by third parties except where the latter is unable to claim allowances himself.

Unlike capital allowances, where the governing feature is the fact that the person incurring the expenditure is liable to tax in the UK, these grants are only payable in respect of expenditure upon assets located in the UK.

Certain areas of the UK have been designated as 'development areas' and others as 'intermediate areas'. Approximately 20 percent of the country's working population lives in the former. Incentives to stimulate development in these areas is provided by means of investment grants and a number of other inducements based upon employment.[2]

Investment grants have the further advantage over capital allowances that normally they are not repayable unless the asset is sold within five years of the expenditure. In the case of capital allowances there is a 'claw-back' if a surplus over the written down value arises on disposal.

It will be apparent that the 100 percent depreciation allowance may cause problems in relation to companies operating abroad since the corresponding write-off in the foreign country is likely to be much less. Where this would result in a loss of double tax relief, the taxpayer is entitled to postpone his claim for the relevant tax allowance.

INCENTIVES TO INVEST ABROAD

The UK provides little by way of direct incentive to invest abroad in the sense of a fiscal or monetary advantage which would not be available in the case of a domestic investment, and perhaps that is hardly to be expected.[3] There are, however, certain exceptions in regard to mining.

Expenditure on abortive exploration may be deducted as revenue expenditure notwithstanding that this would not otherwise be the case, for example, because the exploration is abandoned before the commencement of trading.

Capital expenditure in connection with the working of a mine, oil well or other source of mineral deposits of a wasting nature, or searching for, discovering and testing such deposits, and winning access to them qualifies for an initial allowance of 40 percent. So does expenditure on the construction of certain classes of building which are likely to be of little or no value to a person working the source when he ceases to do so, or when a foreign concession under which it is worked comes to an end.

It is true that, except in the last case, these allowances are equally available in the case of UK mines and also that they amount to 100 percent where they are situated in certain UK areas. In practice, however, their benefit is mainly felt in developing countries since it is in them that the majority of mines owned by UK entities happen to be located.

It is also important to note that in relation to plant and machinery, capital allowances do not depend upon their having emanated from the UK.

In the ordinary way, expenditure on acquiring a site, or rights over it, does not qualify for capital allowances. However, this is not so where the land is outside the UK provided it is likely to become valueless in the circumstances mentioned above.

Another allowance only available where the expenditure is abroad relates to contributions of capital sums towards the cost of (i) mining employees' accommodation and welfare buildings, and (ii) works for the supply of public services. Provided the buildings and works are likely to be of little or no value when the source is no longer worked, writing-down allowances are made over a ten year period.

A substantial tax benefit may arise where a UK company invests in countries (seventeen at 1/3/78) to which tax sparing arrangements have been extended. These are invariably developing countries , and most are members of the British Commonwealth. 'Tax sparing' provisions are based on the view that where a developing country gives a tax incentive, e.g. by way of tax holiday, in order to encourage growth of a particular industry, it would generally be inappropriate for the Revenue of the developed country to take advantage of this to gather in more tax. The contrary view, namely, that a corporation cannot claim relief for tax it has not paid, is held, notably, by the US Government.

More broadly, it can be argued that it is indirectly in the interests of developed countries to encourage those with little more than a pool of labour and some raw materials to undertake some manufacturing activities, and 'tax sparing' arrangements viewed as a kind of aid have the advantage of enabling the donor to take a much more direct hand in controlling the manner in which the benefit is enjoyed than is usually possible. However that may be, 'tax sparing' provides a definite incentive to invest in the country concerned within the given fields. Furthermore, it may well provide a competitive edge over those who operate from within countries which make no such arrangements.

United Kingdom legislation authorizes the Revenue to enter into such arrangements but does not contain a general provision applying them to all similar cases. Each has to be contended for by the developing country during the negotiation of its Double Tax Agreement with the UK and the agreements define with considerable precision the circumstances in which the relief applies.

It is also normal to provide that it will cease in the event of any material amendment to the relevant local statutes. In addition to the direct credit for withholding taxes spared, the indirect credit is usually available for the taxes spared on the corporate income out of which a dividend was paid.

A typical example of a tax sparing arrangement is to be found in the double tax convention between the UK and Jamaica Article 23(2) which provides that for the purpose of allowing a credit against UK tax 'the term 'Jamaican tax payable' shall be deemed to include' Jamaican tax which would have been payable but for an exemption or reduction of tax granted under – and there follows a list of sections from some 15 different Acts dealing with such matters as pioneer industries, films, textiles, hotels, export encouragement and agricultural incentives.

Two other ways in which the UK has encouraged foreign investment remain to be mentioned. In the first place, it has been in the forefront of countries which have sought to remove the disincentives arising from double taxation; hence the whole paraphernalia of double taxation agreements.

In addition, the UK was one of the earliest countries to give an important measure of unilateral relief from double taxation in cases where there is no double taxation agreement, or the agreement does not cover the whole field. This was introduced in 1950 with the specific aim of encouraging overseas trading operations, and provides for credit to be given for foreign taxes upon income in much the same way as is to be found under the normal double taxation agreement. One illustration of its operation arises in relation to New Zealand tax charged on interest arising there to which a UK resident is entitled. This is not covered by the UK/New Zealand agreement, and unilateral relief, by way of credit, can be claimed.

Again, where the earnings of a resident individual are subject to UK tax under Schedule E, credit is given for any foreign tax imposed upon such part of his remuneration as is earned in the foreign (non-treaty) country.

Another important application of these provisions is to the underlying tax suffered by foreign subsidiaries and affiliates. Provided the UK resident company controls directly or indirectly not less than 10 percent of the voting power in the overseas company, foreign tax paid on the latter's profits and attributable to dividends received by the UK company qualifies for unilateral relief. This relief is extended to foreign tax paid in a third country and borne by the foreign affiliate.

DISTRIBUTIONS BY UK CORPORATIONS OF FOREIGN SOURCE INCOME

Whenever a distribution to shareholders is made the corporation must hand over to the Inland Revenue an amount equal to the excess over that distribution of a sum arrived at by grossing up the distribution at the basic rate of tax, 33% following the 1978 Finance Act. The amount so payable is known as advance corporation tax ('ACT') and, as its name implies, is a sum paid on account of 'mainstream' corporation tax. It is not a withholding tax, though its practical effect is rather similar. In particular, an individual recipient who is resident in the United Kingdom obtains a tax credit equal to the ACT and in the hands of a corporate recipient the dividend is treated as having already borne tax.

A number of double taxation agreements have been amended since the system was introduced with a view to extending to non-residents a share in the tax credit, the most common arrangement being that the United Kingdom Revenue retains 15% of the aggregate of dividend plus ACT – see this authority given by Section 497(1)(d) of the 1970 Act.

Where a United Kingdom company has direct or indirect control over not less than 10% of the voting power of a non-resident company, underlying tax paid by the latter is taken into account in calculating the tax credit – see Section 508 of the Taxes Act, 1970, as amended by Section 26 of the Finance Act, 1971.

One result of the imputation tax system in operation since April, 1973, and, in particular, of ACT, is that the credit for foreign tax may be reduced. This arises as follows.

The amount of ACT which can be used by way of credit against the company's liability to corporation tax is limited by Sections 100(6) and 85(2) of the Finance Act, 1972, to the ACT which would be payable on a distribution at the year end of the total trading profits (as adjusted for tax purposes). In effect this leaves mainstream corporation tax at 20% in charge. The purpose of imposing this limitation was that a recipient of a dividend who is not liable to tax, or only liable at a lower rate, can claim repayment of tax on the basis of the credit and the Government wanted to guard against the possibility of having to pay out more than it had received. Any 'surplus' ACT which cannot be used as a result of this rule may be related back to certain earlier periods, that is to say, periods beginning in the two years prior to the commencement of the one in which the surplus arose, or may be carried forward indefinitely, or surrendered to a subsidiary for current use.

Where ACT has been paid and there has also been liability to foreign tax, ACT relief has to be taken first. Subject to this the ACT, may be allocated amongst the various sources of income as is thought fit. It will normally be set against foreign income which has suffered the lowest rate of foreign tax, the balance being set so far as may be, against income taxed at the next lowest rate, and so on. This will maximise the foreign tax relief obtainable. Thus, assuming a company has paid ACT totalling £ 3,750 for a period and possesses trading income of £ 10,000 (assessable under Case I) plus foreign income (assessable under Case V) consisting of (a) a royalty of £ 2,000 (taxed locally at 5%) and (b) a dividend from X Ltd. of £ 4,000 (overseas tax 50%), the allocations and resulting tax liability will be:

(i) On the Case I income the gross corporation tax (say at 50%) will be £ 5,000, less ACT allocation of £ 3,000;

(ii) On the royalty of £ 2,000 the gross corporation tax will be £ 1,000, less ACT allocation of £ 600, and relief for overseas tax of £ 100;

(iii) On the X Ltd. dividend the gross corporation tax will be £ 2,000 less ACT allocation of £ 150 (being the balance of the ACT paid). The remaining £ 1,850 of corporation tax suffered may be set against the foreign tax of £ 2,000, but the remaining £ 150 of credit will be lost. Unlike ACT, it cannot be used in other periods or surrendered to subsidiaries.

1. The capital allowance provisions in regard to industrial buildings are set out in the Capital Allowances Act, 1968, the initial allowance being dealt with in § 1, and the writing down allowances in § 2. The new system of capital allowances for machinery and plant is set out in the Finance Act, 1971, Part III, Chapter 1. The increase in the first allowance to 100% for most items of machinery and plant was effected by § 67 of the Finance Act, 1972. Capital allowances for mines, dredging, agricultural work, and scientific research are dealt with respectively in the Capital Allowances Act, 1968, Chapters 3, 4 and 5 of Part I.

2. The investment grant provision has had an interesting history. Between 1966 and 1970 there was a general system of investment grants in England. This was abolished in 1970, then was reenacted in 1972 for limited types of investment in development areas. The reasons for terminating the investment grants in 1970 and reverting to a system of first year and subsequent year allowances were '(a) that the effects of the grants upon investment had been disappointing, (b) that they were difficult to administer, and (c) that they were available whether the recipient enterprises were profitable or not.' Bracewell-Milnes & Shenfield, LXIa Cahiers de Droit Fiscal International 485 (1976). Professor Prest, in discussing the interaction of the investment grant and the 100 percent initial allowance, pointed out that the post-tax return would exceed the pre-tax: 'Thus an incorporated enterprise with a 10% return before tax, and paying corporation tax at 50% but receiving 100% initial allowances and a separate grant equal to 20% of capital investment would enjoy a post-tax post-benefit return of 16.7%; an unincorporated enterprise paying tax at 75% but otherwise in the same position would find its post-tax benefit rate of return to be 50%!' Prest, Public Finance.

3. *See generally* Tax Treatment of Private Investment in Developing Countries by the United Kingdom of Great Britain and Northern Ireland (UN Sales No. E.72.XVI.2).

United States of America

Robert Anthoine *

TAX PATTERN

United States citizens, wherever resident, and aliens resident in the United States are taxed on their worldwide income. Prior to 1979 an exclusion was allowed up to a maximum of $ 25,000 per annum for income earned abroad. The Tax Reform Act of 1978 substituted for the old exclusion a new regime which provides in general an exclusion or deduction for 'excess' housing, living and educational costs incurred by US persons working abroad, and other peripheral benefits.

Corporations incorporated in the United States, irrespective of location of seat of management or place of management and control, are taxed on their worldwide income. All other corporations (foreign) and non-resident aliens are usually taxed only on income derived from United States sources. Where non-business income is not effectively connected with a permanent establishment, United States income tax is withheld at source at a 30% or lower treaty rate.

Special favorable rules apply to domestic corporations that do business in Puerto Rico and other possessions of the United States which have the effect of exempting them from US income tax on their profits derived from the active conduct of trade or business in the possession. These tax incentives plus the proximity of the United States market and the inapplicability of US customs duties to Puerto Rican imports have had a marked effect upon US investment in Puerto Rico.

Until 1977 US corporations engaged almost exclusively in active business in the Western Hemisphere enjoyed a 14% tax reduction, but this benefit is being phased out of the law pursuant to the Tax Reform Act of 1976.

The current income tax rates for individuals range from 14% to 70% with a maximum rate of 50% generally applicable to earned income. The gain on sale of capital assets held for more than one year is taxed to non-corporate taxpayers at a maximum rate of 28% and to corporations at 28%, plus a possible preferential tax of about 6%. Corporations are taxed at the rate of 17% on the first $ 25,000 of taxable income, 20% on the next $ 25,000, 30% on the next $ 25,000, 40% on the next $ 25,000, and 46% on all over $ 100,000. Shareholders are allowed a $ 100 exclusion for dividends received from US corporations, but are entitled to no credit for corporate taxes paid with respect to the distribution. Various proposals for integration of corporate and shareholder income taxation are under discussion, but no provision is expected to be enacted for some time.

The United States has no foreign exchange or similar regulations although for about ten years prior to 1974 both an interest equalization tax and capital outflow restrictions were in force.

* Winthrop, Stimson, Putnam & Roberts, New York.

GENERAL PROVISIONS FOR TAXING DIRECT FOREIGN INVESTMENT [1]

The income of a foreign corporation is generally not subject to US income tax until distributed as dividends to United States shareholders. An exception to this general rule is provided by 'Subpart F' which taxes certain foreign corporate income directly to US shareholders even in the absence of actual distribution. A foreign corporation is a controlled foreign corporation if more than 50% of its voting stock is owned directly or indirectly by US persons who own 10% or more of the voting stock. Only those US shareholders who directly or indirectly own 10% or more of the voting stock of a controlled foreign corporation are subjected to tax on their pro rata shares of Subpart F income. The Subpart F income which is subject to these constructive distribution rules is generally of the foreign personal holding company type, that is, dividends, interest, rents, royalties and gains from the sale of securities but the tainted income also includes certain active business income derived from base company sales and service activities involving related companies. If less than 10% of the gross income is of the tainted variety, it is ignored; if tainted income exceeds 70% of gross income, all is treated as distributed.

Under the Administration's 1978 Tax Bill, a new regime would have been installed over a three-year period under which the 10% or greater US shareholders in foreign controlled corporations would have been taxed upon their pro rata shares of all foreign corporate income whether or not distributed. The provisions of Subpart F would have been repealed as no longer necessary. The proposal was not enacted in 1978 but is likely to be reintroduced in a subsequent Congress.

Double taxation of foreign source income is mitigated through the application of a broadly based credit for foreign income taxes and foreign taxes imposed in lieu of income taxes. Income-type taxes paid to political subdivisions of a foreign country also qualify. In addition to the credit for taxes directly imposed upon the US taxpayer, the indirect foreign tax credit is also available for foreign creditable taxes paid on the operating income out of which distributions are made by first, second and third tier foreign subsidiaries. The US corporation must own 10% or more of the voting stock of the first tier corporation. In order for second and third tier foreign creditable taxes to be available for the US indirect credit, each foreign parent corporation in the chain connected to the US parent must own 10% or more of the voting stock of its subsidiary and the US parent must have an indirect ownership interest of at least 5% in the voting stock of the second or third tier corporations that paid the foreign tax.

The available foreign tax credit is subject to an overall, worldwide limitation that treats all foreign source income as a single unit. The credit is limited to the amount of US income tax that would be payable on taxable income from all foreign countries in the absence of any credit. A favorable effect of the overall limitation is to enable the US corporation to average foreign income taxes imposed at a rate higher than the US rate with those imposed at a lower rate.

1. For foot-notes 1 to 3, see pages 173 up to and including 175.

INCENTIVES TO INVESTMENT AT HOME AND TAX BARRIERS TO FOREIGN INVESTMENT

United States law provides a number of tax inducements to invest at home. The investment tax credit of 10% is available only for capital expenditure at home. The favorable asset depreciation range system (ADR) cannot be applied to property used predominantly outside the United States. (Under the ADR system, the useful life of various categories of personal property is set up under guideline classes, and the taxpayer may choose a depreciable life which ranges between 20% below to 20% above the guideline life.) And the deferral of tax on export income provided by the Domestic International Sales Corporation (DISC) is not available for foreign produced property. Although the prior deferral of tax on 50% of export earnings has been curtailed by the 1976 legislation by the adoption of an incremental approach designed to limit benefits to those taxpayers increasing their exports, the provision still provides substantial benefits.

Under the Tax Reform Act of 1978, the 10% investment tax credit was made a permanent part of the law and its application was expanded by raising the amount of tax liability which the credit may offset from 50% to 90% by 1982 and by extending it to rehabilitation of existing industrial and commercial buildings and to certain pollution control facilities. The Administration proposed that the DISC provision be phased out of the law so that it would not be applicable at all for taxable years ending after December 31, 1980 but that proposal was not adopted.

The value of the enumerated items under present law is revealed by the estimate of revenue loss contained in the 1979 tax expenditure budget, assuming no change in law:

	Corporations In Millions of Dollars		
Description	*1977*	*1978*	*1979*
Deferral of income of controlled foreign corporations	570	615	665
Deferral of income of DISC	945	1,135	1,335
Asset depreciation range	1,955	2,245	2,640
Investment credit	8,880	10,735	13,320

The only significant 1978 change was in the investment credit, resulting in an increase in the 1979 figure to 14,445.

Apart from the 'positive' incentives to domestic investment which act as a disincentive to foreign investment, there are a number of 'negative' provisions that act as a disincentive to foreign investment. Noteworthy among them is the Section 861-8 regulation which appeared in final form in 1977 after over ten years of vacillation. This regulation allocates a wide variety of expense, such as research and development, to foreign sources, thereby reducing net foreign source income and the utilization of foreign tax credits. Another unfavorable administrative development has been the concerted attack upon the utilization of the foreign tax credit by seeking to establish more rigid criteria that foreign taxes must satisfy in order to qualify as income taxes or taxes imposed in lieu of income taxes, and hence to qualify for the credit.

A recently adopted statutory provision that is onerous to the investor abroad is Section 904(f) which recaptures losses from foreign sources when future income is derived from foreign sources. The technique applied is to treat the subsequent income to the extent of the prior losses as if it were from domestic sources, thereby eliminating foreign tax credits.

Additional tax barriers to foreign investment include the inability of a US parent corporation to file a consolidated federal income tax return with foreign subsidiaries except for a limited class of Canadian and Mexican companies. Within a consolidated group, losses of one company can offset profits of another, and properties can pass untaxed within the group. In addition, the election under Subchapter S which permits certain closely held corporations to be taxed much like a partnership and thereby avoid the corporate tax is not available to corporations that derive more than 80% of their gross income from foreign sources, and percentage depletion is allowed only for domestic production of oil and gas.

On a wholly different front is the recent development of using the tax law to regulate the conduct by US firms of their overseas activities. Both the Tax Reform Act of 1976 and the Export Administration Act contain important provisions dealing with participation in international boycotts. The 1976 Revenue Act also added a provision pertaining to the payment by controlled foreign corporations of amounts that would be illegal under US law. More recently, the Foreign Corrupt Practices Act makes resort to the tax law for some sanctions. In general, the violation of these laws leads to denial of the benefits of DISC, of foreign tax credits, and of absence of US tax on undistributed earnings of controlled foreign corporations – any of which can prove very expensive indeed.

INVESTMENT IN DEVELOPING COUNTRIES

Internal law contains no provisions designed to encourage private investment in the developing countries. Prior to the revenue legislation of 1975 and 1976, there were several provisions of US law that provided marginal benefits to investment in developing countries that were not available to investment at home or elsewhere in the developed world, but all of these have now been repealed. Indeed, the Congress has even eliminated the statutory concept of 'less developed' country from the Internal Revenue Code.[2]

The standard applied by the US government in its tax policy with respect to the taxation of foreign income may be described as 'capital export neutrality', as distinguished from 'capital import neutrality'. The former is achieved when the total rate of corporate tax on foreign profits is the same as it would be on comparable domestic profits. The latter is achieved when firms of all nationalities operating in one industry pay the same total tax rate on profits earned in the country where the industry is located. The application of these standards and the general subject of US taxation of foreign income are discussed in a study prepared in 1976 by the Treasury's Office of International Tax Affairs for the House Ways and Means Committee Task Force on Taxation of Foreign Income, reprinted in the August, September and October 1976 issues of the Bulletin for International Fiscal Documentation. The Treasury study, which does not reflect the Tax Reform Act of 1976, suggests that accepting the principle of, and applying the standard of, capital export neutrality, the US tax law even prior to the 1976 changes was weighted in favor of investment at home rather than being neutral. This trend has been accentuated by the provisions of the Tax Reform Act of 1976 and a major blow to investment in developing countries was avoided thanks to the defeat of the Administration's proposal to tax US persons currently on their shares of the undistributed income of controlled foreign corporations.[3]

TAX TREATIES

The United States presently has in force only six tax treaties with developing countries: Finland, Greece, Iceland, Ireland, Pakistan and Trinidad and Tobago. In view of the hard line taken by the Senate Foreign Relations Committee, through which a treaty must pass enroute to the Senate for ratification, there has been little inducement for a developing country to participate in the treaty process but the US Treasury has an ambitious program underway. Treaties have been signed but not yet ratified with Cyprus, Egypt, Israel, Korea, Morocco and the Philippines.

The United States has occasionally attempted to make concessions to developing countries in tax treaties, but no favorable provision has been ratified. For example, the signed but unratified treaty with Israel contains unusual provisions which favorably treat grants by the Israeli government to US investors and contributed by them to Israeli subsidiaries as contributions to capital and certain loans made as creditable taxes. However, the United States has never consented to the inclusion in a treaty of any provision to encourage major direct private investment in the developing country. No tax sparing provision has been included in any tax treaty negotiated by the United States since 1960 and, of the four treaties that contained such a provision, that with Pakistan became effective January 1, 1959 with a reservation attached by the Senate to the tax sparing provision, and the other three treaties (with India, Israel and the United Arab Republic) were withdrawn from consideration.

However, the extension of the investment tax credit to investment in developing countries was supported by Presidents Kennedy and Johnson. In 1964, a bill was introduced to that effect, but hearings were never held. Moreover, during the Kennedy and Johnson administrations tax treaties were negotiated with Brazil, Thailand and Israel which provided for a credit equal to 7 percent of certain new investments made in the stock of eligible corporations and also of certain reinvested earnings, where the US person owned at least 25 percent of the corporation's voting power. However, these provisions never became effective.

More recently, an article in the treaty with Trinidad and Tobago, signed in January 1970, deferred tax that would otherwise be payable on the transfer in exchange for stock of industrial property rights or technical information to a corporation foreign to the United States. The Senate, in ratifying the treaty, subjected its consent to a reservation concerning this article and issued a statement making it clear that the Committee believed that private American investment abroad should not be encouraged under current economic and political conditions. This position was reaffirmed in 1976 and 1977 in connection with the income tax treaty signed in 1976 between the United States and South Korea and submitted to the Senate Foreign Relations Committee in 1978. The letter of the Department of State to the President, dated August 14, 1976, and the report of the Senate Committee state that in the exchange of notes the United States agrees, when feasible, to resume discussions with Korea with a view toward reaching agreement on a supplementary protocol providing a tax impetus to the flow of US capital and technology to Korea.

The United States is sometimes willing to depart from the OECD model in negotiating treaties with developing nations in order to permit the latter to impose corporate income and dividend withholding taxes up to the maximum effective rate of 46% that can be fully credited against the US tax. An example is the recently negotiated US-Philippines treaty.

SUMMARY OF THE PRESENT US TAX LAW

Under the present US tax law, the income earned by foreign subsidiaries engaged in active operations in the developing countries will not be subject to US tax until remitted to the US shareholders (except in rare cases, for income from certain tax haven trading activities which is taxed to certain US shareholders under subpart F). Accordingly, as long as the subsidiary reinvests its profits abroad, the US tax law will not frustrate any tax incentive provided locally by a developing country. Moreover, since dividend distributions are deemed to be out of the most recently accumulated profits (LIFO), distributions made out of earnings accumulated after the end of a tax holiday period will carry with them a direct credit for any withholding tax and the indirect credit for the underlying corporate income tax imposed by the developing country at its regular rates. The effective rate of income tax on the foreign profits will be the higher of the US or the foreign rate. Indeed, it can be said that as compared with tax sparing, the US system appears to encourage reinvestment of profits rather than rapid remittance and hence to be beneficial to the developing country. This system would of course have been changed if the Administration's 1978 tax proposal noted above had been adopted.

Accommodation between a developing country's tax holiday program which limits tax benefits to income not taxed by the capital exporting country and the US system is suggested by certain provisions negotiated in the US-Egyptian income tax treaty, although the provisions are now obsolete there because of changes in Egyptian law. The idea is to provide that for purposes of the amount of income tax due to the host country, the profits of a local corporation (more than 10 percent of the voting power of which is owned by US residents) from sources other than the United States, which are not actually taxed by the United States, will be deemed not subject to taxation in the United States within the meaning of the relevant article of the investment law until those profits are distributed as a dividend by such corporation to a citizen or resident of the United States. Accordingly, as long as the profits are reinvested during the holiday period, no income tax will be payable. When they are later distributed, local corporate tax will be payable and will be creditable against the US recipient's US tax. In the absence of treaty, such a foreign tax might be attacked as a non-creditable tax on the ground that it is not an income tax by US standards. US policy in this area is unsettled.

UNITED STATES TAX POLICY

It is highly unlikely that the United States will adopt a system of tax sparing or tax exemption for income from the developing world. Moreover United States business has been willing to make investment commitments in developing countries without such provisions. Indeed, in view of the fact that US Enterprises own about one half of the stock of all foreign investments in developing countries, it is clear that the US tax regime has not acted as a significant deterrent to such investments.

In the author's view, as the cornerstone of its international tax policy the United States should continue the foreign tax credit with undiminished vitality and should continue to tax the overseas profits of controlled foreign corporations in the developing countries only upon distribution of dividends to the shareholders, apart from the limited scope of Subpart F which can be modified from time to time to meet changing circumstances. On a case by case basis through individually negotiated income tax treaties the US should extend its investment credit to investment in the shares of subsidiaries that will engage in specified activities in the developing country. Also, in order to facilitate the flow of technology to and technical cooperation with the developing countries, the United States in individual tax treaties and specific cases should permit deferral of US tax on the transfer of technology. [4]

1. For a discussion of the US law prior to the 1976 Act, see United States of America: Income Taxation of Private Investments in Developing Countries (UN Sales No. E.76.XVI.1 (1976)).

2. One provision eliminated by the 1976 Act was the favorable computation of the foreign tax credit with respect to dividends received from less developed country corporations. Since the effective date of the Revenue Act of 1962, a US corporation seeking to credit foreign taxes paid by its subsidiary in the developed world has had to gross up the dividend income received by the amount of the foreign income taxes attributable to such dividend income, resulting in a total tax burden at least equal to that under the US corporate rate. However, until the effective date of the 1976 legislation, the old *American Chicle* formula continued to apply to the calculation of the foreign tax credit on dividends received from less developed country corporations. That computation gave the US corporate taxpayer both a deduction for all of the foreign tax and a credit for a percentage of that tax. As a result, in the case of dividends received from a first tier subsidiary, the effective tax rate on the earnings was less than the US rate, then 48 percent, where the foreign income tax on

the profits distributed was more than zero and less than 48 percent, with the lowest overall effective income tax rate of 42.24 percent being achieved when the effective foreign tax rate was just one-half of the US rate. This benefit, which in truth could not be said to have had any serious incentive effect in inducing investment in the developing world, disappeared on January 1, 1978, after which all distributions from such subsidiaries have to be grossed up in the same manner as dividends from developed country corporations. The 1976 Act also eliminated the use of the per-country limitation in computing the foreign tax credit.

Another provision repealed by the 1976 legislation was the exception for less developed country corporations that existed in section 1248, added by the Revenue Act of 1962. Under that provision, US persons, owning or deemed to own 10 percent or more of the voting power of a controlled foreign corporation during the five year period prior to a sale or exchange, are required to treat gain realized on the shares in the foreign corporation as a dividend to the extent of the earnings and profits of the corporation attributable to those shares accumulated after 1962. Only the balance of any gain is considered capital. As enacted in 1962, section 1248 did not apply to earnings and profits accumulated by a foreign corporation while it was a less developed country corporation as long as the stock sold has been owned by the shareholder for at least ten years before the sale. This exception has been repealed for taxable years beginning after 1975. However, the old exclusion still applies to earnings accumulated before January 1, 1976, whether or not the corporation remains a less developed country corporation and whether the US shareholder had owned the stock for ten years as of that date. It is unlikely that this section 1248 exception had any incentive effect in inducing private capital to flow to the less developed countries. The absence of any foreign tax credit on a capital gain transaction narrowed the tax differential between dividend and capital gain treatment.

A benefit that disappeared in the 1975 legislation was the exception from foreign base company income in section 954 for dividends and interest received from, and gains from the sale of, qualified investments in less developed countries, to the extent that there was an increase for that same taxable year in qualified investments in less developed countries. Qualified investments were defined as stock and debt obligations having a maturity of one year or more of a less developed country corporation in which at least 10 percent of the total combined voting power was owned by the controlled foreign corporation, and the debt obligations of the less developed countries themselves. Those dividends, interest and gains could be reinvested in such qualified investments without being caught under subpart F and included in the gross income of the US shareholders of the base company. The reinvested amounts became taxable to the US shareholders only when the amount of the qualified investment decreased in a later taxable year. The repeal has removed the marginal advantage of being able to transfer profits from one less developed country corporation to another through the base company without the current imposition of US income tax. The advantage was always narrow, and did not apply to income derived from the developed world that flowed through the base company to the developing countries.

An additional marginal, but sometimes helpful, advantage also died in 1975 with the repeal of the minimum distributions method of avoiding subpart F liability: the option to exclude a less developed country corporation under a group election in the calculation of the minimum distribution method of satisfying subpart F liability. This election permitted the advantage of both a group election, where appropriate, and individual treatment of less developed country corporations that would otherwise be within the group, but minimum distributions are no more.

The 1975 Act also removed from the law the provision for percentage depletion of foreign production, introduced limitations upon the foreign tax credit for taxes paid in connection with foreign oil and gas income, provided for the recapture of foreign oil-related losses, and reduced the permissible amount of tainted gross income under Subpart F from the former 30% to the present 10%.

In addition to enacting Subpart F into the law, the Revenue Act of 1962 provided for the treatment of recognized gain from the sale or exchange after 1962 to a foreign corporation of a patent, an invention, model or design, a copyright, a secret formula or process, or any other similar property right as ordinary income rather than capital gain where the sale is made by a United States person who directly or indirectly controls the foreign corporation. The Act also introduced a new and separate limitation upon the foreign tax credit on foreign source interest income and increased the amount taxable upon the receipt by a domestic corporation of a dividend in property from a foreign corporation.

3. See Recommendations of the Task Force on Foreign Source Income, Committee on Ways and Means, US House of Representatives, 95th Cong., 1st Sess. (March 8, 1977). The study contains a discussion of issues and possible solutions with respect to the tax treatment of shipping income, the exclusions from tax of certain earned income of US citizens abroad and of overseas allowances of government employees, state taxation of foreign source income, the limitations on foreign tax credits, and the 'deferral' of tax on income derived by foreign corporations controlled by US shareholders. With respect to the foreign tax credit, the Committee recommends no further changes. Similarly, in connection with the preservation of the 'deferral' principle, the task force decided not to make any recommendations to change the law.

The discussion of the tax 'deferral' principle contains a useful summary of alternative solutions which have been proposed from time to time, and some illuminating statistics. The then current estimate of additional revenue to be obtained from overturning deferral was only $365 million, or 1.5% of total corporate profits from foreign operations of US owned foreign affiliates. (The total tax payments of these affiliates amounted to $12.3 billion of which $10.3 billion was made to foreign governments and $2 billion to the US.) Of the $365 million, over $100 million would be attributable to foreign flag shipping. The balance of less than $265 million would be attributable to manufacturing and other operations overseas. If foreign affiliates in the developing nations were to be excluded, the additional revenue would be far less than $265 million. The report notes that a 1974 survey of 63 countries indicated that 26 countries had an effective corporate and withholding tax rate above the 48% US rate and 37 countries had rates below 48%. Of the 37 countries with rates below 48%, all but 10 are developing countries. Thus, it is mainly in these countries that the impact of ending deferral would be felt.

4. Under present law, gain from the sale or exchange of a patent, an invention, model or design, a copyright, a secret formula or process, or any other similar property right to any foreign corporation by any United States person which controls such foreign corporation is treated as ordinary income rather than as capital gain. Control means, as in Subpart F, ownership of more than 50% of the voting power of outstanding stock. However, such gains will not be immediately taxed where the US transferor owns 80% or more of each class of stock of the foreign corporation provided that it can be established that such transfer is not in pursuance of a plan having as one of its principal purposes the avoidance of income tax.

Summary of Other Developed Country Laws

FINLAND[1]

Finland has been regarded as both a developed and a developing country. In its internal law it does not provide any specific incentives for investment in developing countries or for inward investment. Resident companies, defined as companies that are registered in Finland or have their center of management located there, are subject to national income tax on their worldwide income. The national income tax is levied when foreign branch income is earned and when dividends from foreign sources are received. Companies are also subject to a municipal income tax which after 1979 will be imposed on income from foreign permanent establishments. In the absence of treaty, double taxation is avoided through credits for foreign taxes paid on income subject to Finnish national income tax. In the case of dividend income, to obtain the foreign tax credit the Finnish shareholder must own at least 25% of the capital of the distributing company or 40% of such capital must be owned by residents of Finland. Foreigners receiving non-business income from Finnish sources are subject to withholding taxes of 30% on patent royalties and 25% on dividends[2] but none on interest paid on bona fide indebtedness, unless a lower treaty rate applies.

Through its tax treaty program, Finland on a mutual basis with its treaty partners does provide a tax incentive to investment in each direction by exempting from Finnish tax the income earned by a permanent establishment located in the jurisdiction of the treaty partner, by reducing or eliminating the withholding tax on dividends and royalties paid by Finnish residents to residents of the treaty partner, and by treating dividends from subsidiaries in that foreign country in the same manner as dividends from Finnish companies and hence exempt from tax. In some treaties with developing countries, e.g. Israel, Finland allows a credit for taxes spared.

At present Finland has tax treaties covering income and wealth taxation with the following countries: Austria, Belgium, Brasil, Canada, Czeckoslovakia, Denmark, Egypt, France, the United States, India, Ireland, Iceland, Israel, Italy, Japan, Malta, the Netherlands, Norway, Poland, Portugal, Rumania, Switzerland, the Soviet Union, Spain, Great Britain, Sweden, Tanzania, and West Germany.

During the past decade Finland has attempted to conclude tax treaties which to the greatest possible extent conform to the OECD's model tax convention. Except for certain reservations required because of Finland's special housing companies, Finland has stated a reservation against the OECD's model convention of 1977 only as to art. 9(2) (associated enterprises) and art. 12 (royalties).

These reservations are based primarily on control considerations rather than differing views on issues of principle.

1. From information provided by R. Kenneth Wrede, Attorney at Law, Helsinki.
2. With a few exceptions.

In recent years Finland has gone over to application of the tax credit method, and in treaties with less developed countries Finland has generally accepted the inclusion of provisions concerning the tax sparing credit.

IRELAND

Ireland has a comprehensive system of tax incentives to induce foreign investment. Cash grants may be made generally up to 20% of the cost of new plants in designated areas, with the basis for depreciation not reduced by the grant. Moreover, as in the case of the microchip plant referred to in paragraph 5 of this Reporter's statement, the Irish authorities can stretch their guidelines in order to provide larger grants. The rate of depreciation on a new plant may be selected by the owner. Hence, the plant may be fully depreciated in the first year, and where investment allowances have been made the depreciation will exceed the net cost of the plant.

Of great importance to foreign enterprises seeking to export from Ireland to other members of the Common Market is the total abatement of corporate income tax that would otherwise be payable on export sales. To qualify for the tax relief the goods exported must have been manufactured within Ireland. Complete exemption is provided for profits attributable to exports for the first 15 years with a gradual reduction over the succeeding five years. Under existing legislation, the tax exemption expires in 1990.

In addition to the general tax relief, a special provision pertains to Shannon Airport. Companies that export may enjoy total exemption from corporation tax if they have facilities that operate within the customs free area of the Airport. The exemption applies only to profits from exports and not to profits from trading operations carried on in Ireland outside the customs free area or to profits from the sale of goods to Irish residents. The trading company may enjoy the tax relief even if it is a foreign corporation operating through a branch.

NEW ZEALAND

Under internal law, a New Zealand corporation is subject to tax on foreign branch income as earned. However, there is no New Zealand tax on dividends received by domestic corporations from foreign corporations not exempt from tax, these being regarded as non-assessable income (exemption with progression). Double taxation with respect to all types of assessable income, such as interests, rents and royalties, is avoided by foreign tax credits.

NORWAY

Norwegian residents are taxed on worldwide income. Where a tax treaty does not provide greater relief, a Norwegian corporation is subject to income tax on 50% foreign branch income. Dividends from foreign sources are taxed when received. Withholding taxes paid abroad may be credited against Norwegian taxes but only where a treaty applies does Norway permit the indirect foreign tax credit. Over 30 income tax treaties are in force under most of which foreign income is exempt from Norwegian taxation. In a number of the treaties with developing countries, Norway permits credit for taxes spared on various categories of income.

SOUTH AFRICA

Broadly speaking, South Africa's tax system operates on a territorial basis and income from foreign sources is not included in taxable income. In cases in which inclusion in South African income might arise as a result of disagreement as to the source of the income, for example royalties, unilateral relief is provided by exempting from South African tax the whole or part of the income in question or by application of a foreign tax credit for the taxes incurred abroad.

STATEMENTS OF DEVELOPING COUNTRIES

Argentina

Pedro de Elizalde *

1. At present Argentina does not offer foreign investment tax incentives which would not be available to local investments. Foreign investments and foreign-owned local companies are, however, eligible for promotional benefits and other incentives substantially on an equal basis with local capital.

For example, Industrial Promotion Law No. 21.608 enacted July 23, 1977 authorizes the grant of the following benefits to national as well as foreign-owned local companies:

a) Exemption, reduction or postponement of national taxes; accelerated depreciation of fixed assets for tax purposes;
b) Exemption or reduction of import duties on fixed assets or spare parts therefore, when such assets or parts cannot be manufactured locally under reasonable quality, price or delivery time conditions.
c) Facilities for the purchase or rental of State owned property.
d) Temporary restrictions to the import of competitive goods during the start-up of the project.
e) Import duty relief on the imported content of the goods to be manufactured locally; and
f) Import duty protection against similar imported goods, on a decreasing basis.

The grant of the above incentives is resolved in accordance with specific regional or sectorial regimes and on a case by case basis after evaluation of each project.

The only limitations based on foreign ownership are that in this case the grant must be resolved by an Executive Decree, rather than Ministerial or lower authority resolutions, and that the benefits referred to in a) and b) above must be granted 'based on selective criteria and on the possibility of orientating the foreign investment in accordance with established policies or programs'.

This law marks an important change because the previous industrial promotional system was specifically restricted to locally-owned operations. However, as explained above, it cannot be regarded as a promotion of foreign investment, but rather as a promotion of certain industrial activities irrespective of the nationality of the investor.

2. The specific statute applicable to foreign investment is Foreign Investment Law No. 21.382, together with its regulatory decree No. 283/77 and implementing regulations of the Undersecretary of Foreign Investments. This statute reaffirms the principle of equality discussed above: 'subject to the provisions of this law and those established in special or promotional regimes, foreign investors . . . shall have the same rights and obligations as national investors under the Constitution and the law' (law 21.382, art. 1).

The incentives offered to foreign investors under this law are not of a fiscal nature and may be summarized as follows:

* Allende & Brea, Buenos Aires.

a) The right to repatriate capital after three years from the date of the investment. This right may be suspended only temporarily by the Executive in case of a declared general difficulty in the external payments situation of the country.
b) The right to remit dividends at any time. In case of a declared difficulty as mentioned in a), the investor is entitled to receive Government bonds denominated in the respective foreign currency and bearing international market interest rates, against surrender of the equivalent in local currency. This is an option which has proven of great interest to investors in the past, among other reasons, because it provides a practical possibility of protecting profits available in local currency against devaluation while the inability to remit subsists.

Only the investments registered in accordance with the law qualify for the above benefits. Registration requires the prior approval of the investment either by an Executive Decree or a resolution of the Undersecretary of Foreign Investments, depending on the nature and purpose of the investment. As an exception, the reinvestment of profits on previously registered investments, new investments not exceeding annually 10% of the existing registered investments and to be applied for the same purposes, and the foreign investments already existing in Argentina when law 21.382 was enacted (September, 1976), do not need prior approval for registration.

In all the above cases, the law provides for registration in the currency of origin of the investment.

3. The nature of the remittance rights conferred by law No. 21.382 upon the holder of a registered investment is a rather difficult legal subject.

At times when there are no exchange control limitations upon the repatriation of foreign capital or the remittance of profits, as it is presently the case, said rights have no practical effect since all investors, whether or not registered, may and do in fact obtain foreign currency for such purposes. This situation was clearly recognized by the Minister's message to the President proposing the enactment of the law, which is normally accepted as an important interpretation guideline.

Said remittance rights, therefore, would become effective only when exchange controls restrict the availability of foreign currency for capital repatriation or profit remittances. Yet, if and when controls are imposed, the legal situation will depend upon the laws and regulations imposing the controls rather than upon the Foreign Investment Law, since the regulation of foreign currency transactions is a matter of public policy against which no one may have 'previously acquired' rights. From a practical viewpoint, this is all the more evident because it will in fact be impossible to obtain foreign currency in an exchange controle situation if the exchange control authority does not so authorize.

Nevertheless, it appears to us that based upon the individual right originated by the registration of the investment under law 21.382 and on the constitutional guarantee of property, a foreign investor would be entitled to be compensated by the government for the loss suffered as a result of exchange controls preventing the repatriation of capital or the remittance of profits in accordance with said law. In this respect, however, it should be noted that the law contemplates exceptions in case the Executive Power suspends remittances as a result of a declared 'difficulty in the external payments situation' (see 2 (a) and (b) above); naturally no compensation could be claimed if those exceptions are applicable.

4. The Foreign Investment Law establishes a special tax upon the net profits (i.e. after income tax withholding) paid in excess of 12% of the registered investment base each year, and on the capital repatriated in excess of 12% of the registered investment base.

The rate of the tax is progressive, as follows:

Percentage of profits (or excess over the registered investment base)	*Applicable rate*
From 12% up to 15%, on the excess over 12%	15%
From 15% up to 20%, on the excess over 15%	20%
More than 20%, on the excess over 20%	25%

The excess over 12% in a year can be offset against deffects within the previous five years. Consequently, the tax is not payable when the average over the last five years is below said limit.

The following profit distributions are not subject to this special tax:

i) Stock dividends,
ii) Profits otherwise reinvested in the company,
iii) Profits invested in other companies in compliance with the law,
iv) Profits paid to local foreign capital companies,
v) Profits earned from temporary contributions of capital,
vi) Other profits that may be exempted by decree of the Executive Power.

Furthermore, this tax is not applicable to foreign investments which have not been registered and therefore do not benefit from the remittance and repatriation rights discussed above.

5. Two tax principles or rules of interpretation of interest for foreign investors deserve a special comment:

a. Transactions between a foreign owned local company and its parent or controlling company are considered for all purposes as transactions between independent parties if the respective terms and conditions conform to the normal practice of the market on an arms length basis. Otherwise, such transactions must be treated and taxed in accordance with the rules applicable to capital contributions and profit distributions.

In the case of loans from parent to subsidiary, the 'independent party' treatment will apply only if the terms and conditions thereof have been approved by the Central Bank. In the case of technology transfer transactions between parent and subsidiary such as patent or trademark licenses, technical assistance agreements, etc., the respective instruments must conform to, and be registered in accordance with, the specific legislation governing the transfer of foreign technology.

Until 1976 the Argentine tax authorities, based first on court decisions and later on specific legislation, were entitled to disallow intercompany transactions for tax purposes through an extensive application of the 'economic unit' concept. Thus, a loan from parent to subsidiary, whether or not on normal market conditions, would be treated as a capital contribution and interest thereon as a profit or dividend rather than as a deductible expense. The same happened with respect to royalties or technical assistance payments or even to the supply of goods under certain circumstances.

This is no longer so, although such transactions are still subject to special review in order to determine if arms length conditions are fulfilled.

b. In accordance with article 21 of Income Tax law No. 20.628, no tax exemption or rebate will be effective if the effect of same is to transfer tax revenue to foreign tax collecting agencies. For example: an exemption granted with respect to the regular income tax withholding on interest paid to foreign beneficiaries will not be valid if such interest is taxable in the country of origin of the beneficiary and the beneficiary can take the Argentine tax withholding as a tax credit, because in this case the exemption will only transfer the waived tax revenue to the country of the beneficiary.

This rule applies to income tax exemptions provided for in the Income Tax law as well as in other laws. The only exceptions are (i) the exemption on government bonds and securities, (ii) the exemption on interest on loans to finance industrial equipment imports, and on loans obtained by the government and official banks, and (iii) international double taxation treaties.

The taxpayer has the burden of proving that no transfer of revenue will result from the exemption.

APPENDIX

Income Tax Rates and Mandatory Withholdings Related to Foreign Investment

Basic corporate income tax rate:	33%
Income tax withholding on dividends paid to foreign stockholders:	17.5%
Income tax withholding on general income of any nature paid to foreign beneficiaries, when no specific rate is provided for:	45%
Income tax rate applicable to earnings of branches of foreign companies or permanent establishments owned by foreign beneficiaries:	45%
Income tax withholdings on interest paid on foreign loans (when no exemptions or other special regime applies):	11.25%
Income tax withholdings on copy-rights paid to foreign beneficiaries and on fees of foreign artists retained by the State or certain cultural or charitable institutions:	11.25%
Income tax withholding on royalties, fees or other payments to foreign beneficiaries under registered technology transfer agreements:	18%
Capital gains ('beneficios eventuales') tax on certain real estate transactions not subject to income tax:	15%

Brazil

J. F. Gouvea Vieira *

As a British journalist has stated, 'Brazil is three countries, each more than twice the size of France, wrapped in a continent. One, in the south, is a land of progress; another in the north-east, of lost wealth and poverty and the third in the west, an almost untameable frontier'. These circumstances, plus a population over 110 million, half of which is currently under age 20, go far in explaining the birth of tax incentives in Brazil.

The first incentives were created in 1961 and were intended to favor investments in the poorest geographical areas of the country (the Northeast and Amazon Basin), granting tax reductions or exemptions regarding investments made in these areas. Similar programs have been instituted subsequently for other sections of the economy, such as hotels and motels, fishing, forestation and reforestation, tourism, the aircraft industry and later with respect to a variety of debt and equity securities. Other tax incentives have been enacted for manufacturing concerns and exports.

Brazil is considered to be, today, one of the most attractive jurisdictions for private investment. Besides offering the tax incentives that will be discussed in a more detailed way in the paper hereunder, Brazil has no restrictions upon foreign investments, except in very limited areas such as media communications and navigation, which are reserved for citizens, the oil industry, which is a State monopoly (but which now includes exploration by foreign companies), and certain financial institutions in which foreigners cannot acquire majority ownership and the law provides that foreign and national investors are entitled to the same treatment. However, certain governmental financial incentives are granted only to Brazilian-controlled companies.

Brazil encourages foreign investment by having special rules which have not been changed substantially for years. Foreign investments registered with the Central Bank of Brazil can be remitted up to 12% of the registered investment and capitalized earnings after the payment of a 25% withholding tax. Beyond that limit (12%), earnings can also be remitted after the payment of a supplementary income tax.

Brazilian law is restrictive regarding the remittance in foreign currency of royalties for the use of trademarks, patents, know-how and fees for technical services and technical assistance to non-residents. Royalties for the utilization of patents and trademarks by a Brazilian company to its controlling company abroad are not remittable nor are they deductible to the paying company. Technical assistance fees are remittable, but are considered a distribution of earnings (not deductible for income tax purposes).

It is important to note that Brazil has signed international treaties with 11 countries (Germany, Austria, Belgium, Denmark, Spain, Finland, France, Japan, Norway, Portugal and Sweden) to prevent double taxation, and is presently in negotiation with others. These treaties are important in the scope of tax incentives for private investment in Brazil.

* Escritorio de Advocacia Gouvea Vieira, Rio de Janeiro.

Since March 1967 most items may be fully imported into Brazil, subject only to the obtaining of an importation certificate ('guia de importação') issued by CACEX and to the payment of applicable taxes, which may well be high in the case of luxury items and those items which are 'similar' to items available from Brazilian sources.

Tax incentives are being used as a dynamic instrument for achieving governmental goals and consequently they are sometimes available for a limited time. Presently, the major tax incentives available for private investments in Brazil are directed to the internal production of equipment and machinery, programs resulting in the export of manufactured goods, programs resulting in import substitution together with the investments in the poorest areas of the country (the Northeast and Amazon Basin), forest and reforestation, fishing, tourism and the aircraft industry.

Certain tax incentives may be utilized automatically and others only after the approval of a project by Brazilian authorities. The administrative agencies involved take into consideration the economic feasibility and the advantages to the country (investment in foreign currency, technology, etc.) as well as the shareholders' financial capacity and nationality.

We conclude this introduction recalling that tax incentives are important in an investment decision, but the general picture of the country must also be taken into consideration, such as financing facilities available, political stability, infrastructure, labor and raw materials.

TAX INCENTIVES FOR PRIVATE INVESTMENT IN BRAZIL

Commencing in 1961, the Brazilian Government adopted tax incentive measures. The first sought to encourage investments in the poorest geographical areas of the country: the Northeast and Amazon Basin. Governmental policy consisted of granting tax reductions on part of investments made in these areas.

These early programs have been supplemented from time to time by other programs aimed at other sectors of the economy, such as fishing, tourism, the aircraft industry and later to certain securities. Significant incentives have been granted to exporters.

The following are the most important tax incentive programs. These include regional expansion, capital market and export incentives.

I. Incentives for Regional Development

The main character of incentives for regional development is to benefit economic activities in the Northeast (the Superintendency of Development of the Northeast – SUDENE – is the administrative body of the Federal Government having jurisdiction over this program) and in the Amazon Basin area (this program is administered by the Superintendency for the Development of the Amazon – SUDAM).

Apart from the total or partial income tax exemption to enterprises that are located in these areas, the law also provides special incentives to juridical and physical persons who designate a portion of their income to these areas.

In the case of juridical persons, corporate income tax can be reduced by up to 50% when invested in the SUDENE and SUDAM areas. Funds must be deposited at the Banco do Brasil which will credit 50% in favor of the PIN ('Programa de Intergração Nacional', which was created with the specific purpose of financing the infrastructure works of the SUDENE and SUDAM areas as well as fostering the integration of these areas into the national economy) and the Proterra ('Programa de Redistribuição de Terras e de Estímulos a Agro Indústria do Norte e do Nordeste', which was created with the purpose of promoting the easiest access possible to lands for the people, including agrarian reform in the SUDENE and SUDAM areas) and the balance in the Amazon Basin Investment Fund (FINAM), which is operated by the Amazon Bank, or in the Northeast Investment Fund (FINOR), which is operated by the Northeast Bank of Brazil. The percentage credited to PIN and Proterra is not refundable, and the 50% balance is represented by certificates of deposit which are exchanged within one year by 'quotas' from the funds. These quotas are exchangeable for securities owned by the funds through bids at the stock exchanges. A company or group of companies owning at least 51% of the company beneficiary of the tax incentives in SUDAM or SUDENE areas can exchange their quotas directly for equity in the controlled company through direct negotiations with the banks.

In addition to the Amazon Basin program, a Duty Free Zone has been established in the city of Manaus, Amazon, to encourage its use as an international and domestic warehousing, assembly and manufacturing area.

Physical persons subject to income tax can have similar benefits as those granted to taxable income and sometimes to the tax itself. In gereral, these can be deducted from taxable income up to 42% of the amount thereof if applied to the purchase of registered equity issued by companies considered to be of priority interest to the development of the Northeast and/or the Amazon Basin areas. Investments made in enterprises which are involved in the development of natural resources in the Amazon, as well as donations to special institutions engaged in research, are tax deductible.

II. Incentives to Invest in Specified Securities

These incentives are granted either as a percentage of taxable income or as a credit against tax. Only individuals may benefit from them.

The law provides that individuals can annually reduce part of their income tax liability if the corresponding amount reduced is invested in certain projects of special social and economic interest or in certain types of securities. The limit for reduction established for the calendar year 1977, payable in 1978, is divided by gross income categories, as follows:

Gross Income	Limit of Reduction of Tax Liability
Up to 135,100 Cr.	60%
135,101 to 181,300 Cr.	55%
181,301 to 248,400 Cr.	50%
248,401 to 326,100 Cr.	45%
326,101 to 447,200 Cr.	40%
447,201 to 714,800 Cr.	35%
More than 714,800 Cr.	30%

As an illustration, the following investments are considered to have a special social and economic interest and are eligible for tax reductions if held for a certain number of years:

- the purchase of treasury bonds and securities representing the public debt – the right to a credit of up to 3% of the income tax
- the subscription of shares issued by public issue corporations – the right to a credit of up to 15% of the income tax liability
- the subscription of shares issued by open capital corporations who are engaged in tourism activities – the right to a credit of up to 20% of the income tax liability.

The taxpayer also has the option to compensate for part of his tax liability by purchasing share certificates issued by financial institutions authorized by the Central Bank of Brazil ('Banco Central'). The percentage that individual taxpayer can credit against their income tax liability depends upon the category of gross income declared, and this percentage goes from 24% (if the gross income is 135,100 Cr. or less) to 10% (if the gross income exceeds 714,800 Cr.).

III. Incentives to Other Activity Programs

Provisions similar to those described above have been adopted to benefit other activity programs:

- Forestry and reforestation. Companies and individuals can benefit from these incentives. Companies are permitted to deduct from their income taxes up to 25% and individuals up to 20% for investment in forestry projects approved by the IBDF (Brazilian Institute for Forest Development). Funds must be deposited at the FISET FUND and procedures are similar to those at FINAM and FINOR.
- Companies engaged in the fishing industry are exempted from income tax until 1982. Furthermore, companies can deduct up to 25% of their income tax due to be invested in projects approved by the SUDEPE (Agency for the Development of the Fishing Industry) and individuals can deduct from their gross income the expenses related to research or fishing training in accordance with the agency program.
- As regards tourism, corporate income tax can be reduced up to 12% of the amount invested in tourist projects approved by Embratur. The procedures

for investment are also similar to those for the SUDAM and SUDENE areas, but the funds are deposited in favor of the FISET FUND.

In the aeronautical field it is provided by law that companies can benefit from a reduction of up to 1% on their income tax if they invest the corresponding amount in the purchase of new shares issued by Embraer (the Brazilian Enterprise of Aeronautics) through 1980.

IV. Export Incentives

One of the most widely publicized programs, which was introduced in Brazil in 1964, is the program designed to encourage the exportation of industrialized products. This program is designed not only to improve the Brazilian balance of trade, as a general matter, but also to reduce the traditional dependence of Brazil upon exportation of substantially unprocessed items such as coffee, cotton and cocoa.

The incentive program which has been established to encourage the exportation of industrialized products includes a variety of tax and financial incentives which may be summarized as follows:

A. Income Tax

Corporations will have, through 1980, the option to exclude from taxable income their export sales earnings from industrialized products, plus IPI and ICM from their corporate income tax in Brazil. The amount of export sales earnings is determined as a ratio between total sales and export sales plus IPI and ICM, the same ratio of net profit being exempt from the income tax.

In addition to the income tax exemption upon the company itself, commissions paid to sales representatives abroad are not subject to the normal 25% non-resident withholding tax. Corporate expenses occurring abroad to promote sales and participation in export fairs or in the administration of subsidiaries or sales offices are eligible for income tax deduction.

B. Industrialized Products Tax (IPI)

The Industrialized Products Tax is applicable to the transfer of raw materials and merchandise. In essence it is an added value tax which applies when a different product is evolved from the one which has already paid the tax. Thus it is that a manufacturer, upon acquiring rew materials, would normally have paid the tax on these raw materials and then, upon disposal of the manufacturer's finished products, an IPI tax would be payable by the purchaser.

In the case of the exportation of industrialized products, a tax benefit is afforded the manufacturer of such products as follows:

As to the IPI tax which was paid with regard to the acquisition of raw materials of Brazilian origin, the manufacturer/exporter may receive credit for the materials acquired and incorporated into the exported product in satisfaction of its general IPI tax obligations. In addition, however, in the case of export sales, a calculation is made of the IPI tax which would have been paid if the sale had been made within Brazil, up to the rate of 15%, except for goods for which the Minister of Finance can establish a rate over this limit (even if the product would normally be exempt in the domestic market). This tax, deemed to have been paid but actually not paid, may be used by the manufacturer/exporter as credit against other IPI tax obligations and, to the extent that they have already been absorbed, the credit may be applied against other taxes or the manufacturer/exporter may ask for reimbursement of the amount in question if he has no manner of using the credits in terms of either IPI or other Federal taxes.

If the shipment is made in a Brazilian vessel, the basis for establishing IPI credit is CIF. If in a foreign vessel, the value serving as a basis is the FOB value.

C. Other Tax Incentives

1. ICM

Under Brazilian law a manufacturer/exporter is also exempt from the payment of the tax on circulation of merchandise (ICM) and, in addition, have the credit of this tax as if it had been paid. Recently the Minister of Finance was invested with the power to permit the manufacturer/exporter to credit ICM export credit against the IPI tax.

2. Drawback

Taxpayers can also benefit from a very liberal customs drawback arrangement. Raw materials brought in from abroad and incorporated into Brazilian manufactured products for export are not subject to import duties, IPI and ICM.

3. Services Exports

Income in foreign currency or securities issued abroad and brought into Brazil, derived from technical services, technical assistance or administrative assistance or similar services rendered by a Brazilian company to a foreign company, are exempt from corporate income tax.

4. Ore Exports

Under certain conditions ore exports are deemed to be exports of manufactured goods, and consequently benefit from the same tax incentives, provided that the company is controlled by Brazilians.

5. Sales in the Domestic Market Which Receive the Same Tax Treatment as Exports

In addition, sales in the domestic market for which payment has been made with money from a long-term foreign currency financing, sales of equipment to Petrobras in order to develop certain oil fields and to other companies under contract to Petrobras who are researching oil may benefit from the same export tax incentives.

V. Financing Incentives

In addition to the tax incentives available for exports, exporters can also obtain financing at a real negative cost (taking into consideration the devaluation of Brazilian currency).

I would like to point out that financial incentives other than tax incentives are available in Brazil to companies with the majority of their voting stock owned by Brazilians. The most important is the subscription of non-voting shares by the BNDE (National Development Bank) or one of its subsidiaries (EMBRAMEC, FIBASE, etc.), up to 50% of the shares issued, or through special financing programs which, in fact, constitute a negative financial cost in terms of the dollar due to the devaluation of the cruzeiro.

As mentioned above, these financing incentives are available to Brazilian companies even with foreign shareholders in a minority position; however, BNDE and its subsidiary agree to enter into a shareholders agreement to grant the minority certain benefits.

In addition, some states grant other non-tax incentives to new investments made in their jurisdiction, such as donations of land to build up the industry and infrastructure, as well as financial incentives through their Development Banks.

VI. Incentives for Manufacturing Concerns

A. CDI (Council for Industrial Development)

This is one of the administrative agencies in Brazil which encourages the establishment of both new and expanded manufacturing operations and makes incentives available for this purpose. Two factors which weight heavily in the granting of the incentives are whether the project will result in products which will substitute for importation and whether the resulting products will be exported. The CDI has jurisdiction to both establish general guidelines and to approve specific projects.

Generally speaking, the most meaningful incentive tends to be the importation of foreign source machinery and equipment with a reduction of duty and of IPI and ICM tax-free upon foreign source parts and components during a reasonable interim start-up period, accelerated depreciation for Brazilian source machinery and equipment and eligibility for developmental financing (the last if the company has a majority of Brazilian ownership).

The routine for obtaining incentives under the CDI program can be summarized as follows:

1. The CDI has published a list of products which are eligible for priority treatment. Projects seeking incentives for the manufacture of these items are prima facie eligible for the benefits offered.

2. To apply for the incentive program the CDI has established a standardized application form or procedure.

3. To determine preliminary eligibility of a specific project, the CDI has established a letter of inquiry approach.

4. In some cases the CDI has concluded that the private sector is not moving ahead rapidly enough. In these cases the CDI from time to time establishes regulations with regard to specific products, establishing time periods for the presentation of applications and setting up the minimum percentage in Brazilian content of the final product as well as time periods for its gradual increase. Among the specific regulations which have been executed are those respecting machine tools, radio communications equipment, telex and multiplex equipment, machinery and equipment for the textile industry, motorized saws, agricultural machinery, crawler tractors and other heavy equipment.

In addition to the CDI incentives a manufacturing concern is eligible to benefit from the various export incentives which can be of great significance.

Furthermore, manufacturers of capital goods may be eligible to have certain of their domestic sales treated as if they were exports, with the resulting benefits, as referred to in

B. Special Export Incentive Programs (BEFIEX)

The export incentive program was created by Decree-Law No. 1219 of May 15, 1972 and was amended by Decree-Law No. 1428 of December 2, 1975 and Decree No. 77.065 of January 20, 1976, and is administered by the administrative body BEFIEX.

Before the 1975 amendment companies producing items which had a special program for exportation could be exempted from import duties, IPI and, in certain cases, from the rules of a 'national similar' (waiver or reduction of import duties and other taxes is not given except pursuant to this export incentive program) on machinery, equipment, apparatus and tooling, new or used as well as assembly parts, components and accessories, raw materials and intermediate products. The value of the goods imported annually with the exemption could not be greater than one-third of the net value of the average annual exportation of manufactured goods. Tax exempt imports under this law, together with other importations carried out under the system of drawback or other special systems, could not exceed 50% of the FOB value exported by the company and also by a group of companies participating in the program.

After the 1975 amendment, BEFIEX may grant a reduction of 20% to 90%

in the import duty and in the tax upon industrialized products upon the importation of machinery, equipment, apparatus, instruments, accessories and tooling necessary for the carrying out of special exports approved by the Minister of Industry and Commerce. In these cases, the importation of components, raw materials and intermediate products carried out within the scope of Decree-Law No. 1219 of May 15, 1972, may enjoy a reduction of 50% on import duty and in the tax upon industrialized products.

In the case of export programs which are considered to be of relevant national interest, analyzed by the Commissioner for the granting of fiscal benefits for BEFIEX export programs in which the benefitted company obligates itself to present, annually, during the period of the duration thereof, a positive balance in exchange (taking into account exchange costs of every nature), exemption from import duties and from the tax upon industrialized products may be proposed to the President of the Republic in an Interministerial Position paper, which will be signed by the Ministry of Industry and Commerce, the Minister of the Treasury and by the Chief Minister of the Secretariat of Planning of the Presidency of the Republic.

C. Exports Commitments (CIEX)

Decree-Law No. 491 of March 5, 1969, as amended by Decree-Law No. 1428 of December 2, 1975, together with Decree No. 77.065 of January 20, 1976, grant powers to the Minister of the Treasury to grant a reduction of up to 90% on the import duties and on the tax upon industrialized products on the import of machinery, equipment, apparatus and instruments directed to the implementation, expansion and re-equipping of industries which have a program and assume a commitment to export. Those incentives are available, in addition to those available to export, and may only be granted to companies whose program of imports and exports permits a financial and exchange plan which contributes positively, each year, to the improvement of the Brazilian balance of payments.

D. Registration of Contracts Involving Transfer of Technology into Brazil (INPI)

Income tax and the exchange control laws require that all contracts involving transfer of technology have to be registered at the INPI (National Institute of Industrial Property) in order for the corresponding remuneration to be considered tax deductible and/or to be transferred in foreign currency abroad (after registration of the contract at the Central Bank).

In the registration procedures INPI makes, in fact, a distinction between the transfer of technology involving Brazilian companies and foreign companies with provisions to remunerate the technology in foreign currency. However, when the transfer of technology involves the obligation of payments in foreign currency, the INPI studies the contract closely and takes the following into consideration:

1. the availability of similar technology in Brazil;
2. reasonableness of the services' price and/or technology;
3. the capacity of the licensee to absorb the technology;
4. restrictive clauses in the contract;
5. the overall advantages that the technology will bring to the country (reduction of imports, increase of exports, etc.); and
6. the relationship between the licensor and licensee.

It is important to point out the the INPI requires prior consultation (through a consultation letter) before the execution of any contract involving the transfer of technology.

ANNEX I

THE TAX SYSTEM IN BRAZIL

We can define the Brazilian tax system as being 'rigid', meaning that only those taxes prescribed in the Federal Constitution can be enforced.

The Brazilian Constitution divides the country in three fiscal jurisdictions: Federal, State and Municipalities, which results in the following system:

I. The Federal Tax System

The two major taxes under Federal jurisdiction are the income tax and the Industrialized Products Tax (IPI), which is an excise-added value tax. We will discuss the individual income tax, the corporate income tax, the special rules with respect to taxpayers with residences abroad, the Industrialized Products Tax and other taxes.

A. Individual Income Tax

This tax is similar in certain aspects to the corresponding US income tax. All residents of Brazil who earn a gross income of more than 47,300 Cr. are subject to individual income tax. Also individuals showing external signs of wealth (that is, having an indicated net worth) must file a special income tax return.

Income is classified into eight different categories depending upon the source (income from public bonds, income from private bonds, wages and salaries, income derived from the liberal professions, income from real estate, income distributed by companies, agricultural profits and other income). For each of these categories (except for agricultural profits, which are taxed in accordance with 'presumed profit', and those distributed by companies), taxpayers may deduct, up to certain limits, expenses necessary for realizing the income.

Certain deductions are permitted from the gross income of various categories.

These deductions are allowed for purposes of encouraging public savings and investments in certain areas of the country, certain economic activities (which we will discuss later in the tax incentives section) and for personal and family expenses.

Family expenses can be deducted up to fixed amount which is indexed annually (this year 10,700 Cr. for each family dependent). The law considers a family dependent any person who is in fact dependent on the taxpayer (ascendants, sons under 21, unmarried daughters, widows or divorcees, adopted children and foster children, among others).

The deduction of the total amount of medical fees; life insurance premiums, interest paid for personal borrowing and expenses incurred in the education of dependents, up to a specified limit, are also permitted.

Net income calculated as described above is taxed on a progressive basis. Taking into consideration the continuing devaluation of Brazilian currency, tax rules provide that individual income tax paid in advance is entitled to a discount. Late payments are penalized with monetary correction.

Taxpayers also have the alternative of reducing part of their income tax due by tax incentives procedures, as discussed below.

Certain income is subject to withholding tax, as follows:

- wages and salaries which the withholding tax is levied on at a progressive rate, from 5% to 30%;
- income from 'Bills of Exchange' (securities issued by a financial institution). The rate varies from 7% to 10%, depending on the maturity date of the security;
- interest paid on treasury bonds; 20% to 14% is withheld if the bonds were issued after July 23, 1974, and 30% to 20% if they were issued after January 1, 1977. This withholding tax is due only on interest and not on the principal arising from monetary correction;
- certain dividends (see INFRA Section B with respect to corporate income tax);
- income to residents abroad (see Section C concerning non-resident income tax);
- commissions paid to salesmen, travelling salesmen, brokers or independent commercial representatives who are not employees (7%); and
- commissions, bonuses, fees and copyrights exceeding certain amounts in Cr. paid monthly by companies to individuals and civil partnerships other than to directors, partners or employees (8%).

Withholding tax is credited against the taxpayer's income tax for the taxable year.

Individual Progressive Income Tax Rate for the Calendar Year 1977, Payable in 1978

Net Income	*Rate*
Up to 47,300 Cruzeiros	0%
47,301 to 55,500 Cruzeiros	4%
55,501 to 66,400 Cruzeiros	6%
66,401 to 80,100 Cruzeiros	9%

80,101 to 95,500 Cruzeiros	12%
95,501 to 115,600 Cruzeiros	15%
115,601 to 140,100 Cruzeiros	18%
140,101 to 169,300 Cruzeiros	23%
169,301 to 203,800 Cruzeiros	27%
203,801 to 244,800 Cruzeiros	31%
244,801 to 297,600 Cruzeiros	35%
297,601 to 358,500 Cruzeiros	39%
358,501 to 433,200 Cruzeiros	42%
433,201 to 564,200 Cruzeiros	45%
564,201 to 910,000 Cruzeiros	48%
Over 910,000 Cruzeiros	50%

B. Corporate Income Tax

1. Taxpayer

This tax is imposed on any entity domiciled in Brazil which has made a profit. It is important to note that corporate income tax is due from all companies, even if they are not legally organized, and by branches or agencies of foreign companies engaging in commercial activities in Brazil through representatives. Sole proprietorship companies whose gross income is less than 69,800 Cr., educational institutions, non-profit corporations and unions are exempted from corporate income tax; nevertheless, they must file income tax returns.

2. Taxable Income

Income tax is due on the business profit or on the presumed profit or imputed profit.

a) Business Earnings

Taxation upon busines earnings is mandatory for corporations ('sociedades anônimas'), limited liability companies ('sociedades por quotas de responsabilidade limitada') or branches of foreign companies.

Business earnings are equal to the difference between the gross receipts and the expenses necessary for the maintenance of income production. It is important to note that one must add to the business profit the following:

- capital gains and the net result of random transactions; and
- the remuneration of directors, top management and partners, as well as bonuses to employees exceeding a specified amount which is non-deductible. (This amount is adjusted annually by the Minister of Finance to compensate for monetary inflation.)

b) Presumed Earnings

Companies whose capital and gross income do not exceed a given amount establishment by the Minister of Finance can have their earnings taxed on a presumed basis. In this case, taxable earnings will be deemed to be 12% of the gross income.

c) Imputed Earnings

Companies' earnings can be imputed if books are not kept in accordance with the existing law, or if the company refuses to exhibit them to the tax authorities. The imputed earnings which will serve as the basis for calculation of the income tax can be established, in accordance with the law, at 30% of the total amount of the fixed assets (cash and receivables) or from 15% to 50% of the capital or gross revenues at the discretion of the tax authority.

3. *Tax Rate*

The corporate income tax rate is 30%. This rate is reduced to 17% in the case the concessionaires of public service companies whose profits do not exceed 12% of the capital, and 6% in the case of agricultural and livestock companies.

4. *Distribution of Earnings. Issue of New Capital Stock. Directors, Top Management and Partners' Remuneration. Employees' Bonuses*

Through 1978, distribution of earnings under any form is subject to a 5% income tax payable by the distributing company. 'Open' companies (public issued companies) are exempt from this tax. In addition, distribution of earnings is subject to a withholding tax depending on whether the beneficiary (payee) is an individual or a corporation.

a) Individuals

If it is not a registered stockholder (e.g., if bearer shares are involved), the corporation paying the dividend must withhold 25% for income tax. If the payer company is a listed company (open company) this rate is reduced to 15%.

If one is a registered stockholder there is an option of paying the withholding tax at the rate indicated above, or of including the amount of the dividends received in one's personal tax return. Dividends up to 7,000 Cr. (in 1977) paid by an open company are exempt from income tax. If the payee is a non-resident, dividends are subject to a 25% withholding tax, which is generally reduced in the case of tax treaty recipients.

b) Juridical Persons (Companies)

There is no withholding tax concerning earnings on registered or endorsable shares and registered bearer stock held by juridical persons.

Directors, top management and partners remuneration is not considered to be tax deductible if the amount paid exceeds seven times the individual amount annually authorized, and if the total remuneration paid by the corporation to directors, top management and partners of a 'limitada' or similar entity exceed 30% of the taxable income before the deduction of this remuneration has been made. The monthly tax-deductible payment permitted in 1978 per person is 38,500 Cr.

C. Non-Resident Income Tax

The general rule is that all income credited, placed at the disposition of, or remitted abroad to a non-resident physical or juridical person is subject to a Brazilian non-resident income tax at the rate of 25%.

The 25% withholding tax is also applicable to dividends, profits, fees for the use of patents or trademarks, payments for technical services, technical assistance, administrative assistance or any other income paid to a non-resident of Brazil.

When a representative in Brazil has general powers of representation, sales realized in Brazil through him and invoiced directly to the buyer are subject to an arbitrary tax which assumes that profit represents 20% of the total amount of the sale.

It is important to note that when remittance of earnings which exceed an average of 12% per annum upon registered investment and reinvestment (capitalized earnings), averaged over a 3-year period, are exceeds, a supplemental income tax is applicable at the following rates:

From 12% to 15%:	40%
From 15% to 25%:	50%
More than 25%:	60%

It is also more important to note that fees paid by a Brazilian company for technical assistance received can be deducted as operational expenses in the calculation of the net income up to a limit of 5%, depending upon product classification, of the gross sales of the product during the first five years of production or from the introduction of a new industrial process under the following conditions:

- the contract must be registered with the INPI (National Institute of Industrial Property) and at the Central Bank of Brazil;
- the annual fees do not exceed the limits fixed by the Minister of Finance by product classification; and
- the Brazilian company paying the fees (payer) is not controlled by the beneficiary of the payment (payee).

If these conditions are not met, expenses for technical assistance cannot be deducted from taxable income. These expenses then will not only be taxed at the corporate level rate of 30% (normal income tax rate), but also will be subject, through 1978, to the supplementary income tax of 5% due on distributed income.

All fees paid, credited or placed at the disposition of a non-resident are subject to a withholding tax of 25%.

Income derived from the distribution of imported movies is subject to special taxation. When it concerns distribution on a percentage fee basis, the fraction to be remitted (not more than 70% of the gross income) is subject to a 25% withholding tax.

Tax Treaties

Brazil has signed and ratified tax treaties to avoid double income taxation with eleven countries: Germany, Austria, Belgium, Denmark, Spain, Finland, France, Japan, Norway, Portugal and Sweden, and it is presently negotiating others. Each of these tax treaties grants tax reductions and advantages to residents of both countries, such as the avoidance (in general) of the effects of double income taxation, and, in most cases, reduces the Brazilian income tax rate applicable to non-residents. Most of the countries grant 'matching credits' on the withholding tax due on dividends, interest and royalties at a higher rate than paid in Brazil; other countries, such as Japan, Norway and Belgium, grant a 'tax sparing' by granting a tax credit to a tax not paid in fact because of a specific tax incentive as mentioned herein.

Dividends – Brazilian withholding tax has been reduced to 15% in most cases, except in the treaties with the Scandinavian countries (Denmark, Finland and Norway) with respect to whom the withholding tax is still 25% when it concerns partnerships, and is reduced to 15% respecting companies, and with Japan, in which case the rate is reduced to 12.5%.

Taxation in the recipient country of dividends received from Brazilian sources varies from treaty to treaty. Some countries grant a matching credit on the Brazilian withholding tax at a higher rate (Portugal, France and Japan), others adopted a system of exemption together with granting a 'matching credit'. However, in each case it is essential to check the specific treaty provisions and the domestic law of each of these countries.

D. Industrialized Products Tax (IPI)

This tax was enacted in 1966 and has many common points with the European tax VAT (Value Added Tax). It is a non-cumulative tax in the sense that the system is to deduct from the tax due the amount already paid as in the prior stage of industrialization. At the same time, the IPI tax is selective in that its rate varies in accordance with the product. It is applicable both to imported and domestic products.

Industrialization means all operations which modify the nature, the functioning, the utilization, finishing or product presentation, except upon machinery belonging to third parties and packing only for transportation of the product.

The taxable event for imported products is clearance through customs. For domestic products it is the physical transportation of merchandise from one place to another.

In the first case, the tax is calculated on the value of the product increased by the import duties plus other taxes that the product is subject to on import, together with the other expenses for the account of the taxpayer. In the second case, it is calculated at the product price when transferred from one place to another, increased by the ICM tax or by referring to the gross market price.

The tax rate depends upon the nature of the goods (ranging from 0.4% up to 365.63%). The law makes a distinction between indispensable goods and luxury articles. The standard rates are 16% to 17%. Tobacco is in a special category of 365.63%.

Brazilian Withholding Tax Applicable to Royalties

	Germany	Austria	Belgium	Denmark	Spain	Finland	France	Japan	Norway	Portugal	Sweden
Copyright	15	10	10	15	10	10	10	12.5	15	10	15
Movies	25	25	25	25	25	10	10	15	—	10	25
Trademarks	25	25	25	25	15	25	25	25	15	15	25
Others	15	15	15	15	15	15	15	12.5	15	15	15
Paid to Controlled Companies	15	15	15	25	15	15	—	12.5	15	15	15

'Matching Credit' Concerning Royalties From Brazil

Regular Credit	– Portugal	Ownership up to 50% of the Brazilian Company stock	– Austria 25% – Germany 25%
Credit of 25%	– Denmark, Spain, Finland, Japan, Norway, Sweden	Ownership over 50% of the Brazilian Company stock	– Austria – exemption – Germany – 20%
Credit of 20%	– France	20% Deduction	– Belgium

Brazilian Withholding Tax Applicable to Interest

	Germany	Austria	Belgium	Denmark	Spain	Finland	France	Japan	Norway	Portugal	Sweden
Interest in General	15	15	15	15	15	15	15	12.5	25	15	15
Interest paid to Individuals or Partnerships	10	15	10	15	10	15	10	12.5	25	15	15
Interest on Bank long term Financing for Purchase of Equipment	15	15	15	15	15	15	15	12.5	25	15	25

'Matching Credit' Concerning Interest from Brazil

Regular Credit	– Portugal
Credit of 25%	– Austria, Denmark, Finland, Norway
Credit of 20%	– Germany, Spain, France, Japan, Sweden
20% Deduction	– Belgium

Certain goods are exempted from the IPI. Besides goods exported from Brazil, essential goods (foodstuffs, insecticides, etc.), certain samples, raw materials for the petrochemical industry, agricultural goods, industrial equipment, war equipment and industrialized goods at the Manaus Duty Free Zone are also exempted. Goods purchased directly from a domestic manufacturer whose payments have been made in local currency originated from the exchange of foreign currency, dividends from long-term financing given by an international financial institution or foreign government are also eligible to receive an IPI exemption.

The amount of the IPI to be paid is calculated by deducting from the total amount to be paid the amount already levied on the products purchased by the establishment during the same period. Accumulated tax credits can be transferred to the following period.

E. Import Duties

The Brazilian import duty system is largely an 'ad valorem' system. The value upon which the duty applies is the CIF value, which consists of the normal price (generally the wholesale price) of merchandise in the country of origin plus the cost of freight and insurance.

Certain importation items as samples or spare parts not for resale are exempted from the obligation to obtain the import certificate. Import certificates are, however, required if the product is benefitted by exemption or reduction of import duties or is a financial importation. Import certificates are normally issued after the presentation of certain information to CACEX respecting price and all other information considered applicable. Importation certificates are normally issued after the filing of the application without excessive delay and are valid, as a general rule, for 180 days.

The payment to the foreign supplier can be made any time after the importer has possession of the shipment documentation. Imported goods, however, can be cleared before the purchase of foreign exchange. In principal, payment cannot be made after 180 days after the issue of the import certificate, but with a special authorization from the Central Bank of Brazil, this payment can be extended up to 360 days.

In order to discourage the utilization of commercial credits to products considered to be unessential, the purchase of foreign exchange before the issue of the import certificate is required. Exchange contracts can stipulate if payments will be at sight or at term. Exchange contracts at sight must be settled in 48 hours and at term up to 180 days.

To protect transfers of contracts at term, banks generally require a collateral deposit. The percentage of this deposit depends upon the client. Interest of 2% is generally charged by the bank on the percentage not guaranteed by the deposit.

Since 1975, due to the Brazilian balance of trade and balance of payments situation, the Central Bank has established a list of products for which a previous deposit in the same amount as its CIF value is required as a condition to the issue of the import certificate. In general, the list of products includes only products that are subject to import duties over 37%.

A special system is in force concerning oil imports (State monopoly of petroleum), wheat and newsprint paper, which are imported through Banco do Brasil, and imports of basic products and essential raw materials for which domestic production is insufficient: coal, lead, aluminium, amianthus, fertilizers and insecticides.

Concept of national similar goods – Brazilian law considers 'similar' to imported goods, goods manufactured in Brazil, taking into consideration the following:

- equivalent quality, quantity and adequate specification for its utilization purposes;
- price not exceeding the import cost, computing the regular price and import duties and other import expenses; and
- delivery time normal or current for the same kind of goods.

Exemption or reduction of import duties are available only for import goods without similarities to national goods, except imports made in connection with a special export program approved by BEFIEX.

In general, the existence or not of a national similar good will be decided before the issue of the import certificate. Importers can, in certain circumstances, make an agreement with the domestic manufacturer stating the goods which will be manufactured in Brazil and those to be considered without national similar. This 'participating' agreement must be ratified by CACEX in order to be enforced.

F. Other Taxes

The Financial Operations Tax ('Imposto sobre as operações financeiras') – Credit and insurance operations of financial institutions or insurance companies are subject to the IOF. Many types of operations are exempt from this tax, including export credits. The tax basis in financial operations is the total amount of the operation (principal and interest). In insurance operations, the tax basis is the insurance premium. The tax rate for credit operations is 0.3% monthly and for insurance operations 2% monthly. Part of this tax is designed to cover Central Bank expenses and the balance is designed to constitute monetary reserves.

There exists a Federal Services Tax on Transportation, and Communication and also a Sole Tax on Minerals levied on operations concerning the production, importation, circulation, distribution and consumption of lubricants, combustible liquids and gas combustibles, electric energy, minerals and mineral waters.

There is also a tax on rural property which is to provide incentive to agrarian reform. This tax is levied on the value of non-utilized land as declared by its owner and approved by the fiscal authority. This tax generates a very small source of income which is transferred by the Federal Government to the municipalities.

II. State and Municipal Taxes

A. State Taxes

1. ICM

The Tax on the Circulation of Merchandise (ICM) is the most important state tax. As the IPI, it is an added value tax. It has a non-cumulative characteristic and the taxpayer can deduct the tax already paid in the previous stage. In contrast with the IPI, the ICM has a uniform rate for all goods and States (14% for transactions within a State and 13% for transactions among States). The taxable event occurs when the merchandise is transferred from a commercial, industrial or agricultural establishment or when it concerns imported goods, when they are delivered to the establishment.

Tax is calculated for domestic goods on the sales prices of the merchandise (without the IPI) and for imported goods at customs value including import duties, the IPI and other import expenses. ICM exemptions are roughly the same as the IPI.

2. Real Estate Transfer Tax

The real estate transfer tax basis for taxable transfers is the market value of the property transferred; for inheritance tax, the value established for the property by the court. Tax rates for taxable transfers have been fixed by the Federal Government at 1% and inheritance tax at 2%, no matter what the relationship is between the 'de cujus' and the heir. Property transferred by gift is also taxed at a 2% rate.

B. Municipal Taxes

1. Tax on Rendering of Services (ISS)

The taxable event is the rendering of any services which are listed in the law by a company or by an independent professional. The tax is levied on the price of the services. Some services are exempt from this tax, such as those rendered by a civil construction enterprise to juridical persons of public law, including companies which are concessionaires of public services and other administrative agencies.

The tax rate varies a good deal in accordance with the kind of services and from municipality to municipality. As an illustration, we can indicate the following in Rio de Janeiro:

2% maximum for civil construction;
10% for games and shows;
5% maximum in other cases.

2. *Urban Building and Property Tax*

The tax system in Brazil makes a distinction between the Urban Building and Property Tax and the Tax on Rural Property, which is a Federal tax which has already been discussed.

The Urban Building and Property Tax is an annual tax based on an assessed evaluation of the property as declared by the taxpayer or evaluated by tax authorities based on technical data. The rate is 0.8% in Rio de Janeiro.

A supplementary tax of 0.5% must be added, which concerns services rendered by the municipality, The tax rules stipulate that this tax must be paid by the landlord, but very often it is paid by the tenant.

ANNEX II

EXCHANGE CONTROL IN BRAZIL

The administrative bodies that are involved in the mechanisms of exchange controls and in a more general way in the foreign commerce and foreign finance are:

A. National Monetary Council ('Conselho Monetario Nacional')

Since the extinction of SUMOC (Superintendency of Money and Credit) at the end of 1969, the National Monetary Council was vested with the duty of define the general exchange and foreign commerce policy. The Council is vested with powers to 'regulate the exchange rate of the Brazilian currency and the question of the balance of payments with the purpose of a national utilization of foreign currency'. The Minister of Finance is the Council's chairman, and it is formed by the Ministers of Planning, and Industry and Commerce, the President of the Central Bank, the President of the National Development Bank, the President of Banco do Brasil, the President of BNH (National Housing Bank) and by three outstanding persons nominated by the President of the Republic.

1. Central Bank of Brazil

It is the Central Bank which is vested with the power to execute the governmental exchange policy. Supervised by the board of directors, a specific director is particularly responsible for exchange and foreign capital and is in charge of two special departments: the GECAM and the FIRCE.

a) The GECAM (Foreign Exchange Department) issues the regulations and controls foreign exchange operations.

b) The FIRCE (Fiscalization and Registration of Foreign Capital) is the department in charge of the registration of foreign capital in Brazil. The FIRCE approves foreign financing and registers foreign investment in accordance with the law.

2. Other administrative bodies (CACEX and CPA)

The general policy of foreign trade is formulated by the National Council of Foreign Trade ('Conselho Nacional do Comércio Exterior – Concex'), but it is CACEX (a department of Banco do Brasil) that is in charge of its activities. CACEX issued the rules that enforce the Council's policy. CACEX is also empowered to issue import licenses or import certificates, verifying that the appropriate price is being charged for the item to be imported, its weight, and it also carries out the classification of the item if an import license is required. CACEX is particularly in charge of enforcing the law known as 'national similar'.

The Customs Policy Council ('Conselho de Politica Aduaneira', or CPA) is entrusted with the power to amend import duties and their application. The Council also has the power to charge the minimum import value fixed by CACEX for import duty purposes.

B. Importation into Brazil

Since March, 1967, most items can be imported, subject only to the obtaining of an Importation Certificate ('guia de importação') issued by CACEX and to the payment of applicable taxes (which may well be high, however, in the case of luxury items and items which are 'similar to' those which are available from Brazilian sources).

C. Exportation from Brazil

Besides certain products which, for reasons of national interest, are prohibited to be exported, exports in Brazil are free, in most cases subject to an export form, generally issued automatically.

Control by CACEX exists on various products in order to supervise export prices and the specific governmental rules applicable to the matter.

Prior authorization by CACEX is required when exports are payable in non-convertible currency ('ou de conta'), export on consignment, re-export, and export without payment.

In most cases, in order to export, it is first required to apply to CACEX for an export form ('guia de exportação). The obtaining of this document (not transferable) follows the execution of a contract closing the foreign exchange within a period fixed by the banks, except when coffee or other products payable in 'moeda de conta' or in non-convertible currency are concerned. However, it is important to point out that the shipping of the product must be carried out within 15 days from the issuing of the export license, and that the payment thereof must be accomplished 20 days after shipping. For products that require inspection at the port of destination, CACEX tacitly accepts the disregard of this period. Special waiver can also be granted by CACEX. CACEX may also finance the exporter through special government funds to finance export of machinery and equipment.

Credits granted by CACEX cannot exceed 80% of the total export value. If the financing period is longer than one year, it can be totally refinanced if the exporter gives a collateral guarantee. Credit term depends upon the amount of the contract and on the condition of the international market.

Exchange contracts generally are not subject to prior approval by the Central Bank. It is up to the authorized banks to ask for the necessary guarantees. The law stipulates that the bank signature on the export certificate constitute not only a guarantee that the exchange contract is in order, but also a guarantee on the exporter itself.

Coffee exports follow a rather complex regime, the outlines of which are as follows:

The Brazilian Coffee Institute ('Instituto Brasileiro do Café-IBC') does not authorize exports if the price is not at least equal to the fixed floor price which is revisable periodically and varies depending on the quality of the product and port of shipment.

Upon the corresponding export sale, the exporter must contribute a quota to the coffee defense fund. This quota is fixed as a function with the floor price fixed in cruzeiros by the IBC and with the foreign exchange rate fixed by Banco do Brasil. The exporter receives the amount of the sale less the quota of contribution. However, the bank can keep the export currency balance to freely negotiate in the market.

Soluble coffees are not subject to the contribution quota, but are subject to an export tax which varies with the market of destination.

An export tax of 15% is applied to cocoa exports. The withholding is reduced to 5% when it concerns a cocoa by-product and the amount is reserved to financing of regulations and ameliorations of the cocoa agriculture.

Special rules are applicable to lumber export, oil products, fuel and lubricants to ships and aircraft in transit, and in operations with countries with which Brazil maintains bilateral trade agreements (East Germany, Bulgaria, Greece, Hungary, Israel, Poland, Rumania, and Yugoslavia).

D. Currency Transfer

1. Foreign Investment Law

Foreign investments in Brazil are regulated by Law no. 4131 of March 3, 1962, amended by Law no. 4390 of August 29, 1964 and by Decree no. 55,762 of February 17, 1965.

In general terms, foreign direct investment in Brazil is free. However, loans from abroad must be approved in advance by the Central Bank. For certain types of loans, namely those involving foreign governmental agencies, or guaranteed by the National Treasury, prior authorization is required by the Commission of Foreign Loans (CEMPEX). In all cases, repatriation of investment earnings made in Brazil are not eligible to be transferred abroad in foreign currency unless it has been registered at the Central Bank. The formality of registration of an investment and investment at the Central Bank continues to be a prerequisite to ability to remit earnings and to repatriate capital.

Foreign investment is defined by law (Law no. 4131, Article 1) as the property, machinery and equipment which entered the country without initial exchange expense, destined to the production of goods or services, as well as financial or monetary resources intended for application in economic activities, provided that they belong, in both cases, to physical or juridical persons, resident or domiciled or with head office abroad.

For the purpose of foreign investments' registration, they are classified as direct investments or loans, in accordance with the form of their entry into the country. Foreign investments that are not incorporated into the equity capital of the enterprise nor participate directly in the business risk are considered as a loan. Also, all foreign credit obtained abroad for the purchase of capital assets granted by the manufacturer or by a third party is considered a loan. Loans are considered to be made in currency when the financial or monetary resources enter into Brazil.

Proof of the entry of foreign investment in Brazil must be presented to the Central Bank in order to get the registration.

The registration of foreign capital shall always be carried out in the currency which actually entered the country and in the case of financial importation and investment in the form of assets, in the currency of the domicile or head office of the creditor or investor, respectively, or in special cases, in the currency of the source of the assets, provided that the prior approval of the Central Bank of Brazil is obtained, which shall take into account as well, the convenience of the balance of payments.

In order to register loans, credits, or financing, it is necessary to assure that the interest rate established in the contract corresponds to the rate in force in the financial market from which the loan, credit, or financing is forthcoming, on the date of its realization of operations of the same type and conditions.

The registration concerning direct foreign investment is made in foreign currency. Earnings realized by companies established in the country and attributed to residents and persons domiciled there, which are reapplied in the same enterprise as the one in which they originated or in another sector of the national economy, are considered as reinvestment. The registration of reinvestment is carried out simultaneously in national currency and in currency of the country to which the income could have been remitted.

Conversions for the purposes of this provision are made at the average exchange rate in effect between the date of determination of the profits in the balance sheet and the date of the realization of the reinvestment. The average exchange rate shall be established on the basis of the quotation during the period in question in the exchange market through which the reinvested earnings could have been remitted abroad.

Contracts involving transfer of technology with financial remittances for the payment of royalties due by reason of patents, trademarks, and other property of the same type, technical, scientific, administrative, or similar assistance shall also be registered at the Central Bank after being registered by the National Institute of Industrial Property.

Financial remittances for these payments must be made in the currency of the country of the domicile or head office of the beneficiary of the remittance.

Transfers of interest and the amortization of loans and financing are not subject to further authorization if they are in conformity with the conditions of the contract as registered at the FIRCE.

Transfer of earnings, dividends and interest are subject to a normal withholding tax of 25% if they do not exceed the average of 12% per annum upon registered investment and reinvestment (capitalized earnings) over a three-year period. Excess remittances are subject to a significant supplemental income tax (see the taxation above).

The Brazilian exchange control legislation also provides that whenever there occurs a serious disequilibrium in the balance of payments, or there are serious reasons to contemplate the imminence of such a situation, the Board of Directors of the Central Bank of Brazil may impose restrictions for a limited period of time, upon importation and upon remittance of earnings from foreign capital (the latter power has never been used). These shall not be, however, restrictions upon the remittance of interest and repayment of principal set forth in duly registered loan agreement.

In the case of foreign capital applied in active production of goods and services of a luxury nature, the remittance of profits abroad is limited annually to 8% of the capital registered with the Central Bank of Brazil. However, those activities have not been defined, and consequently this restriction does not exist.

Royalties for the utilization of patents, trademarks, and know-how by a Brazilian company to the benefit of a physical or juridical person that controls directly or indirectly the majority of voting shares are non-remittable. However, in case of payment for technical assistance, they are remittable, but are considered to be a distribution of earnings and therefore are charged off against the 12% upon registered investment and reinvestment, which can be remitted free of the supplemental tax described above.

In accordance with a Central Bank resolution dated September 19, 1965, remittances of royalties of a non-related company to a foreign licenser, as well as royalties for technical assistance, are limited to from 1% to 5% of gross sales. This is the same percentage as can be deducted as business expenses for income tax purposes.

In the area of technical assistance, the law presumes that an adequate period of time for such an arrangement is five years, and permits an extension for an additional five years only if it can be shown that the technology used is the appropriate one (i.e., that new technology is involved).

In the patent license area, the relevant period of effectiveness of the agreement is the shorter period of the patent in the country of origin and in Brazil. In addition, patent royalty payments cannot be made except upon evidence that the patent is in force in the country of origin and in Brazil.

2. Special financial operations

In accordance with Resolution 63, enacted on August 21, 1967, commercial banks and investment banks were authorized to deal in exchange and, after Resolution 64 was enacted (August 23, 1967), the National Bank of Economic Development ('Banco Nacional de Desenvolvimento Economico') was authorized as well to borrow foreign currency (generally from foreign financial institutions) and then relend the funds thus received to Brazilian borrowers to finance assets or working capital. However, such relending is accompanied in Brazilian currency, by a specific undertaking that the risk of exchange is to the account of the Brazilian borrower. Each bank is subject to a risk for this kind of operation which cannot be exceeded.

This limit is twice the Bank's paid-in capital and reserves. Borrowing under the terms of Resolution 63 is subject to a previous authorization of the Central Bank which by its terms makes its decision, taking into account the amount involved, terms and conditions of the loan. Actually, as the policy of the Brazilian monetary authorities is to limit the annual amount of Brazilian engagement abroad, Central Bank is authorizing such individual operations only when its amount and maturity period can be fitted into the overall scope of the Brazilian industries abroad. Central Bank also exercises control over the market rates in order to verify if they are the best obtainable in the international market.

3. Other invisibles

In general, transfer of invisibles (other than those mentioned above) to meet current transactions are subject to previous authorization of GECAM (Department of Central Bank). They are normally authorized upon presentation of documents proving good faith transactions.

Foreigners can freely bring into Brazil cruzeiros, foreign travellers checks, or foreign currency. However, when leaving the coutry, they are allowed to purchase foreign currency only in the amount of one-third of the amount sold.

Residents in Brazil can purchase freely up to the corresponding amount of US $1,000 each time they leave the country. Exceeding that limit is subject to previous Central Bank authorization.

Sale of airplane tickets to residents in Brazil is payable in cruzeiros.

E. Exchange Market and Non-Resident's Bank Accounts

In 1967 the system of two exchange markets was abolished. All operations are now carried out at a uniform exchange rate determined by the monetary authorities. The uniformity of the official and the infra banking authorized to deal with the foreign exchange rate is guaranteed and assured by the monetary authorities, who permanently purchase from the banks foreign currency at the offered rate and also sell to them the amount needed to meet their authorized transactions.

The cruzeiro rate is determined in connection with the US dollar and the rate of other foreign currencies is determined in connection with their rates in the international market.

In 1968 Brazil adopted a policy of flexible exchange rate system, meaning that the worth of the cruzeiro is fixed in consequence of the inflation rate in Brazil and in the rest of the world.

Market operations are assured by the Central Bank, Banco do Brasil and banks authorized to deal in exchange and other authorized establishments.

However, bank accounts can be opened in cruzeiros in Brazil for non-residents.

Private compensation (exchange of foreign currency, property, or valuables against Brazilian currency, property or valuables in Brazil) is forbidden by Brazilian law except with a special authorization granted by the Central Bank.

Greece

George N. Stathopoulos *

INTRODUCTION

Greece, being a developing country in the industrial sense, rather than fully developed as for instance the US, Germany, France, etc., is principally a capital inflow country that is a country primarily interested to attract foreign capital in the form of direct and indirect investments as well as know-how and technology in order to develop its industrial infrastructure.

In this respect, its tax regime and more particularly its tax incentives are geared mainly in the direction of attracting foreign capital into Greece rather than instituting tax provisions that would encourage the outflow of capital from Greece to other countries.

This, at least, has been the up to now trend which can be traced back as a starting date to 1953 with the passage of Law 2687/1953, 'Reinvestment and protection of foreign capital'.

Since 1953 there have been other tax laws favorable to investments as well but not specifically only for foreign investments as Law 2687. These other Laws include Law 4171 of 1961 as amended entitled 'General measures to assist the development of the country's economy' and several other more recent laws, which have been instituted with the view of decentralizing industrial and tourism development away from the Athens-Piraeus zone by giving the country a more balanced and spread out geographical economy. The method for achieving this is through certain tax incentives for investment outside the capital area by setting up certain industrial zones which benefit from tax and other incentives.

These latter 'general' laws with favorable tax provisions are equally applicable to foreign investors. Consequently they too affect the net inflow of capital from abroad.

Laws 89/67 and 78/68 were enacted in order to set up Regional Offices or Headquarters Offices in Greece for commercial and industrial enterprises as well as for shipping companies for their activities outside Greece. Even though, in the true sense of the word, they are not stimulating the inflow of direct investments, i.e., productive investments, they will also be covered in this paper as they do bring into Greece foreign exchange to cover office expenses, employee payments, etc., which merit due consideration. The resulting effect is less tangible vis-a-vis foreign capital inflow than that of direct productive investments but to a country such as Greece requiring foreign exchange, these Laws play an important role and will do more so in the future with the attraction of additional foreign companies setting up regional offices in Greece, primarily for activities in the Middle East and Africa.

In this whole circle of tax provisions affecting flows of private capital from developed to developing countries the tax treaty ramifications are most significant in provinding mechanism for avoiding double taxation of income between

* Attorney at Law, Athens.

the country from which the capital flows (the capital exporting country) to the host or recipient country where the investment is put to use in the form of productive investment. The double taxation treaties in this respect encourage the flow of capital from the developed to developing countries and in this respect the tax treaty provisions particularly as they apply to dividends, royalties and interest will be stressed here in order to indicate the significant role that they play in encouraging capital flows.

With this introduction the text that follows touches on the main tax provisions which encourage the attraction of foreign capital into Greece and thus facilitate the flow of foreign investment.

MEASURES TO ATTRACT FOREIGN CAPITAL

I. National Laws

1. Law 2687/1953 'Reinvestment and Protection of Foreign Capital'

As mentioned previously this is the basic law which attracts foreign capital into Greece.

Law 2687 defines what is foreign capital and sets forth the various procedural requirements for importation of capital, and provides for certain tax measures, foreign exchange provisions which affect and facilitate the inflow of foreign capital. The main tax provisions of this law are the following:

(a) The income tax rates existing at the time the act of the investment of approval has been issued will remain unaltered for a periode up to ten years with provisions for adjustment to lower rates of any such lower rates are enacted.
Alternatively, for a like period, income tax may be imposed at a fixed percentage on net or gross earnings, which percentage may be lower than the tax rates currently in force.

(b) Reduction of exemption from the payment of customs duties, contributions or other taxes and charges on imports of machinery, accessories, spare parts and tools for a period not exceeding ten years.

(c) Reduction or exemption from the payment of any tax, charge or contribution imposed by any local authority (municipalities, communities, etc.) harbour authorities or other organizations for a period not exceeding ten years.

(d) Reduction or exemption from the payment of charges and dues of any kind for the registration of a mortgage or the constitution of a pledge as a security for imported foreign capital, as well as from the charges connected with the execution of the respective contracts.

No retroactive imposition of taxation may be made on enterprises constituted with foreign capital imported in accordance with the provision of the present enactment. Such prohibitions shall also apply to similar enterprises or to enterprises established with capital provided otherwise.[1]

1. For foot-notes 1 to 20, see page 224.

Law 2687 also provides for certain provisions for the repatriation of capital, profits and interest payments to foreign investors. This is an important area since Greece is considered as a 'strict' foreign exchange nation in the sense that outflows of capital are very closely watched and special approvals are necessary in order to remit funds abroad. In this sense, Law 2687 guarantees the foreign investor that if he invests certain funds in Greece, he will be allowed in due course to repatriate both his imported capital as well as a substantial part of the profits and make certain interest payments on contracted loans.

The foreign exchange provisions of Law 2687 are the following:

1. No capital may be repaid before the expiration of one year from the date on which the enterprise begins to operate productively and, in any case, no such repayment may be made before the expiration of one year from the date on which the capital was imported into Greece. The amount of foreign currency granted for the repayment of the capital may not exceed 10% p.a. of the amount of the capital imported.[2]
2. The amount of foreign currency granted for the payment of interest or profit may likewise not exceed 12% [3] p.a. of the amount of imported capital for the payment of profits, and 10% p.a. for the payment of interest in case the capital has been imported in the form of a loan. If, during any one year, the amount of foreign exchange which has been remitted for the above-mentioned two purposes is less than the amount specified in the act approving the importation such difference may be remitted in subsequent years i.e. it gives cumulative effects of payments abroad for dividends and interest.
3. Both the original capital, as well as any capital imported subsequently for investment, is considered as capital imported from abroad. The Ministerial Act approving the importation of foreign capital may, however, specify that a part or the whole of the profits realized from imported foreign capital shall be considered as foreign capital, within the terms of the present enactment, provided such profits are reinvested in the enterprise from which they originated or are invested in any other enterprise specified in the act of approval.

2. Law 3171/1961 'General Measures to Assist the Development of the Country's Economy', as Amended

This Law, as mentioned in the introduction, is not specifically geared for the foreign investor but applies both to Greek and foreign investors. It was enacted for large scale investments, investments in excess of 150.000.000 Drs., and Drs. 50.000.000 in the case of extension of installations, etc. on the original investments. The intention of Law 4171 was to encourage, large scale investments in order to meet the international competition particularly with Greece's forthcoming entry into the EEC. The principal tax provisions included in this Law are the following: [4]

The following items shall be exempted from any and all taxes [5] duties, dues, stamp taxes, contributions levies and any other charges assessed for the benefit of the Government or any third party (municipality, community, fund, organization or other corporation public or private) whether such items are produced or not by local industry, and provided they are necessary or useful for carrying out surveys, studies, construction work and erection of initial plant facilities, any general or specific provision to the contrary notwithstanding.

(a) Machinery, accessories, spare parts, tools, electronic computers imported either permanently or for free use; also in the case of manufacturing and mining industries, all of their plant equipment, provided all the above equipment is new. Excluded from this exemption shall be the office equipment of the investing enterprise as well as its passenger and freight transport carriers, telephone exchanges with their accessories, converters, telephone apparatures, television sets, elevators, with capacity up to four persons, and their accessories.

(b) Research, testing, measuring and control instruments for the requirements of the investing enterprise, and

(c) Cranes and transport vehicles for moving supplies and products within the site of the enterprise including motor trucks.[6]

For a period of ten [7] years from the end of the year during which the enterprise went into operation (a) income tax rates on undistributed profits of the enterprise in effect at the time when the joint ministerial decision (which placed the investment under Law 4171/61) was issued, shall not be altered, (b) no tax shall be imposed on the property of the enterprise.

For a period of ten [7] years from the end of the year during which the enterprise commenced its production activities, all taxes, dues, contributions, levies and any other charge (except charges as might be assessed for services rendered) in favour of municipal or communal authorities, organizations, funds or any other legal entity, of public or private law, in effect at the time when the joint ministerial decision is issued, shall not be altered.

Any existing exemptions from the foregoing third party taxes on the products and the property of the enterprise shall also be deemed not modifiable.

Finally, Law 4171/61 in addition to the general favorable tax provisions as noted above, provides for the facility of remitting abroad royalties for technical assistance granted to Greek firms by foreign more advanced firms.

The following two provisions deal with the foreign remittance rights of royalties and provides for a tax break in the firm of assessing the taxable base of Government approved royalties, in applying to such the normal income tax rate.

These favorable provisions are as follows:

To effect payment abroad of royalties accruing from the use in Greece of copyrights, patents, research findings, designs, secret manufacturing processes and formulas or any other property rights or services as well as for technical administration, approval shall be given for making available the necessary amount of foreign exchange required annually. These amounts are to be determined by decision of the Minister of Coordination [8] upon the opinion of the Committee set up under Art. 3 of L.D. 2687/53. The ministerial decision shall specify (a) the amount of remuneration to be paid (in total amount and percentage) (b) the amount of foreign exchange to be remitted abroad, and (c) all necessary pertinent details.[9]

For the purpose of assessing income tax on the rights referred to in the preceding paragraph, the net income shall not be deemed to exceed 35% of the amount paid in accordance with the respective decision of the Minister of Coordination, subject however, to application of provisions contained in agreements for avoidance of double taxation by which the net taxable income is otherwise determined or by which a tax rate applicable to the gross income is provided for.[10]

3. Regional Development Laws (Law Decree 1377/1973, etc.) [11]

Law Decree 1377/1973 concerning new measures in support of regional development is the existing basic Law which deals with the encouragement for local capital to invest in Greece and more particularly in the various regions outside of the Capital that is the Athens-Piraeus area in order to arrive to a more balanced regional development in Greece.

For the purpose of Law 1377/1973 Greece is divided into the following regions: [12]

Region A: An area covering the Nome of Attica except the Deme of Lavrion.

Region B: An area covering the Deme of Lavrion, the Nomes of Thessaloniki, Boeotia, Euboea, Corinthia and the province of Chalkis.

Region C: Alle other areas in the country. (From this region Areas D and E were later formed as enumerated below).

Region D: By an Act of the Council of Ministers: (a) industrial zones may be determined within the Nomes of Aetolia and Akarnania, Arcadia, Arta, Grevena, Drama, Dodecanese (except the islands of Cos and Rhodes), Hevros, Eurytania, Zakynthos, Thesprotia, Ioannina, Kastoria, Cephallonia, Kilkis, Cyclades (except the island of Mykonos), Lakonia, Lesbos, Levkas, Messinis, Xanthi, Pella, Preveza, Rhodopi, Samos, Serrai, Florina, Chios, the island of Thassos and the province of Scopelos and included in Region D hereby created.[13]

Region E: The following border areas are included: Nomes of Evros, Xanthi, Rhodopi, and the islands of Lesvos, Chios, Samos, and the Dodecanese.[14]

The reinvestment allowances from net profits for domestic industrial or handicraft enterprises installed or moved or established in the above mentioned Regions are set forth below as follows: [15]

(a) in Region B which realizes new productive investments within the period from January 1, 1973 to December 31, 1977 is entitled to deduct from net profits an amount equal to fifty percent (50%) of the value of the expenses involved thereof,

(b) in Regions C and D which realize new productive investments within the period from January 1, 1973 to December 31, 1982 is entitled to deduct from their net profits an amount equal to one hundred percent (100%) of the value of the expenses involved thereof, and

(c) in Region E, the deduction for net profits in increased to one hundred and fifty percent (150%) for investments realized within five years from the date of filing their application to be subject to Law 289/1976.

In addition to the above tax free deductions from net profits for investments, enterprises as above are allowed deductions as well from net profits for working capital as follows:
(a) up to 10% for enterprises in Region B
(b) up to 20% for those in Regions C and D
(c) and 25% for those in Region E.

The rates of employer's and employee's contributions [16] to the Social Security Organization (IKA and other auxiliary funds, as determined on each occasion for the period from January 1, 1973 to December 31, 1982 in respect of personnel of any kind shall be reduced: (a) by twenty percent (20%) for facilities of domestic industrial or handicraft enterprises established in Region C or on the islands of the Nome of Attica, for domestic mining enterprises and domestic iron and steel industries equipped with steel rolling facilities and for plants of automobile tire and tube industries located outside the Nome of Attica; (b) by forty percent (40%) for facilities of domestic industrial or handicraft enterprises located in the areas referred as Region D above; (c) by fifty percent (50%) for industries and craft industries located in Region E.

Turnover tax prescribed by current provisions shall be [17] reduced: (a) by twenty five percent (25%) for industrial or handicraft enterprises installed, moved or established in regions of the Deme of Lavrion, the Nomes of Boeotia, Corinthia and Thessaloniki, the islands of the Nome of Attica and the province of Chalkis; (b) by fifty percent (50%) for industrial or handicraft enterprises installed, moved or established in regions other than those referred to in item (a) or in the remaining part of the Nome of Attica and also for automobile tire and tube producing industries located outside the Nome of Attica.

To the above provisions on tax and other contributions (reinvestment allowances from net profits, reductions in employer-employee contributions and turnover tax reductions) should be added certain accelerated depreciation allowances offered to firms as well by Law 1377/73 which depend on the firms geographic region of establishment as well as the number of shifts it uses in the firm.

4. Law 89/1967 concerning 'Establishment in Greece of Foreign Commercial and Industrial Companies'

As mentioned in the introduction this law (although strictly speaking does not attract foreign direct investments) provides for certain tax provisions for attracting the establishment of foreign companies in Greece. Due to the exist--ence of a tax holiday from income and other taxes for such Law 89 companies establishing in Greece (and which transact business outside of Greece) this important tax provision had led to many of the well know multinationals and international companies to establish their regional headquarters in Greece, particularly so since the 1975 civil war in Lebanon.

The basic tax provisions of Law 89/67 provide for the following[18]:

Foreign commercial and industrial companies which have obtained an establishment permit shall, without any other formality, be entitled to the following facilities concerning customs duties, taxation and other matters, provided they are exclusively engaged in commercial activities whose objects lie *outside Greece*.

(a) They shall be exempt from customs duties, import taxes, stamp duties, contributions, turnover tax, luxury taxes and any other duties or charges in favour of the State, now existing or that may be imposed in the future, on any imported article necessary for equipping their offices in Greece.

(b) They shall be exempt from *income tax*, as well as any other tax, charge or contribution in favour of the State or any third party, now existing or that may be imposed in the future, on income derived from activities whose objects lie outside the Greek territory.

The above focuses briefly on the provisions affecting the reception of private foreign investment form abroad and while in the case of 2687/1953 and Laws 89 and 389, they are strictly applicable to foreign investments. Other Laws such as Law 4171/671 and Law 1377/1973 apply both to the Greek and to the foreign investors; the latter laws do play an important role as well in attracting foreign capital.

II. The Role of Tax Treaties

Having examined the national laws which provide for the above basic tax facilities, we now turn to the international tax agreements for the avoidance of double taxation between the exporting capital country and the host recipient country, and in our case, Greece.

Greece has concluded double tax treaties with the following countries: The United Kingdom, the US, Austria, Germany, France, Sweden, Italy, India, Cyprus and Belgium. Several other important tax treaties with developed countries are now in the process of being concluded.

The main tax provisions included in the double taxation agreements and which facilitate particularly foreign capital flows concern the tax provisions for royalties, dividends and interest.

The chart below [19] summarizes the Greek Tax Treaty network and notes the applicable tax rates for these three categories i.e. royalties, dividends and interest.

Tax Treaty Country	*Royalties*	*Dividends*	*Interest*
Non Treaty rate	17.25%	38% or 41% or 43% or 47% [20]	43.4%
Italy	no tax due	25%	10%
Belgium	5%	25%	15%
Austria	(10% if Austrial Co. owns more than 50% of Greek Co.) No income tax if less than 50% ownership	Non Treaty rates	0 (10% if Austrian Co. owns 50% or more of Greek Co.)

Tax Treaty Country	*Royalties*	*Dividends*	*Interest*
France	5%	Non Treaty rates	10%
Germany	no tax due	25%	10%
Sweden	5%	Non Treaty rates	10%
Cyprus	no tax due	25%	10%
UK	no tax due	Non Treaty rates	0
USA	no tax due	Non Treaty rates	(a) Effective rate 43.4% if the US company controls more than 50% of the voting power of a Greek Co. (b) 43.4% effective rate on excess of 9% p.a. interest if it has 50% or less of voting power in Greek Co.
India	17.25%	Non Treaty rates	43.4%

OUTFLOW OF LOCAL CAPITAL

Greece being yet a developing country, and in need of foreign capital investment, and foreign technology in order to accelerate its economic and industrial development is primarily interested in instituting tax and other incentives in order to attract foreign capital, i.e. flows of private capital into Greece rather than the reverse of encouraging Greek investments abroad. This picture however may begin to change now as Greece becomes a full member of the EEC.

There are no specificic tax incentives in Greece for instance as those offered by Germany, in order to invest abroad. The only incentives offered today by the Greek Government is to facilitate the Greek technical companies to undertake projects abroad particularly in the Middle East area and this is primarily in the area of banking facilities that is guaranteeing the good performance bonds and facilitating the financial transactions of those companies operating abroad.

Although there are no specific national tax laws that encourage the outlaw of Greek capital the role of the Tax Treaties in this respect should not be overlooked as with the Tax Treaty network that Greece has established the facility is there for Greek investments to be made abroad and to take advantage of lower dividend rates for profits earned in another tax treaty country where the investment take place.

Looking a bit into the future and particularly so after Greece's entry into the EEC, then some Greek industrial companies will start shyly to set up manufacturing facilities outside Greece. It is quite possible then that the Greek Government will institute certain tax measures to encourage investment abroad in areas where for instance labor rates are lower or/and profits will be higher (than local profits) which in turn will repatriate more profits in the form of foreign exchange. This trend could very well be facilitated with Greece's entry in the EEC whereby Greece will have to adopt and harmonize itself with the various EEC regulations on foreign exchange or capital flows which will lead to an easing up of the various regulations. Thus, the restrictions and red tape that a Greek company meets today in order to invest abroad will become simpler and the EEC Treaty provisions on the free flow of capitalgoods and persons will be the rule to follow.

In addition to the Tax Treaty network, Greece offers unilateral tax relief to non-Tax Treaty countries. Thus, if there is no Tax Treaty between Greece and another country, any taxes paid abroad by a Greek Company for instance, this will be deducted up to the amount that the tax would have been paid had the income been earned in Greece. In this manner double taxation for the same income (which is earned abroad) is avoided. It should be pointed out here that Greece applies the worldwide income principles of taxation, and therefore it has to report in Greece income earned abroad from activities outside Greece. This unilateral relief provision is an important stimulus to investments outside Greece and will become more useful once Greek investments start to go abroad.

SUMMARY

It may be summarized here that the basic tax provisions which are in effect today in Greece, deal with the attraction of capital flows from developed countries or more industrialised countries into Greece rather than the reverse. There is a logical reason for this as Greece is interested in attracting foreign capital which is often accompanied with foreign technology, a necessary ingredient for its industrial and general economic development.

The basic laws which have significant tax provisions for facilitating the inflow of foreign capital is Law 2687 of 1953, instituted for the attraction and protection of foreign capital as well as the other laws such as Law 4171/1961 as amended and the developmental laws for investing at Greece and particularly so in areas outside the Athens-Piraeus district. The latter laws were intended to reach in Greece a more balanced economy from a geographical point of view.

With Greece's entry into the EEC certain major tax changes will have to be instituted particularly as it concerns the incentives area, e.g. the existing tax-free reserves from net profits for investments, etc.

Generally the position taken in the EEC is that this sort of incentive should gradually be abandoned as they result in certain disruptions of the rules of competitions.

Ireland which has been one of the three subsequent countries to enter the EEC, through a special protocol no. 30 to the Accession Treaty has been allowed, however, to keep its tax holiday offered to exports during the transition period. Thereafter, the equivalent amount of the incentive offered shall be allowed but in the form of direct grants to export companies. Ireland based its argument on the fact that this incentive at least for the duration of the transitional period was necessary for its regional development.

It is expected that Greece will come to a similar type of an agreement with the EEC as it concerns regional development and the tax incentives in existence today. It should finally be pointed out that a special Committee is studying this very problem of existing tax incentives and their harmonization with EEC rules.

1. Article 8, Law 2687/1953.
2. Article 5, Law 2687/1953.
3. It should be pointed out that the 12% on imported capital of foreign exchange allowed on profits is net after taxes withheld. Thus, the gross dividend annually related to imported capital is approximately 18%.
4. Article 2 of Law 4171/1961, as amended.
5. Turnover tax included (Article 12, para. 2 of L.D. 4486/1965 as interpreted by judgment of the Council of the State).
6. The provisions of para. 1, art. 2 appear as amended by para. 1, art. 2 L.D. 916/1971.
7. The above-mentioned maximum period of time was fixed by para. 6, art. 2 L.D. 916/1971 while a maximum period of time of fifteen years was originally allowed.
8. As amended by para. 1, art. 1 L. 159/1975.
9. The provisions of para. 4, art. 7 appear as amended by para. 3, art. 6 L.D. 916/1971.
10. Article 7, para. 5 of Law 4171/61 as amended.
11. Legislative Decree 1377/1973 amendment and supplementation of L.D. 1078/1971 concerning 'Tax and other Measures in Support of Regional Development' and of L.D. 1312/1972 concerning 'New Measures in Support of Regional Development'.
12. Article 1 Law 1377/1973.
13. Article 10 Law 1377/1973.
14. Article 1, Law 289/1976 Re 'Incentives for the Development of Border Areas and related Provisions'.
15. Article 2, Law 1377/1973.
16. Article 10 L.D. 1377/1973.
17. Article 11, Law 1377/1973.
18. Article 2, Law 89/1967.
19. The above chart is taken from the Book 'Investing in the Eastern Mediterranean' (1977), Chapter on Greece, page 33, by J. F. Chown and G. N. Stathopoulos.
20. Article 15 of Law 452/1977 sets the following dividend rates for dividends distributed as of January 1, 1977 and thereafter: (a) Dividends for shares on the Stock Exchange: (i) order shares 38% (ii) bearer shares 41%. (b) Dividends for shares not on Stock Exchange: (i) order shares 43% (ii) bearer shares 47%.

Guatemala

Sergio Garcia Granados *

This concise study was originally planned to comprise all of the five Central American countries: Guatemala, El Salvador, Honduras, Nicaragua and Costa Rica. But as the study was being made, we realized that it was very difficult for us to obtain reliable information as to the application of the law from the other four countries excluding Guatemala. In consequence, the study will be concentrated on Guatemalan law, with references to the other Central American countries.

GENERAL OUTLOOK

In general, the Guatemalan legislation and government look favorably upon foreign investment into the country. There are a few exceptions, mainly professional services provided in Guatemala by foreign professionals, internal transportation, communications, and a few other. Generally, the public approves of foreign investment as well, except in the case of very large investments, in which case it is feared that large investments might exert a strong political influence on the government. In the case of extractive industries, the government grants a concession valid for a certain number of years. Usually the concession follows bases previously set by law. The government, for example, has recently authorized an oil company and a nickel concern to set up operations of exploitation. As concerns smaller ventures, a large number of foreign companies operate either directly in Guatemala or in the Central American Common Market from another Central American country. A very high percentage of commerce of industrial goods and services in Central America is formed by products or services produced by branches or subsidiaries of foreign corporations or foreign-local joint ventures.

The tax laws do not differentiate between foreign and local investors except: 1) In the case of credit to non-residents of profits, dividends, royalties or interests where a special remittance tax, discussed below is payable (usually between 11% and 12%). 2) In the case of the granting of tax incentives under the Central American Treaty for Tax Incentives to Industrial Development. This treaty provides that tax incentives should not be granted to a company when the company's home country legislation would made ineffective the tax reduction thus granted. This is the case for companies of most of the developed countries, as the recognition of the tax credit without tax sparing makes ineffective the tax reduction recognized by the Central American country. This, however, in practice, has not been applied in Guatemala. It has not been possible to receive information concerning the application of this rule in other Central American countries.

In general, the outlook for investments is the same in the rest of the Central

* Saravia y Munoz, Guatemala City.

American countries, although the Governments of Nicaragua, and Costa Rica actively encourage foreign investment in their respective countries. Costa Rica not only presents a favorable governmental attitude, but also promotes the country as a tax haven for operations outside of Central America.

Although there is an exchange control in some of the Central American countries, foreign exchange does not constitute a problem worth giving special attention. Once the investment has been registered in the Central Bank, where this is requested, there is a guarantee of obtaining foreign exchange both for remittance of profits and for repatriation of capital. Register of investment in the Central Bank does not signify an authorization to operate; rather, a company registers a transaction after the investment has been made. However, it is always advisable to request local legal advice as to the possible implications of the investment, before making any substantial transfer of funds into a recipient country.

REMITTANCE OF DIVIDENDS AND BRANCH PROFITS

Dividends and branch profits are not taxed in Guatemala when paid to residents of Guatemala. In the case of residents of other countries, an eleven percent tax is payable by the recipient of a dividend or branch profit. This amount is withheld by the entity paying these dividends or branch profits. The amount paid is considered a definitive payment as income tax of the recipient.

The situation in other Central American Common Market countries is the following: In the case of Costa Rica, the payment made to residents is taxed at a five percent flat rate. In the case of dividends or branch profits paid to non-residents, the tax payable at withholding is fifteen percent flat.

In El Salvador, a differentiation is made between branch profits and dividends paid to individuals or to corporations. In the case of corporations, both branch profits and dividends are liable to a withholding tax of 38 percent. In the case of individuals, dividends are taxed at a 38 percent withholding and branch profits at the rate of 28 percent.

Honduras does not have a tax on dividends and branch profits paid to residents, and in the case of dividends paid abroad, the withholding tax is 5 percent.

In the case of Nicaragua there is no withholding tax on dividends for residents or non-residents.

It must be pointed out that these withholding taxes are applied for remittance of profits or dividends in the same scale for payments out of the Central American area or for payments within the Central American area.

PAYMENT OF INTEREST ON FOREIGN LOANS

In Guatemala there is no limitation in the receiving of foreign loans by Guatemalan residents. Neither is there any limitation for the deductability of these loans up to an interest which does not exceed a certain limit. The present limit is fifteen percent per year.

The taxation of the interest received by a foreign entity or individual is the same as local income tax, which goes up to an effective rate of 52 percent on amounts exceeding $500,000 in one year. However, the minimum rate applicable to interest is eleven percent, which has to be withheld by the paying party.

In the case of loans which are payable and actually paid in a term exceeding eighteen months, the payment of income tax on the interest is waived completely, and no tax is payable on the interests received abroad.

In the rest of Central America the situation is as follows:

In El Salvador interest paid to non-residents is taxed as income of a resident. In Honduras, the tax is five percent withheld at source. In Nicaragua, the tax is also income tax as paid by a resident and in Costa Rica the interest paid to non-residents is exempt. We could not obtain information concerning special incentives or waivers of the tax in the rest of the Central American countries.

TAXES ON ROYALTIES AND OTHER INTANGIBLES

The amount that can be deducted by a company in relation to the transfer of technology or the use of patents, trademarks, or other intangibles in Guatemala is limited to 15 percent of gross turnover of the entity deducting it. In all cases the deduction must be authorized by the Ministry of Economic Affairs.

Concerning the payee of the royalties, a withholding tax is withheld at source at the rate of eleven percent. The rate is higher when the amounts paid in one year exceed 21,500 US Dollars, in which case income tax is payable by the recipient.

In the rest of the Central American countries the situation is the following:

In El Salvador: Income tax is payable on the amount received and a withholding of a 38 percent is made. In Honduras: A ten percent tax is paid on remittance of the royalties abroad. In Nicaragua: Income tax is payable by the recipient of the royalties and in Costa Rica a withholding tax of 20 percent is payable. We could not find reliable information for the rest of the Central American countries concerning limitations to the deductability of the royalties paid abroad.

TAXATION OF CAPITAL GAINS ON PROPERTY

In Guatemala there is no special tax on capital gains or any special treatment for them, and the full amount of the capital gains are added to the income tax of the taxpayer in the year when the capital gains are realized. This creates a heavy tax burden on the realization of capital gains, as often the addition of these gains takes the taxpayer to the highest brackets in the scale (a maximum effective 52%). This high tax though, can be avoided by careful tax planning at the moment of the realization of the capital gains.

In addition to the local income tax, the difference between the amount remitted or credited to the non-resident and the amount originally paid for the property sold, would be subject to a withholding tax which is a definitive payment of 11% when credited or remitted.

We have no information available as to the treatment of capital gains of non-residents in the rest of the Central American countries.

TAX INCENTIVES

The Treaty for Common Tax Incentives for the Industrial Development exists within the framework of the Central American Common Market. At present the treaty is applied in Guatemala, El Salvador, Honduras, and Costa Rica and with limitations in Honduras. The treaty does not allow any other incentives to industry than the ones provided for in the treaty. In the case of special activities like tourism development, hotels, forestry, etc., which are not considered industrial, there are several laws in the different countries promoting these and other non-traditional activities.

The tax incentives granted on the Central American treaty for industrial development are as follows:

For the purposes of the incentives, three groups of business enterprises are distinguished:

Group A:
- industries using raw materials at least 50 percent of which originate from Member Countries; and
- enterprises which manufacture either machinery or semi-finished products to be used in industry.

Group B:
- industries which do not qualify for Group A, but which have a favorable influence on the combined balance of payments of the Member States.

Group C:
- enterprises whose main purpose is cutting, packing, bottling or assembling, using raw materials of which less than 50 percent originate from Member States.

The privileges granted are:
- exemption from import duties with respect to machinery and equipment for 10 years (Group A), 8 years (Group B) and 3 years (Group C);
- 80 percent reduction from import duties with respect to raw materials for 5 years (Group A) and 3 years (Group B), and a reduction by 50 percent during 5 additional years (Group A) and 2 additional years (Group B);
- exemption from import duties and fuel (except gasoline) for 5 years (Group A) and for 3 years (Group B) (the latter Group is granted a 50 percent exemption for 2 additional years);
- exemption from income tax for 8 years (Group A) and 6 years (Group B); and
- exemption from taxes on net worth or property for 10 years (Group A) and 6 years (Group B).

TAX TREATIES

Except for the Central American treaties on the Central American Common Market (rules that mainly refer to indirect taxes), there are no general tax treaties with foreign countries. Honduras has signed a tax treaty with the United States but at present it is not being applied.

India

Vasant P. Mehta *

1. The direct taxes are (i) Income-tax, (ii) Wealth-tax, (iii) Gift-tax and (iv) Estate Duty.

2. Income-tax includes tax on capital gains and is a tax on the income of every person for each assessment year beginning from 1st April and ending on 31st March during the previous year which might be the financial year ending on 31st March, calendar year or any year ending between 30th June and 31st March each year. A person has been defined under the Act to include individuals, Hindu undivided families (HUF's), Association of persons, body of individuals, firms, companies, local authority and every form of artificial judicial person.

3. Income is computed and assessed under the following heads:

(1) Salaries
(2) Interest on securities
(3) Property income
(4) Income from business, profession or vocation.
(5) Capital gains
(6) Income from other sources including dividends and interest income.

4. The basic principles are similar to those governing the British system of taxation.

5. India is a sovereign democratic Republic having a population of over 600 million people and geographical area of 32,80,000 sq. kilometres consisting of over 21 States. The unit of currency is Indian Rupee. At the present rates of exchange £1 sterling is equal to Rs. 15/- and 1 US dollar is about Rs. 9/-.

6. Under the Constitution of India, the Parliament has exclusive power to tax income other than agricultural income. Only the State Legislatures have the power to tax agricultural income. Further, they have also power to levy taxes on income from profession, trades, callings or employment for the benefit of the State of not exceeding Rs. 250/-. Amongst the indirect taxes, sales-tax is both a Central and a State tax. Excise and customs duty are Central levies. Stamp duties are levied by the State Legislatures.

7. Agricultural income is taxed differently in different States and several States including the State of Gujarat do not tax it at all. In the State of Maharashtra, the agricultural income is totally exempt upto Rs. 36,000/- per year per person. The income above that limit is taxable on a slab system with a maximum of 50 per cent.

COMPUTATION OF INCOME

8. Individuals are classified as resident and ordinarily resident, resident but not ordinarily resident and non-resident. Firms, Hindu undivided families

* Attorney at Law, Bombay.

(HUF's) and companies are classified as residents or non-reesidents applying the test of management and control.

EXEMPT INCOME

9. (1) Official remuneration of embassies and consular staff.
   (2) Remuneration of UNO employees.
   (3) Income of approved sports associations.
   (4) Income of approved medical institutions.
   (5) Casual and non-recurring receipts upto Rs. 1,000/-.
   (6) Part of income from lotteries.
   (7) Educational scholarships.
   (8) Remuneration of foreign technicians on fulfilling certain conditions.
   (9) Interest on certain government loans, savings certificates, bank deposits.
   (10) Interest on non-resident external accounts.
   (11) Income of charitable organisations fulfilling certain conditions.
   (12) Income of certain members of scheduled tribes.

10. Deductions upto Rs. 3,500/- are allowed against salary income and per quisites are calculated as per special rules.

11. Expenses incurred in earning interest from securities and income from other sources like interest and dividend income are allowed as deduction against each specific head of income.

12. Deductions allowed in computing income from business, profession or vocation are:

(1) Rent of premises.
(2) Current repairs.
(3) Interest on borrowed capital.
(4) Insurance premia on assets of the business.
(5) Depreciation on the reducing value allowed at specific rates. In certain cases initial depreciation and extra shift allowance are also given.
(6) Salaries, bonuses, commission.
(7) Payment of gratuity, provident fund, superannuation funds, etc. on fulfilling certain conditions.
(8) Contribution for family planning.
(9) Expenditure on scientific research, whether of a capital or revenue nature. Research expenses are entitled to deduction at 100% even on capital expenditure u/s 35(1) and at 133% on research at an approved research institution u/s 35(2A). Income of a business house being a company in India by way of fees for supply of technical knowhow abroad is exempt from Indian tax u/s 80-0, if the conditions thereunder are fulfilled.
(10) Entertainment expenditure to a limited extent.
(11) Investment allowance at specified rates for selected industries on fulfilling certain conditions.
(12) Export market allowance – weighted deduction at 133% or 150% on specific export expenses not being freight and insurance incurred in India.
(13) Amortisation of preliminary expenses every year for 10 years.

(14) Any expenditure not being capital expenditure or personal expenditure incurred wholly and exclusively for the purpose of the business.

(15) Patent and copyrights – capital expenditure on patent and copyright is allowed deduction in 14 equal instalments spread over 14 years.

(16) Trade or professional association subscriptions are not taxable. 50 per cent of its net income is taxable at appropriate rate.

(17) Advertising expenses are fully allowed.

(18) Agricultural development allowance – 120 per cent of expenditure incurred is allowed as a deduction to a company engaged in agriculture, animal husbandry or dairy farming.

(19) Preliminary expenses upto certain limit incurred on project reports, market surveys and consultancy services is allowed as a deduction in 10 equal instalments over 10 years.

(20) The plantations and mining operations have special provisions for deduction of expenses.

(21) Tax holiday: Income equal to 7½ per cent of the capital is exempt for 5 years in case of income of a new industrial undertaking, ship or a hotel.

(22) Donations to organise charities – About 50% of the amount donated to charities upto a limit of Rs. 5 lakhs or 10% of the total income which ever is less is to be allowed in computing taxable income of an assessee.

(23) Under sec. 80MM, 60 per cent of the income of a company supplying technical knowhow to a company in India is exempt from tax.

(24) Under sec. 80M – Inter Corporate dividends – income of an Indian company is exempt upto 60%. It is exempt upto 100% if derived from a company engaged exclusively in the manufacture of certain articles specified in the Ninth Schedule.

(25) Under sec. 80-0, income derived by way of foreign exchange by an Indian company for supply of technical knowhow is totally exempt from tax.

(26) Interest paid on monies borrowed for payment of tax is allowed as a deduction in computing taxable income under sec. 80V.

(27) There are several other similar reliefs and deductions such as educational expenses, income of persons, income of co-operative societies to a limited extent, etc.

CAPITAL GAINS

13. Capital gains are charged on the transfer of a capital asset. If the asset is held for more than 36 months, it is charged as long-term capital gains while if the asset is held for a period less thans 3 years, it is taxed as short-term capital gains at the rates applicable as if it were income of that year. The computation of long-term capital gains is done on the basis of sale price minus the cost subject to certain exceptions. In cases of assets held earlier than 1964, the market value of the asset as on 1st January 1964 can at the option of the assessee be substituted for its cost. In cases of shares or other assets held by foreign companies, the selling price is subject to approval of the Central Government or the Reserve Bank of India. The price so fixed would be taken into

account while computing the capital gains. For other assessees there is a provision for taking the fair market value on the date of transfer instead of the actual selling price if the sale price is lower than the market value and then computing the capital gains. However, this notional selling price is subject to various conditions and unless there is evidence that there is some attempted concealment, the same will not be taken into account. There are various provisions in respect of residential houses and land used for agricultural purposes whereby if the amount of capital gains is reinvested in the same form of assets and kept so invested for a further period of 3 years, there will be no liability to capital gains. After the recent amendment, long-term capital gains arising on sale of assets will not be liable to tax if the entire consideration is reinvested in certain specified assets which include shares of public limited companies. Under sec. 80T, no capital gains is chargeable where the long-term capital gains do not exceed Rs. 5,000/- and in case the capital gains exceed Rs. 5,000/- if it is in respect of a capital asset being building or land, 25% of the said capital gains will be excluded and if it is any other form of asset, 40% of the said capital gains will be excluded and the balance amount would be taxed as income of the assessee.

14. In the case of widely held companies having taxable income not exceeding Rs. 1 lakh, capital gains will be charges at 40% while in excess of the same would be charged at 50%.

15. Agreements for relief from double taxation can be broadly divided into two groups as under:

(a) The agreements with Sweden, Denmark, Norway, Finland, Austria and to some extent the agreement with West Germany are based on the method of exclusion, i.e. the income from sources allocated to one country is not taxed in the other country, though it can be taken into account for purposes of determining the rate of tax, if the laws of that country so require.

(b) The agreement with Japan, and to some extent the agreement with West Germany are based on the method of tax credit, i.e. the tax in the two countries is levied according to their respective laws but credit for the tax payable in one country is provided for by the other in respect of income from sources allocated to the first country. These agreements provide for giving credit for tax that would have been paid in India but for certain tax incentives.

16. Collaboration agreements between India and other countries importing technical knowhow and technical showhow into India are approved by the Government of India in terms of guidelines issued by the Government.

17. There is no agreement for relief of double taxation between India and UK or USA. Satisfactory agreements exist with Germany, France and Japan. The most satisfactory agreement exists with Japan. Illustrative charts of taxability of collaboration agreements with Japan and West Germany and with countries with whom India has no agreement for relief of double taxation are annexed hereto.

18. Under sec. 9, income accruing to a foreign company where the supply of technical knowhow is made outside India and the payment has also been made outside India, is now deemed to accrue or arise in India and would be taxable at 20% without allowing any deduction. However, in cases where there

is agreement for relief from double taxation and under the agreement the foreign income is not taxable under the Indian law, it is possible that such foreign income for supply of technical knowhow abroad will not be taxable in view of the agreement for relief from double taxation.

LUMPSUM PAYMENT

19. (1) Lumpsum payment if made under a collaboration agreement abroad would be taxable at 20%.

(2) Royalties for exploitation of knowhow from a foreign company in India would be taxed at 40% without allowing deduction of any expenses.

(3) Fee for technical assistance will also be taxed at 40% without allowing any deduction of expenses.

(4) Head Office expenses are allowed for agreements signed and approved before 1st April 1976.

(5) Payments made in kind to foreign collaborator by way of equity participation will be taxed according to the illustrations in Charts 'A', 'B', and 'C' depending on whether the payment is for technical knowhow or showhow. However, they will not be taxed on the basis that payment is in India as the shares are in India. A copy of the minutes of the Direct Taxes Advisory Committee meeting clarifying the position is annexed hereto.

TAX ADMINISTRATION

20. (1) Income-tax Officer.
(2) Commissioner (Appeals) – 1st Appeal.
(3) Income-tax Appellate Tribunal – 2nd Appeal.
(4) High Court – References on questions of law.
(5) Supreme Court on appeals from judgments of the High Courts. There are 17 High Courts all over India and the Supreme Court in New Delhi over all the High Courts.
(6) Alternative to appeal to the Tribunal, an assessee can go in Revision to the Commissioner of Income-tax.
(7) Writs challenging the constitutional validity of any provision of taxs laws can be filed in the High Courts and/or in the Supreme Court.
(8) Administratively, the Commissioners of Income-tax work under the Central Board of Direct Taxes. There is a Finance Secretary and a Finance Minister at the apex of the tax hierarchy.

INTEREST, PENALTIES AND PROSECUTIONS

21. There are different penalties for defaults in filing returns, payment of taxes and concealment of income. In some cases prosecutions are launched

particularly for concealment of income which are independent of the penalty proceedings. Interest is charged at 12 per on delayed payment.

22. Recently a Committee has been appointed to give a report on simplification of the lax laws. The report is expected by end of December 1977.

WEALTH-TAX ACT

23. There is a Wealth-tax Act which taxes the net wealth of every individual or HUF on the valuation date for each assessment year. There is no wealth-tax on companies and foreign companies holding shares of Indian companies would not be liable to wealth-tax. The wealth-tax is levied on the annual net wealth after allowing various deductions for certain exempted asset which include shares, securities, bank deposits, etc. not exceeding Rs. 1,50,000/-, self-occupied or rented properties upto Rs. 1 lakh and basic exemption of Rs. 1 lakh.

GIFT-TAX ACT

24. Under the Gift-tac Act transfers without consideration or for inadequate consideration or deemed transfers are liable to tax at appropriate rates. Gifts upto Rs. 5,000/- per year are totally exempt from gift-tax. Gifts upto Rs. 50,000/- made to a pouse is exempt from gift-tax. There is now a provision for aggregation of gifts made after 1st June 1973. There are also deeming provisions for levying gift-tax where the transfer of an asset has occurred at a price lower than the market value and therefore for inadequate consideration, unless the said price is a price fixed by the Central Government or the Reserve Bank of India in cases of transfer of shares by foreign companies.

FOREIGN EXCHANGE REGULATIONS ACT

25. Exchange control exists in the form of Foreign Exchange Regulations Act, 1973 and is based on a corresponding Act in England. As far as a foreign company is concerned, it cannot establish a place of business in India without obtaining permission from the Reserve Bank of India under sec. 29 of the Foreign Exchange Regulations Act. Permission is required to carry on in India or establish in India a branch office or other place of business for carrying on any activity of a trading, commercial or industrial nature, the permission would be granted after applications are made in the specified forms. Any general Equity participation upto 40% will be permitted on such terms and conditions that the Reserve Bank will make for repatriation of dividends and capital on sale of assets and stocks or shares.

26. There is restriction on acquisition, holding, etc. of immovable properties by a foreign company and the same requires prior approval of the Reserve Bank of India under sec. 31 of the Foreign Exchange Regulations Act.

27. Foreign nationals taking up employment in India do not require permission of the Reserve Bank under the Foreign Exchange Regulations Act if they do not seek repatriation of the income from India, although they will be required to obtain appropriate permission to be permitted to stay in India for indefinite periods under the immigration and other laws.

ANNEXURE I

Classification and Amplification of Guidelines Issued for Administering Section 29 of Foreign Exchange Regulation Act, 1973

1. Section 29(2)(a) of the Foreign Exchange Regulation Act, 1973, inter alia provides that branches of foreign incorporated companies operating in India and Indian companies having more than 40 per cent non-resident interest have to seek Reserve Bank of India's approval for continuing their existing activities in the country.

2. Under the existing guidelines for administering Section 29 of FERA, 1973, placed on the Tables of both the Houses of Parliament on 28th December 1973, Indian Companies having more than 40 per cent foreign share holding, and branches of foreign companies, can continue their existing activities after increasing, within a specified period, Indian participation to not less than 26 per cent of the equity of the company (in the case of branches after converting themselves into Indian companies), if they are engaged in production of items specified in appendix I of the Industrial Licensing Policy, 1973, or engaged in a predominantly export-oriented industry (minimum export being 60 per cent of total production) or are engaged in manufacturing or other activities which need sophisticated technology or specialised skills or are engaged in tea plantation activities. All other companies whether engaged in manufacturing or trading activities are required to bring down foreign share-holding to the level of 40 per cent. The functioning of branches of Air and Shipping companies operating in India are, however, to be decided on the basis of reciprocity. It has also been stipulated in the existing guidelines that where a company is engaged in multi-activity operations, a total view will have to be taken of all the activities in which a company is engaged while considering the question of allowing it to carry on business. The proportion of output covered by Appendix I industries of the Industrial Licensing Policy 1973, and those falling outside this will be a material consideration. If activities outside Appendix I industries constitute only a minor part of the total activities of the company (not exceeding 25 per cent of the ex-factory value of the annual production, or Rs. 5 crores whichever is less), it will be allowed to continue on the basis of existing approvals, provided Indian participation is not less than 25 per cent of the equity of the company.

3. The rationale behind the above provisions of the guidelines in allowing non-resident equity holding of more than 40 per cent was to give due consideration to a company being predominently engaged in activities in the priority

or export oriented sectors which contribute to the nation's economic and industrial development.

4. There were, however, cases of companies which are engaged in such priority or export-oriented sectors in various proportions which, when taken together, would come to 75 per cent. While dealing with such applications under Section 29(2) of FERA, 1973, the need for clarification of the guidelines was felt. It was, therefore, considered appropriate to spell out clearly that, if the activities of a company under Appendix I industries combined with activities requiring sophisticated technology and exports, accounted for not less than 75 per cent of the total annual turnover, such a company would be allowed to continue its activities subject to the condition that it would increase Indian participation, within a specified period, to not less than 26 per cent of the equity capital of the company.

5. Under the existing guidelines, no distinction has been made between companies substantially engaged in priority or export-oriented sectors (where the extent of such activities is less than the prescribed limits in the guidelines) and other companies engaged in purely trading activities or other manufacturing activities in non-priority areas, since all such companies are required to reduce their foreign shareholding to 40 per cent. To give due weightage to activities which are in the interest of country's economic development and which form a substantial part of the total output, it was felt that an intermediate resting point might be allowed in such cases. It has, therefore, been decided that companies, whose Appendix 1 activities together with activities requiring sophisticated technology and exports, account for not less than 60 per cent of total annual turnover, should be treated on a different footing; such companies will now be required to associate Indian equity participation of not less than 49 per cent. Keeping in view paramount need to encourage exports, a condition will also be stipulated that the company concerned should undertake to export a minimum of 10 per cent of its total annual turnover within a period of two years commencing from the date of approval by the Reserve Bank of India.

Similarly, companies with exports exceeding 40 per cent of their total turnover will now be required to associate Indian participation to not less than 49 per cent of the equity of the company. Cases of companies coming up with proposals of substantial exports would be considered, on merits, for higher level of equity participation.

6. By the above decisions which have been brought about as a result of experience gained in operating the guidelines, these have been clarified and amplified to the extent necessary, in tune with the spirit of the existing guidelines.

7. The annexure to this statement shows how the provisions of the guidelines have been clarified and amplified.

(This note was laid on the Table of the Parliament on 15th April, 1976.)

a) If the activities of a company under Appendix I together with activities requiring sophisticated technology and exports, account for not less than 75% of total annual turnover, such a company will be allowed to continue its activities subject to the condition that it will increase Indian participation, within a specified period, to not less than 26% of the equity capital of the company.

b) If the activities of a company under Appendix I together with activities requiring sophisticated technology and exports account for not less than 60% of total annual turnover, such a company will be allowed to continue its activities, subject to the condition that it will increase within a specified period, Indian participation to not less than 49% of the equity of the company. In such case a condition will be stipulated that the company concerned should undertake to export a minimum of 10% of its total annual turnover within a period of two years commencing from the date of approval by the Reserve Bank of India.

c) If the exports of a company account for more than 40% of the total annual turnover, such a company will be allowed to continue its activities subject to the condition that it will increase, within a specified period, Indian participation to not less than 49% of the equity of the company.

d) Cases of companies coming with proposals for substantial exports could be considered, on merits, for higher level of equity participation, provided such participation is in the overall interest of the economy of the country.

e) The limit of Rs. 5 scrores referred to in Explanatory Note (ii) of the existing guidelines will be applicable only in the case of trading activities of multi-activity companies. Thus the limit of Rs. 5 scores will not be applicable to the non-Appendix I manufacturing activities of multi-activity companies.

f) The ceiling of 25% referred to in Explanatory Note (ii) will be raised to 40% and 60% respectively in the types of cases mentioned in (b) and (c) above.

Notes

(i) The item treated as being covered by Appendix I or sophisticated technology will not be again counted towards exports while clubbing the three together in (a) to (c) above.

(ii) The above clarification and amplification of the guidelines *will not be applicable to the drug industry.*

ANNEXURE II

Guidelines for Collaboration Agreements

i) The Indian Company should be free to sub-licence the technical know-how/product design/engineering design under the agreement to another. Indian party, should it become necessary. The terms of such sub-licensing will, however, be as mutually agreed to by all the parties concerned including the foreign collaborators and will be subject to the approval of Government.

ii) The deputation of technicians either way shall be governed by specific approval to be granted by the Government on application in terms of members, period of assistance and training, rate of allowances to be paid, travelling charges and other items of expenses etc.

iii) Import of capital equipment and raw material would be allowed as per import policy prevailing from time to time.

iv) Foreign brand names will not ordinarily be allowed for use on the products for internal sales although there is no objection to their use on products to be exported.

v) Exports shall be permitted to all countries except where the foreign collaborator has existing licensing arrangements for manufacture. In the latter case, the countries concerned shall be specified.

vi) The duration of the agreement shall be for a period of five years from the date of agreement or five years from the date of commencement of production provided production is not delayed beyond three years of signing of agreement, (i.e. a maximum period of eight years from the date of signing of agreement). Within this period, the Indian company should develop and set up their own design and research facilities so that continued dependence on foreign collaboration beyond this periode will not be necessary.

vii) In case the item of manufacture is one which is patented in India, the payment of royalty/lumpsum payments made by the Indian Company to the Foreign collaborator for a period of agreement mentioned in condition (vi) above shall also constitute full compensation for use of the patent rights till the expiry of life of the patent and the Indian company shall be gree to manufacture that item even after the expiry of the collaboration agreement without making any additional payments. A specific provision in this regard must be incorporated in the collaboration agreement to be entered into between the two parties.

viii) In case any consultancy is required to execute the project, this should be obtained from an Indian Consultancy Engg. firm. If foreign consultancy is considered unavoidable, an Indian consultancy firm should nevertheless be the prime consultants.

ix) The Indian company should submit a return about the progress of the undertaking as in the form enclosed, showing the position as on 31st December, each year. This return should be submitted by the 31st January, the following year annually till the date of expiry of foreign agreement. The return should be addressed to the following authorities:

a) The Ministry/Department administratively concerned with the field of collaboration.
b) The Directorate General of Technical Development, Udyog Bhavan, New Delhi-110 011 (to be sent in duplicate).
c) The Secretariat for Industrial Approvals (Foreign Collaborations – II Section), Ministry of Industry, Department of Industrial Development, Udyog Bhavan, New Delhi-110 011.
d) Ministry of Finance (Department of Economic Affairs) North Block, New Delhi-110 011.
e) The agreement shall be subject to Indian laws.

ANNEXURE III

Minutes of the Seventh Meeting of the Direct Taxes Advisory Committee Held on the 17th December 1965 at New Delhi

Collaboration Agreements for Supply of Machinery and Technical Know-how

It was explained to the Committee that where shares in an Indian concern were allotted to a non-resident in consideration for transfer abroad of technical know-how or services, or delivery abroad of machinery and plant, the existing instructions were that no attempt should be made to charge the profit of the non-resident to tax in India merely on the ground that the shares were situate in India. Where the consideration for the transfer outside India of know-how is paid in cash outside India, the position is that the profits would normally be treated as arising outside India to the non- resident and would not be liable to tax in India, except to the extent that such profits are attributable to services rendered in India by the non-resident, under the terms of the agreement.

The Committee was also informed that in respect of payment of fees for technical services made to a foreign company under a pre-1.3.1964 agreement, the rate of tax to be deducted at source under the Finance Acts of 1964 and 1965 was 65%.

Foreign Collaboration Transactions

The suggestion was that the value of equity shares given to a foreign collaborator for technical know-how should not be subjected to income-tax as income for capital gains, if the contract is entered into and the know-how is also supplied abroad. The Committee was informed that payment for know-how delivered abroad was not treated as income arising or received in India if the payment was also made abroad. However, if from an agreement it appeared that is also contemplated rendering of services in India, the income attributable to such services would fall to be treated as arising in India. In so far as transaction of sale between parties as principal to principal are concerned, no liability arises on accrual basis to the non-resident on such profits.

CHART A.
TAX IMPLICATIONS OF COLLABORATION AGREEMENT WITH JAPAN

Consideration	Indian Tax Liability	Japan Tax	Remarks
1. Payment for supply of machinery	Not taxable	Yes	
2. Payment for services in selecting machinery	–do–	Yes	
3. Lump sum payment for supply of know-how if supplied and paid outside India	20%	½ at 40% 28% 30%	
4. License user fees	40%		
5. Technician's remuneration	Not taxable if conditions fulfilled.		
6. Technical fees for erection	Not taxable if conditions Article II(1) (i) (ii) fulfilled.		
7. Double Taxation relief	Article XI		

Notes:
1. Payment under 4 will be deductible.
2. Payment under 1, 2 and 4 can be capitalised.
3. Payment under 3 may not be deductible but will be allowed depreciation and investment allowance.
4. Indian party should not agree to pay Indian taxes of Japanese collaborator.

CHART B.
COLLABORATION BETWEEN FEDERAL GERMAN REPUBLIC AND INDIA

Consideration	Indian Tax	German Tax	Remarks
1. Lump sum payment	Over 20%		
2. Royalty	40% net	Not taxable	Full credit in Germany

	Consideration	*Indian Tax*	*German Tax*	*Remarks*
3.	Sale of Machinery	No tax	Taxable	
4.	Technical Assistance	Taxable in India 40%		Full credit in Germany
5.	Technician salary	Not taxable in fulfils conditions in Section 10 (iv)		
6.	Sale of technical know-how outside India	Not taxable		

Notes:
1. There is agreement for relief from double taxation between India and Germany.
2. Lump sum payment for supply of 'know-how' where supply and payment are outside India will not be taxable in India because of the agreement. Under the amended law, it is liable to 20% Indian tax if there was no agreement: This aspect will be clarified by the Central Board of Direct Taxes.
3. Under article XVI(3)(b)(cc) of the agreement Indian tax paid on royalties will be allowed full credit in Germany.
4. Corporation tax in Germany is on a split rate. 51% on undistributed profits and 15% on distributed profits.
5. Indian tax on income from technical services in India is 40%.
6. Dividend income from India – 73.5% tax.

CHART C.

	Consideration	*Agreement entered after 29.2.1974 and before 1.4.1976*	*Agreement entered into after 31.3.76*	
		Tax rate	*Tax rate*	
A.	Royalties & Fees for Technical Services (Excluding lump sum payment)			S.40 D
	Rate of deduction for expenses	20%	Nil	
	Tax payable	52.50%	40%	
	Rate of deduction of tax at source	52.5%	40%	

Consideration	*Agreement entered after 29.2.1974 and before 1.4.1976*	*Agreement entered into after 31.3.76*
	Tax rate	*Tax rate*
B. Industrial Know-how Lump sum payment:		
Rate of deduction of expenditure	—	Nil
Tax payable	—	20%
Rate of deduction of tax at source	—	20%
C. On balance income	73.5%	73.5%

CHART D.
PROFITS AND GAINS OF BUSINESS OR PROFESSION S. 44 C

A. Head Office expenses deduction	a. 5% of adjusted total income b. average head office exp. c. as attributable to business in India	Whichever is less

In the case of every individual or Hindu undivided family or unregistered firm or other association of persons or body of individuals, whether incorporated or not, or every artificial juridical person referred to in sub-claus *(vii)* of clause (31) of section 2 of the Income-tax Act, not being a case to which Sub-Paragraph II of this Paragraph or any other Paragraph of this Part applies.

Rates of Income-Tax

(1) where the total income does not exceed Rs. 8,000	*Nil:*
(2) where the total income exceeds Rs. 8,000 but does not exceed Rs. 15,000	15 per cent, of the amount by which the total income exceeds Rs. 8,000;
(3) where the total income exceeds Rs. 15,000 but does not exceed Rs. 20,000	Rs. 1,050 *plus* 18 per cent, of the amount by which the total income exceeds Rs. 15,000;

(4) where the total income exceeds Rs. 20,000 but does not exceed Rs. 25,000	Rs. 1,950 *plus* 25 per cent, of the amount by which the total income exceeds Rs. 20,000;
(5) where the total income exceeds Rs. 25,000 but does not exceed Rs. 30,000	Rs. 3,200 *plus* 30 per cent, of the amount by which the total income exceeds Rs. 25,000;
(6) where the total income exceeds Rs. 30,000 but does not exceed Rs. 50,000	Rs. 4,7000 *plus* 40 per cent, of the amount by which the total income exceeds Rs. 30,000;
(7) where the total income exceeds Rs. 50,000 but does not exceed Rs. 70,000	Rs. 12,700 *plus* 50 per cent, of the amount by which the total income exceeds Rs. 50,000;
(8) where the total income exceeds Rs. 70,000 but does not exceed Rs. 1,00,000	Rs. 22,700 *plus* 55 per cent, of the amount by which the total income exceeds Rs. 70,000;
(9) where the total income exceeds Rs. 1,00,000	Rs. 39,200 *plus* 60 per cent, of the amount by which the total income exceeds Rs. 1,00.000.

Surcharge on Income-Tax

The amount of income-tax computed in accordance with the preceding provisions of this Sub-Paragraph shall be increased by a surcharge for purposes of the Union calculated at the rate of ten per cent, of such income-tax.

Taxable Income	*DOMESTIC COMPANY*						*FOREIGN COMPANY*			
	Where the public are substantially interested		*Where the public are not substantially interested*				*Royalties & Fees* [1]		*On the balance if any of the total income*	
			INDUSTRIAL COMPANY		*OTHER THAN INDUSTRIAL COMPANY*					
	For use where the taxable income exceeds Rs. 1,40,000		*For use where the taxable income exceeds Rs. 2,50,000*							
	I.T. @55%	*S.C. @5% of I.T.*	*I.T. @60%*	*S.C. @5% of I.T.*	*I.T. @65%*	*S.C. @5% of I.T.*	*I.T. @50%*	*S.C. @5% of I.T.*	*I.T. @70%*	*S.C. @5% of I.T.*
Rs.	*Rs.*	*Rs.*	*Rs.*	*Rs.*	*Rs.*	*Rs.*	*Rs.*	*Rs.*	*Rs.*	*Rs.*
250000	137500	6875	150000	7500	162500	8125	125000	6250	175000	8750
300000	165000	8250	180000	9000	195000	9750	150000	7500	210000	10500
400000	220000	11000	240000	12000	260000	13000	200000	10000	280000	14000
500000	275000	13750	300000	15000	325000	16250	250000	12500	350000	17500
600000	330000	16500	360000	18000	390000	19500	300000	15000	420000	21000
700000	385000	19250	420000	21000	455000	22750	350000	17500	490000	24500
800000	440000	22000	480000	24000	520000	26000	400000	20000	560000	28000
900000	495000	24750	540000	27000	585000	29250	450000	22500	630000	31500
1000000	550000	27500	600000	30000	650000	32500	500000	25000	700000	35000
2000000	1100000	55000	1200000	60000	1300000	65000	1000000	50000	1400000	70000
3000000	1650000	82500	1800000	90000	1950000	97500	1500000	75000	2100000	105000
4000000	2200000	110000	2400000	120000	2600000	130000	2000000	100000	2800000	140000
5000000	2750000	137500	3000000	150000	3250000	162500	2500000	125000	3500000	175000
6000000	3300000	165000	3600000	180000	3900000	195000	3000000	150000	4200000	210000
7000000	3850000	192500	4200000	210000	4550000	227500	3500000	175000	4900000	245000
8000000	4400000	220000	4800000	240000	5200000	260000	4000000	200000	5600000	280000
9000000	4950000	247500	5400000	270000	5850000	292500	4500000	225000	6300000	315000
10000000	5500000	275000	6000000	300000	6500000	325000	5000000	250000	7000000	350000

1. Royalties & fees received for technical services in pursuance of an agreement made after 31st day of March, 1961 and 29th day of February, 1964 respectively but before the 1st day of April, 1976, as approved by the Central Government.

Royalties or fees for technical services received by a foreign company from an Indian concern in pursuance of an agreement made by it with the Indian concern after 31st March, 1976 and approved by the Central Government is chargeable to tax under section 115A at the following rates:

(*a*) on income by way of royalty consisting of lump sum consideration for the transfer outside India of, or the imparting of information outside India in respect of, any data, documentation, drawing or specification relating to any patent, invention model, design, secret formula or process or trade mark or similar property, at the rate of 20 percent of such income;

(*b*) on other income by way of royalty and fees for technical services, at the rate of 40 percent.

From the assessment year 1977-78 and onwards, the inter-corporate dividends received by foreign company is liable to income-tax at a flat rate of 25%. This is because deduction under section 80M is not allowable to foreign companies on and from the assessment year 1977-78.

Income-Tax and Surcharge for Private and Public Limited Companies Assesment Years 1977-78 & 1978-79

Taxable Income	DOMESTIC COMPANY										FOREIGN COMPANY			
	Where the public are substantially interested				Where the public are not substantially interested									
					INDUSTRIAL COMPANY									
	For use where the taxable income does not exceed Rs. 1,40,000		For use where the taxable income exceeds Rs. 1,40,000		For use where the taxable income does not exceed Rs. 2,50,000		For use where the taxable income exceeds Rs. 2,50,000		OTHER THAN INDUSTRIAL COMPANY		Royalties and fees		On the balance if any of the total income	
	I.T. @45%	S.C. @5% of I.T.	I.T. @55%	S.C. @5% of I.T.	I.T. @55%	S.C. @5% of I.T.	I.T. @60%	S.C. @5% of I.T.	I.T. @65%	S.C. @5% of I.T.	I.T. @50%	S.C. @5% of I.T.	I.T. @70%	S.C. @5% of I.T.
Rs.	Rs. P.	Rs. P.	Rs. P.	Rs. P.	Rs. P.	Rs. P.	Rs.	Rs. P.	Rs. P.	Rs. P.	Rs.	Rs. P.	Rs.	Rs. P.
10	4.50	0.23	5.50	0.28	5.50	0.28	6	0.30	6.50	0.33	5	0.25	7	0.35
20	9.00	0.45	11.00	0.55	11.00	0.55	12	0.60	13.00	0.65	10	0.50	14	0.70
30	13.50	0.68	16.50	0.83	16.50	0.83	18	0.90	19.50	0.98	15	0.75	21	1.05
40	18.00	0.90	22.00	1.10	22.00	1.10	24	1.20	26.00	1.30	20	1.00	28	1.40
50	22.50	1.13	27.50	1.38	27.50	1.38	30	1.50	32.50	1.63	25	1.25	35	1.75
60	27.00	1.35	33.00	1.65	33.00	1.65	36	1.80	39.00	1.95	30	1.50	42	2.10
70	31.50	1.58	38.50	1.93	38.50	1.93	42	2.10	45.50	2.28	35	1.75	49	2.45
80	36.00	1.80	44.00	2.20	44.00	2.20	48	2.40	52.00	2.60	40	2.00	56	2.80
90	40.50	2.03	49.50	2.48	49.50	2.48	54	2.70	58.50	2.93	45	2.25	63	3.15

100	45	2.25	55	2.75	55	2.75	60	3	65	3.25	50	2.50	70	3.50
200	90	4.50	110	5.50	110	5.50	120	6	130	6.50	100	5.00	140	7.00
300	135	6.75	165	8.25	165	8.25	180	9	195	9.75	150	7.50	210	10.50
400	180	9.00	220	11.00	220	11.00	240	12	260	13.00	200	10.00	280	14.00
500	225	11.25	275	13.75	275	13.75	300	15	325	16.25	250	12.50	350	17.50
600	270	13.50	330	16.50	330	16.50	360	18	390	19.50	300	15.00	420	21.00
700	315	15.75	385	19.25	385	19.25	420	21	455	22.75	350	17.50	490	24.50
800	360	18.00	440	22.00	440	22.00	480	24	520	26.00	400	20.00	560	28.00
900	405	20.25	495	24.75	495	24.75	540	27	585	29.25	450	22.50	630	31.50
1000	450	22.50	550	27.50	550	27.50	600	30	650	32.50	500	25.00	700	35.00
2000	900	45.00	1100	55.00	1100	55.00	1200	60	1300	65.00	1000	50.00	1400	70.00
3000	1350	67.50	1650	82.50	1650	82.50	1800	90	1950	97.50	1500	75.00	2100	105.00
4000	1800	90.00	2200	110.00	2200	110.00	2400	120	2600	130.00	2000	100.00	2800	140.00
5000	2250	112.50	2750	137.50	2750	137.50	3000	150	3250	162.50	2500	125.00	3500	175.00
6000	2700	135.00	3300	165.00	3300	165.00	3600	180	3900	195.00	3000	150.00	4200	210.00
7000	3150	157.50	3850	192.50	3850	192.50	4200	210	4550	227.50	3500	175.00	4900	245.00
8000	3600	180.00	4400	220.00	4400	220.00	4800	240	5200	260.00	4000	200.00	5600	280.00
9000	4050	202.50	4950	247.50	4950	247.50	5400	270	5850	292.50	4500	225.00	6300	315.00
10000	4500	225.00	5500	275.00	5500	275.00	6000	300	6500	325.00	5000	250.00	7000	350.00
20000	9000	450.00	11000	550.00	11000	550.00	12000	600	13000	650.00	10000	500.00	14000	700.00
30000	13500	675.00	16500	825.00	16500	825.00	18000	900	19500	975.00	15000	750.00	21000	1050.00
40000	18000	900.00	22000	1100.00	22000	1100.00	24000	1200	26000	1300.00	20000	1000.00	28000	1400.00
50000	22500	1125.00	27500	1375.00	27500	1375.00	30000	1500	32500	1625.00	25000	1250.00	35000	1750.00
60000	27000	1350.00	33000	1650.00	33000	1650.00	36000	1800	39000	1950.00	30000	1500.00	42000	2100.00
80000	36000	1800.00	44000	2200.00	44000	2200.00	48000	2400	52000	2600.00	40000	2000.00	56000	2800.00
100000	45000	2250.00	55000	2750.00	55000	2750.00	60000	3000	65000	3250.00	50000	2500.00	70000	3500.00
120000	61000*†	3050.00	66000	3300.00	66000	3300.00	72000	3600	78000	3900.00	60000	3000.00	84000	4200.00
140000	77000*†	3850.00	77000	3850.00	77000	3850.00	84000	4200	91000	4550.00	70000	3500.00	98000	4900.00
160000	—	—	88000	4400.00	88000	4400.00	90000	4800	104000	5200.00	80000	4000.00	112000	5600.00
180000	—	—	99000	4950.00	99000	4950.00	108000	5400	117000	5850.00	90000	4500.00	126000	6300.00
200000	—	—	110000	5500.00	110000	5500.00	120000	6000	130000	6500.00	100000	5000.00	140000	7000.00
220000	—	—	121000	6050.00	126000†	6300.00	132000	6600	143000	7150.00	110000	5500.00	154000	7700.00
240000	—	—	132000	6600.00	142000†	7100.00	144000	7200	156000	7800.00	120000	6000.00	168000	8400.00
250000	—	—	137500	6875.00	150000†	7500.00	150000	7500	162500	8125.00	125000	6250.50	175000	8750.00

Morocco

*Seddik Zaari**

Area and Population

The Kingdom of Morocco is the most western of the three North African countries. It has two coast lines, one on the Atlantic Ocean and the other one on the Mediterranean Sea where the width of the Strait of Gibraltar, 7,5 miles only, separates it from Europe.

With an area of some 172 000 square miles, Morocco may be considered as the center of an axis connecting Africa, Europe and America.

The moroccan population reached 17.300.000 in 1974, of the total 57% are under 20 years old.

Casablanca is the largest city in Morocco with approximately 2 Millions inhabitants. The other important towns are: Marrakech (population: 450.000) and Rabat (population: 440.000) which is the administrative Capital.

Government

Morocco has been independent since March 1956, and has been governed by King Hassan II since February 1961, when he succeeded his father, Mohammed V.

In the present constitution which was promulgated on March 10, 1972, it is stated that Morocco is a constitutional Monarchy, with Islam as the State Religion.

The King has the power to appoint and dismiss the Prime Minister and he presides over the Cabinet. He may put forward legislation passed by the Parliament and has the power to dissolve the House of Representatives. He is impowered to declare a state of emergency and to initiate revisions of the constitution. In addition, the King is the Commander in chief of the Armed Forces, makes appointment to civil and military posts, and presides over the Council for National Development Planning and the Supreme Judiciary Council.

Parliament consists of a single assembly, the House of Representatives, with members for a four year time and of whom two-thirds were elected in April 1977 by direct universal suffrage and one-third by an electoral college composed of councillers in local government and employees' representatives.

The government is responsible to the King and the House of Representatives. The Prime Minister is impowered to initiate legislation and to exercise statutory powers except when these are reserved to the King.

For internal administration purposes, the country is divided into 30 Provinces, each with a provincial governor appointed by the King and elected regional assemblies, and two Prefectures, Casablanca and Rabat-Salé.

* Attorney at Law, Casablanca.

Membership in International Organizations

Morocco is a member of the United Nations and its specialized agencies, a member of the International Monetary Fund, the International Bank for Reconstruction and Development (World Bank) and its affiliated bodies.

Morocco is a member of the Arab League and the Organization of African Unity. Morocco is also a member of several of the newly incorporated Arab and African Institutions, including the Arab Fund for Economy and Social Development, the Islamic Bank and the Arab Fund for Development in Africa.

Economy

Morocco has various soils with good agricultural potential and important mineral ressources. There is an emerging industrial sector and the beginnings of an industrial labour force. The economic infrastructure is at an advanced stage.

The infrastructure status is widely developed:

- Road network: 15.786 miles (25.400 Kms);
- Railway network: 1100 miles (1.770 Kms);
- Port Network: There are six principal ports, the weight handled by them is over 20 Millions metric tons per year;
- Airport network: There are five principal airports, which handle over 1,5 million passengers per year.

Between 1963 and 1969, the average annual rate of growth of Domestic Product was 3,9%, with the fastest growth being recorded in mining and industry (4,3%).

Since the introduction, in 1968, of the first Five-year Development Plan, the Country's rate of growth has substantially increased (averaging between 1968 and 1972: 5,6% annually against 3,9% before and the planned rate of 4,3%).

The moroccan economy operates essentially on the principles of a mixed economy system in which both the private and the public sectors have important roles to play. The government economic role is implemented through a number of autonomous public agencies.

The government influences the level and nature of private investment in the most important economic activities by granting the concessions required for regulated enterprises and by providing fiscal incentives.

For this purpose, new legislation texts establishing incentive measures for investments were enacted in 1973. These texts were promulgated so as to encourage the promotion of private investments by creating an 'investment code' providing a number of advantages and guarantees and making the granting of these advantages efficient and automatic.

Before dealing with the investment codes which include common provisions to all sectors (industry, sea based industries, handicrafts, mines, tourism as well as export oriented enterprises and specific measures for each particular sector), one has to consider the common law taxation system of firms established in Morocco.

TAXATION OF FIRMS IN MOROCCO

The common law taxating system of firms established in Morocco includes the following major taxes.

Stamp and Registration Duty

Payable at the creation or the modification in the structure of the equity of firms.

Registration Duty

Includes tax on simple and pure transfer at a fixed rate of 1,5% to which is added a surtax on transfer of buildings at a rate of 2 to 3,5% and on transfer of business (exclusive of goods) 1,5 to 3%.

Notarial Tax

Assessed on the registered capital, the two first pieces of 3,000 DH (667 45 Dollars) and taxed respectively of 1% and 0,5% the surplus of 20%.

Stamp Duty

Fixed at a rate of 1% assessed on the nominal value of shares and bonds plus an issuing premium.

Urban Tax

Assessed on the value of buildings or panels and machinery. Its rate varies between 7,5% and 13,5%.

Building Tax

Assessed on the rental value and it varies between 1% and 8% according to locality.

License Duty

It is payable by any person engaged in an industrial or commercial activity and not exempted by a Dahir (law).

It includes:
- a proportional tax assessed on the gross rental value. Its rate varies from 10 to 30%
- a tax for each employed person. It varies between 10 to 24 DH. per person (2,25 to 5,30 US dollars)
- a variable tax which depends on the characteristics of different professions.

Business Profit Tax

Assessed on the result of the whole operations of all kinds made by the company after the deduction of the accepted charges.

Its rate varies as follows:
- 40% on profits from 1 to 500,000 DH. (111 112 US Dollars)
- 44% on profits from 501,000 to 2,000,000 DH. (444 445 Dollars)
- 48% on profits over 2,000,000 DH. (444 445 Dollars)

Products Tax

Payable on products at sale and at the importation. Its average rate is 15%. It varies from 6,38 to 20% according to the level of necessity of the considered product.

Service Tax

It applies to all rendered services. Its normal rate is 7,5%.

INCENTIVE MEASURES

In order to encourage local and private foreign investments, new legislative texts providing several fiscal exonerations and other specific advantages to each particular sector were enacted in 1973.

These legislative texts establishing incentive measures consist of 6 separate Codes:
- Industrial Code
- Maritime Code
- Mining Code
- Tourism Code
- Handicraft Code
- Export Code

Industrial Code

In order to benefit from the advantages made available under this code, the investor must meet the following conditions:

- The investment program must encompass equipment valued at at least 100,000.00 DH. net of tax.
- The enterprise must belong either to Moroccans or to corporations the capital of which is at least 50% held by Moroccans or Moroccan companies.

The several advantages granted to local and private foreign investments are governed by the following provisions which relate to:

a) Customs Duties

The enterprises are entitled to benefit from exoneration from customs duties on new material, machinery, and equipment, on second-hand equipment when importation is authorized by the Minister responsible for industry. However, there will be no exoneration from customs duties in the case of material, machinery and equipment that can supplied by Moroccan industry as long as the local price is not over 20% more, and equivalent in quality and time of delivery.

b) 'Tax on products'

Equipment, machinery and material imported or acquired locally shall benefit from an exoneration from the 'tax on products'.

c) Registration Tax

The percentage charge on the registration of equity capital is fixed at 0,5% whether for the creation of new corporations or for increases of capital.

d) Profits Tax ('IBP')

Total exoneration from profits tax is granted during the first ten consecutive years of operation to all new enterprises established in the Provinces of Tangier, Tetuan, Al Hocema, Taza, Nador, Oujda, Ksar Es Souk, Ourzazate, Tarfaya and the district of Essaouira.

A profit tax reduction of 50% during the first ten consecutive years of operation is granted to new enterprises established in areas other than those listed above and other than within the city limits of Casablanca.

In order to be entitled to the above-mentioned advantages, the enterprises must calculate normal depreciation starting from the first year of the tax exemption.

However, in determining the taxation base, new enterprises established within the city limits of Casablanca, or existing enterprises establishing extensions, no matter where located, may include accelerated amortization as deduction. This accelerated amortization is applicable to new capitalization realized in conformity with the investment program, and may be up to twice the rate normally admitted.

e) Licence Tax

During the first five consecutive years of their operation, all new enterprises shall be completely exonerated from the licence tax.

Existing enterprises which extend their operations by new investments are entitled to total exoneration from the licence tax on activity or elements relating to this extension for their first five consecutive years of operation.

f) Exchange Control Regulation

The retransfer of the proceeds of liquidation is guaranteed up to the amount of capital invested by a foreigner as follows:

- For capital inflows effected through a transfer of convertible currencies to the Banque du Maroc or through learing accounts
- For capital investment derived from draw-down of a capital account over a minimum of five years
- Retransfer of after-tax dividends for distribution to non-residents is quaranteed without limitation.

g) Refund of Interest

Enterprises are entitled to a refund of two points off the interest rate payable on loans granted by the Banque Nationale pour le Développement Economique (BNDE) which is specialized in granting medium and long term loans to the industrial sector.

h) Conventional System

All new enterprises with a planned investment exceeding 30 million DH., as well as those intending to operate or to extend their operations in one of the sectors defined by decree, may not benefit from any of the incentive measures described above, except in the framework of agreements concluded with the Government which may in turn grant additional advantages.

Maritime Code

Under the provisions of this Code, shipping enterprises are entitled to benefit from the following advantages provided that:

- the investment applies to construction, and outfitting of commercial vessels (for transport of goods or passengers) or fishing vessels
- Such shipping enterprises belong either to Moroccans or to corporations in which at least 50% of the capital is held by Moroccans or Moroccan companies.

The advantages granted under this code and relating to: the Registration tax – the Exchange Control Regulation – and the Refund of interest are similar to those provided for in the Industrial Code:
- Registry tax reduced to 0,5%
- Guaranteed retransfer of capital invested and transfer of dividends
- Reimbursement of 2% of the interest charge on loans extended by the BNDE in addition to the reimbursement available through maritime credit.

Provisions Relating to the Profits Tax and the Licence Tax

In determining the taxation base for the profits tax, shipping enterprises may include accelerated amortization as a deductible charge up to twice the rate normally admitted on the amount of new investment made in conformity with the investment program.

These enterprises are completely exonerated from the licence tax for a period of five years.

Aside from the above-mentioned incentive measures, shipping enterprises are entitled to benefit from:
- An equipment bonus of 15% for the purchase of cargoes and/or passengers ships whether new or second-hand under five years of age, certain fishing vessels of more than 50 tons and all other types of fishing boats over 100 tons whether they are new or second-hand under four years of age.
- A selectivity bonus (of 15% or 5%) which is added to the equipment bonus for the purchase of specialized ships.

Mining Code

In order to benefit from the advantages provided for in this code:

The mining investor must be moroccan individuals, cooperatives, public agencies specialized in mining, corporations in which at least 50% of capital is held by Moroccans or by moroccan companies duly authorized to carry on research, exploitation and beneficiation of mineral ores in a specific mining sector, in accordance with mining regulations in force;

The mining investment must include expenditures of at least 100,000.00 DH. on equipment for mining research and production.

The advantages granted under this code and relating to: Customs duties - Tax on products - Registration Tax - Exchange Control Regulation - and Refund of interest are similar to those provided for in the Industrial Code:
- exemption from customs duties;
- exemption from products tax;

- reduced registry tax of 0,5%;
- guaranteed retransfer of capital invested and transfer of dividends;
- reimbursement of 2% of the interest charge on loans approved by BNDE.

In determining the taxation base for the Profits tax, mining operators may include accelerated amortization as a deduction. This accelerated amortization is applicable to new capitalization made in conformity with the planned investment program, and may be up to twice the rate normally admitted.

These mining operators are completely exonerated from the licence tax during the first five consecutive years of operation.

It is to be stated that governmental financial assistance can be granted under the following conditions:

Mining operators who undertake investments for the extraction and benefications of mineral ores and whose investment program includes production equipment valued at at least DH. 500,000 and creation of at least 50 new jobs, are entitled to benefit from governmental financial assistance relating to expenses for infrastructure.

Government participation will be equal to 50% of the total infrastructure expenses approved by a commission, the composition and internal regulations of which are defined by decree. This assistance may not exceed 15% of the total investment program .

For investments exceeding 30 million DH., mining investors may obtain specific privileges through special agreements negotiated with the State of Morocco.

Tourism Code

In order to encourage tourist investments tourist enterprises which comply with the conditions described below are entitled to benefit from:

- an exemption from the products tax
- a reduced registry tax of 0,5%
- the transfer of dividends and the retransfer of capital invested
- an exemption of 50% to 100% of profits tax depending upon the region of investment.

Newly established enterprises engaged in tourist transportation are granted total exoneration from the profits tax during the first five years of operation.

Newly established tourist enterprises other than those engaged in tourist transportation and which are located in one of the area defined by decree are granted total exoneration from profits tax during the first ten consecutive years of operation.

A reduction of 50% of the profits tax is granted to all new enterprises other than those described above.

- Accelerated amortization. Existing tourist enterprises which extend their operations by new investments may accelerate amortization up to twice the rate normally admitted.
- Exoneration from the licence tax during the first ten consecutive years of operation, except for enterprises engaged in tourist transportation, which

are only entitled to this exoneration for a period of five years.
- Refund of interest. Refunds of interest will be paid by the government to the Credit Immobilier et Hotelier (which grants loans for hotel development) in order to bring its interest rate to 4,5% for all loans granted to tourist enterprises.

Aside from the above-mentioned provisions, state advances may be granted to some tourist enterprises:

All new tourist enterprises of Class 1, 2, 3 or 4 stars which can prove that they have themselves already invested at least 20% of the capital for the planned investment are entitled to an interest-free advance equal to 15% of the value of this investment.

This advance, which is granted by the Credit Immobilier et Hotelier on behalf of the State is reimbursable over a period of ten years starting from the sixth year after it is made.

Tourist enterprises with a planned investment exceeding 30 Million DH. may be granted special privileges through agreements concluded with the Government.

Tourist enterprises entitled to benefit from all the incentive measures described above are those which are involved in all kinds of activities aimed at promoting tourism, such as:
- construction, management, equipment of hotels, motels . . .
- administration of guest-houses, . . .
- repair and refurnishing of hotels not yet classified,
- tourist transportation, operation of pleasure boats, organization of hunting or fishing activities for tourism . . .

Handicraft Code

Under the provisions of this Code, the investment must meet the following requirements:

The average amount of investment per employee must not exceed 5,000.00 DH.

The handicraft factories must belong to Moroccans or to corporations the capital of which is held completely by Moroccan individuals and/or by corporations, the capital of which is completely held by Moroccan individuals or by 100% moroccan owned corporations.

The main advantages are as follows:
- exoneration from customs duties and from the tax on products;
- reduced registry tax of 0,5%;
- total exoneration from profits tax during the first ten consecutive years of operation and total exoneration from licence tax during the first five years of operation for all new handicraft factories;
- retransfer of capital invested and transfer of dividends.

Handicraft factories are entitled to a refund of five points off the interest rate on loans granted by the Banque Centrale Populaire.

For investments exceeding 5 million DH. special advantages may be granted through agreements negotiated with the Government of Morocco.

Export Code

It applies to exporting enterprises exercising an industrial or handicraft activity in sectors defined by decree.

The following advantages are cumulative with those provided for in the Handicraft Code and Industrial Code.

- total exoneration from the tax on profits earned from export sales during the first ten years of operation of a new enterprise and during the first ten years following the publication of this Code for existing enterprises.
- endowment of foreign exchange equal to 3% of export receipts. Exporting enterprises are entitled to an annual authorization to buy foreign currencies up to 3% of their total export business.
- Retransfer of invested capital and transfer of after tax dividends.

While encouraging private investment either local or foreign, the Government of Morocco has granted substantial advantages to private investors.

The investment Codes provide many fiscal advantages which may be summarized as follows:

- Total exoneration from taxes on 'patentes' for ten years for investments in tourism and five years for the other sectors,
- Exoneration from taxes on products for all sectors with the exception of the maritime sector,
- Cuttingdown on the registration fees to 0,5% for the creation of new corporation and the increase of their capital,
- Total or partial exoneration from taxes on profits, or its reduction by the practice of accelerating amortizations.

In addition to the above incentives, foreign investors are given the guarantee of the State of Morocco for the transfer of dividends and the retransfer of capital up to the amount invested.

Finally, attention should be drawn to the fact that for investments over 30 million DH (6,6 Million US Dollars) other advantages may be negotiated under a convention to be agreed upon between the investor and the State of Morocco.

Spain

Dr. Bernardo Ma Cremades *

A. INVESTMENT AT HOME

1. Spain encourages investment in certain geographical areas and in different industrial sectors by means of tax benefits which may affect Transfer Tax, Registration Fees, Tax on Income from Capital, Company Tax and business License Tax, as well as certain local taxes.

Foreign investment is in general, with certain exception in given sectors, permitted up to 50% participation in a company as long as it is carried out through the provision of capital from abroad or by other specially authorized means. It should be emphasized that foreign participation is allowed up to 100% in the case of investment in industrial companies dedicated to the production of certain capital equipment, creating capital exceeding 100,000,000 ptas., and a specified amount of employment. These majority investments may be effected by means of fairly simplified procedures, whereas all other majority investments require the prior authorization of the Board of Ministers. Branches of foreign companies likewise require administrative authorization.

2. Company tax is paid on the taxable profits of the company, generally at the rate of 36% per annum. This tax affects companies under Spanish law (subsidiaries) and also, for the operations carried out on Spanish territory, branches of foreign companies, and other forms of so-called 'permanent establishment'.

Apart from rebates and special exemptions applying to different sectors or investments, there are important possibilities for amortization, according to plans approved by the Exchequer. Special reserves may also be set up, such as the Fund for Future Investment (up to 50% of non-distributed profits) and Reserve for Investment in Exports (up to 50% or more, depending on the case, of the profits obtained from exportation).

3. Withholding Tax is paid at the rate of 15% on the dividends paid by a Spanish company to its shareholders, whether Spanish or foreign, at 14% on payments for royalties and similar and at 6% in the event of the commencement of new technological processes. Interest payments on loans pay 24% under this Tax.

This tax is also paid on the dividends paid out by a foreign company to its shareholders when the former has a branch in Spain according to the proportion of profits which it is estimated correspond to operations effected on Spanish territory. Tax treaties may provide otherwise.

4. There is a series of new regulations in the internal system which permit tax credit for income in the form of dividends paid by affiliated companies in which the mother company owns more than 25%. In this case, 58% of the dividend income is deductable. A similar regulation is applicable to foreign subsidiaries.

* Attorney at Law, Madrid.

There is also the possibility of a group of companies being conjointly taxed for the Company Tax, if application is made. The different companies of the group are taxed through the dominant company (which must possess more than 50% of the remaining companies of the group in question).

With regard to taxable income originating abroad, where this has been subject to a tax analagous to Company or Income Tax, almost full tax credit is provided for.

There is no special tax credit for capital income received by persons or bodies non-resident in Spain, with the exception of certain stipulations in different tax treaties.

5. Spain has tax treaties with 14 countries, of which 10 are capital exporting and 4 are developing countries.

B. FOREIGN INVESTMENT

1. Principally a receiver of foreign investment, it is only in recent years that Spain has projected itself commercially and also with industrial investment in the less developed countries, above all South America (due to the historical, language and ethnic bonds) and Africa (geographical proximity). In reality, there are no special regulations expressly offering tax credits for investments in countries in the course of development. Thus, the general rules on group treatment, the 58% deduction with respect to dividends received from an affiliated company, and credit for taxes paid abroad are applied. In addition, certain treaties of technological, scientific or industrial cooperation may have indirect repercussions.

2. Regulations on tax benefits in this respect are still oriented towards commercial exports. In this sector, investment can provide the benefits of amortization and anticipated reserves which constitute tax credits for the Company Tax. Decided support is provided for the creation of sales points abroad. Additional support to exportation is provided by means of tax rebates which can be major of importance.

3. By means of the consolidated declaration and the corresponding group treatment with regard to Company Tax, a Spanish mother company is able to utilize the losses of a branch abroad when it has more than 50% participation in the latter's capital. It should be emphasized that, after prior application, the Spanish tax permits the free amortization of the losses of one business year throughout the five successive business years.

When the said regime of group treatment is authorized, exemption from the Tax on Capital Income is obtained for the dividends paid by the companies of the group among themselves. It is expected that all these rules will be regulated in more detail in the near future above all with regard to their international repercussions.

Yugoslavia

Miodrag P. Popovic *

Foreign firms may be obliged to pay taxes in Yugoslavia on the basis of one of the following:
a) financial investment in domestic companies,
b) carrying out investment work in Yugoslavia, and
c) transport of passengers and goods to Yugoslavia.

In the first two cases, taxes are levied on profits realised while in the third case taxes are levied on the income realised by the transport of goods and passengers. Accordingly, reasons for payment of taxes are economic – if the planned profit or income should not come up to expectations the reasons for collecting taxes are also lost.

With regard to the aim of this study we shall consider the taxation of foreign firms which have invested capital in domestic companies only. In this sense we shall first of all indicate the legal sources and basic characteristics of the appropriate taxation material; the second part will be devoted to the regulations concerning investment of foreign capital, leading in the third part to an explanation of the tax system accompanying this investment of capital.

Legal sources are as follows (hereafter in the text they will be referred to by the corresponding Roman numerals):

I) Law on financial investment by foreign persons in domestic organisations of associated labour; Official Gazette of the SFRY, No 22/1973;

II) Regulation on the conditions for financial investment by foreign persons in domestic organisations of associated labour; Official Gazette of the SFRY; No 26/1976;

III) Law on taxation of foreign persons; Official Gazette of the SR Bosnia & Hercegovina, No 36/1972;

IV) Law on the taxation of profit made by foreign persons; Official Gazette of SR Montenegro, No 21/1975;

V) Law on the taxation of foreign persons; National News of SR Croatia, No 5/1973;

VI) Law on the taxation of foreign persons; SR Macedonia Official Gazette, No 15/1973;

VII) Law on the taxation of foreign persons; Official Gazette of SR Slovenia, No 3/1973;

IX) Law on the taxation of foreign persons; Official Gazette of SR Serbia, No 22/1973;

X) Law on the taxation of foreign persons; Official Gazette of the Autonomous Province of Vojvodina, No 3/1974 and 18/1976.

A quick glance at the legal regulations is enough to conclude that the Yugoslav legal (and taxation) system is federal. In the domain of the material which most interests us it is important to notice two things:

* Popovic, Popovic, Mikijelj & Popovic, Belgrade.

- that the Federation determines the conditions and regulates the legal regime of investment of foreign capital in domestic companies, and that
- republics and provinces pass the legal regulations on the taxation of profit gained from the invested capital (for which they are authorized by I, Art. 17).

This means that the conditions of investing foreign capital are determined equally for the whole of the legal territory of Yugoslavia while in the domain of taxation various differences may exist which are a result of the different economic characteristics and fiscal situation of the republics and provinces. As we shall see later, the principles of taxation policy are however fairly similar with the existence of differences in the amount of tax in order to attract the investment of foreign capital to the underdeveloped parts of the country.

It is of advantage at this point to note one more difference between the legal regime concerned with the investment of foreign capital and that which is concerned with the tax to be paid. As a contract on mutual investment has been signed and registered, the foreign investor is protected from changes in the law; he may decide whether the contract on investment will come under the regulations of the new law or whether the regulations of the law in force at the time of signing the contract and registering it will apply. However should the legal regulations concerning tax on profits from mutual investment change then there is no choice – the new law only applies from the moment it comes into force.

Yugoslav companies have a compound organizational structure (basic organisation of associated labour, work organisations, compound organisations of associated labour etc.); in order to avoid confusion we shall simply refer to them as domestic companies.

The investment of foreign capital in domestic companies is carried out in order to reach mutual business aims with mutual risk (mutual operations). However, in order to register the contract on foreign investment it is necessary that the intended mutual operations are of advantage to the domestic economy. This contribution to domestic economy is primarily fairly widely fixed (I art. 12, point 4, 2) in the sense of increasing production, productivity and export or in introducing new techniques and organisation of production or, even, in the advancement of scientific-research work. Later, by a regulation (II art. 1) the government postulates that in the contract on the investment of foreign capital the export of the product must be taken into account, i.e. the result of the investment, in amount, worth and corresponding currency in order to ensure payment of profit to the foreign investor and the repayment of the invested means.

Certain fields exist in which it is not permissible for foreign capital to be invested. These are: banking, insurance, internal transport, trade, communal and public service activities. Exceptionally the Federal Executive Council is authorised to permit the investment of foreign capital in these field if this will contribute to the faster development of these branches of economy or activities (I art. 3).

The value of foreign capital invested in domestic companies cannot be more than the worth of the means which are invested by the domestic company, nor equal to the total amount of those means. Which means, that foreign capital can be invested at the most by 49% of the total value of invested capital. Exceptionally the investment of foreign capital can cross this mark if in the development of a particular branch of economy there is a special interest for the investment of foreign capital, which is confirmed by an act of the Federal Assembly.

Foreign investment can be made in various forms: equipment and machinery, raw material and material for processing, foreign currency, technology, industrial property, knowledge and experience, services. With regard to the shape of the invested foreign capital certain limitations exist:

- if the foreign investor invests equipment into the domestic company, its worth cannot be more than one third of the value of foreign capital; the second condition is that this equipment is not produced in Yugoslavia or it is not of a suitable quality (II art. 2)
- if the foreign investor invests into the domestic company real industrial property, or knowledge and experience, the value of the investment must not be more than one tenth of the sold product resulting from this investment; the second condition is that this same real industrial property or knowledge and experience have not been given at the same time to some other domestic company under another contract (II art. 3).

When we come to non-financial investment of foreign capital (patent rights, licences, technology, etc.) then we must mention that the contract on investment of foreign capital will not be registered if the contribution by the foreign company is unrealistically estimated i.e. if it is given too high a value.

The top limit of a foreign capital investment is not fixed in contrast to the lower limit which cannot be beneath Din 1,500.000 (US $ 85,000).

Relations between the foreign company and the domestic company on the occasion of mutual capital investment are defined by a contract which of course has to be in writing. This means that the contract is formal, though a special form of written contract has not been set by law. However, the law does state that registration of the contract on mutual capital investment is obligatory, this is carried out by the Federal Committee for Energetics and Industry, which should also be informed of the intended contract before its signing (this is done by the domestic company).

Before describing the difficulties which can occur in registering a contract on the investment of foreign capital, we must first make one circumstance clear. Yugoslav law does not define in detail all aspects of the mutual investment contract but, on the contrary, sets only the legal frame. This leaves the business partners a wide field for negotiations and treating for the mutual business. However at the same time this legal flexibility imposes on the contracting parties a certain caution because it is imperative that all aspects of the business relations be precisely defined in the contract on mutual investment.

The law defines that, as a general limitation, the foreign company may not have other or greater rights than the domestic company (I art. 5). Apart from that there are some precisely defined impediments to the registration of contracts on mutual investment (I Art. 12, II art. 2-5):

- the mutual investment of means must be of advantage to domestic economy in the sense of increasing productivity, manufacture or export, or in introducing new techniques and work organisation, or in promoting scientific-research work,
- from the manufactures which are the result of the mutual investment must

come the export of the goods to the value necessary to ensure profits and secure the return of the capital invested by the foreign company,
- the amount of invested capital must be sufficient to enable the aims above to be reached and may not be below Din 1,500,000 (about US $ 85,000),
- business cooperation must be in accordance with the usual conditions by which such cooperation is realized in international economic relations; apart from that it must not violate the equality of the domestic company and domestic economy,
- the contribution of the foreign firm in non-financial forms of capital investment (real industrial property, knowledge and experience) must not be unrealistically estimated and the value of this must not be more than one tenth of the total sale of the products arising from this investment,
- the value of equipment invested by the foreign firm may not be more than one third of the invested foreign capital,
- the business board, as a mutual organ of the foreign investor and the domestic company, may not decide on the following questions relating to the domestic company: on planning and general self-government acts, on the administration of public funds, on the confirmation and division of the income of the company and the division of personal income, on the conclusion of credit contracts and organisation of work relations, as well as on the amalgamation, ownership and division of domestic companies.

On the above questions the business board may give its suggestions only to the work council of the domestic company. Domestic companies, in which foreign means are invested, are administered by their work councils. However, in the contract on mutual investment of means, the forming of a business board to decide on mutual rights arising out of the investment may be agreed on.

The law does not define the division of functions between the business board and the work council but this is left to be regulated by the contract on investment. Apart from general regulations that in the contract on investment the method of training the business board, its field of authority and method of work are confirmed, the law only states questions which fall exclusively within the authority of the work council of the domestic company (which we have listed above).

The contract on mutual investment becomes valid after it has been entered in the register, and on the day of its signature. There are no time limits as regards the duration of the contract except that by law the contract on investment should be long-term. The contract can be concluded for a certain period of time but this, of course, may not be less than the time necessary for reaching the mutual business aims.

The contract on mutual investment may cease to be valid before the termination of the time limit. However, the contracting parties are not allowed to break the contract by mutual agreement before the contractual limit. The right to break the contract arises only from one of the following two reasons (I art. 11):
- if during two consecutive years of mutual business losses have occurred or if the business results are to a great measure below the expected, and
- if the other party does not fulfill its obligations as undertaken by the contract.

In the contract on mutual investment the competent court or arbitration for resolving disputes between the foreign company and the domestic company, resulting from the contract on mutual investment, must be foreseen. A special arbitration which the contracting parties train on the basis of the contract may be chosen or even a foreign arbitration. If nothing is defined in the contract on investment, then disputes will be resolved by the competent economic court in Yugoslavia.

Because of the compound structure of Yugoslav companies, special care must be given when concluding a contract on mutual investment to the question of responsibility. As foreign capital can be invested in a work organisation (which is made up of two or more basic organisations of associated labour) or in one of the basic organisations of associated labour (and each of these has its particular legal character with independent responsibilities even when it is found in a work organisation which also has its own legal character) we must differentiate these two cases:

- when the foreign capital is invested in a work organisation obligations arising from the mutual business operations are carried equally by all the basic organisations of associated labour of which it is formed. An exception from this rule exists if by the act on forming the work organisation it is in any case prevented from any responsibilities for its basic organisations of associated labour in its business operations - which must be entered into the legal register;
- when the foreign capital invested in one of the basic organisations of associated labour for obligations of mutual business corresponds to that basic organisation only (usually to the amount of means at its disposal). However, it is possible in the contract on investment to foresee subsidiary responsibilities of the other basic organisations of associated labour in the make-up of the work organisation but in this case they must give their prior consent to the contract on investment.

Otherwise, the basic organisation of associated labour in which the foreign capital is invested is not responsible for the responsibilities of the other basic organisations or work organisations in whose make-up it belongs, unless this form of responsibility is foreseen in the contract on investment (I art. 14).

The foreign company may totally or partly transfer its part in foreign capital to another foreign firm as well as to the domestic company in which it has capital invested or some other domestic company. Conditions for such a transfer are twofold:

- the foreign firm must first offer the transfer of its part of the capital to the domestic company into which the capital is already invested, in writing. If the domestic company rejects or fails to reply within 60 days, the foreign firm may offer the transfer of its share to another domestic or foreign company, and
- the domestic company in which the foreign capital is invested and the other investors (if there are any) which have their share in the mutual investment must give their consent to the transfer of rights and obligations from the contract on investment. The domestic company in which foreign capital is invested may not withhold its consent if the conditions for the transfer of rights and obligations are the same as in the offer which the foreign investor has previously made to it.

The right of transferring rights and obligations of the investor may be excluded from the contract on investment of foreign capital.

The foreign investor has the right to transfer the invested means, that is the remainder of the invested means (I art. 19). This right of transfer relates to the invested capital and differs from the right of the foreign investor to transfer profits issuing from the invested foreign capital. Conditions for realising this right are:

- either the contract has ceased because the business aims have been realised, that is the termination of the agreed term of the contract,
- or the contract has been broken for reasons foreseen by law,
- or in the contract on investment the possibility for the foreign investor to partly withdraw his invested capital during the term of the contract has been foreseen.

The right to transfer the invested capital includes the right to transfer the amortisation of invested installations and equipment in accordance with the degree of its fall in value. The law foresees for the domestic company a minimum degree of amortisation and this has to be applied analogously in the case of mutual investment. However, the maximum degree of amortisation has not been defined, so that it is for the business partners to confirm the degree of amortisation in their negotiations. In other words, in the contract on investment, all legal questions connected with the transfer of amortisation of invested capital in connection with installations and equipment must be arranged. The law merely postulates that this transfer must be carried out in compliance with the regulations on currency operations.

If the foreign investor has invested capital in a financial form, the right to transfer the invested means guarantees the repayment of annuity. However all modalities of this type of transfer must be explicitly foreseen in the contract on investment.

The foreign investor has the right to participate in the profits gained by the mutual investment of means. This participation in the profits, regardless of in what form it is realised, represents the profit of the foreign investor. The right to transfer the profit is not limited. Namely, previously the foreign investor was obliged to reinvest a part (20%) of the profit gained into a domestic company. Such an obligation does not now exist, so that the foreign investor can choose in what way the profits will be used as follows:

- to transfer it, wholly or partly,
- to increase its share in already invested capital for mutual business,
- to invest in another domestic company by making a separate contract of investment of foreign capital, or
- to dispose of these means in Yugoslavia in some other way in compliance with existing regulations.

Instead of the obligations of reinvesting part of the profit realised by the foreign investor, Yugoslav law now foresees tax reductions for investing profits in domestic companies (which will be detailed later).

The transfer of profits is carried out according to the contract on investment and in compliance with currency regulations.

Contractual regulation of all questions connected with the mutual investment of capital is of special interest here, in a double meaning:

First, the law does not define the criterium for the division of the total income, that is, the method of accounting the profits is not defined. This has been left to the contracting parties. In this sense their agreement with regard to the expenses which occur during the mutual business operations is important, because profit is the difference between the total income and the contractually defined business expenses. In other words, the first problem the contracting parties must solve is defining the method of accounting the total sum of profits.

The other question relates to the division of the already confirmed profits between the foreign investor and the domestic company. The law does not foresee the obligation that the share in the profits is defined by the proportionate shares in mutual capital. This means that the contracting parties are free to decide the share each of them has in the profits gained from their mutual business operations.

Although in the contract on investment the conditions and method of annexing the profits of the foreign investor are regulated, there nevertheless exists a basic limitation in the sense that the division of profits must ensure that the domestic company has enough means to cover personal incomes and mutual expenses as well as means for the proportionate accumulation of its contribution to the realisation of that income (I art. 8).

The right to annex profits can be carried out by the foreign investor only during participation in mutual business through his capital investment.

As has been mentioned before, the legal material on taxation of foreign firms investing capital in domestic companies for mutual business operations is regulated by the republican and provincial legal regulations (laws listed under III to X in the first part of the text). However, there are no great differences between them. What is more, we can say that as far as the principles of taxation policy are concerned there are no differences. The taxation areas can however be separated according to republics and provinces by the different degrees of taxation where the one thought has been to make the investment of foreign capital attractive in the less developed economic areas.

Foreign capital which is invested in a domestic company is not taxable, but the profit gained by the foreign investor through investing his capital in mutual business operations is liable for taxation. This means that tax is paid on the income which the foreign investor realises by investing his capital.

Normally, if there is no income forthcoming from the investment of foreign capital in any one calendar year the foreign investor will not have any taxation obligations. A situation of loss, however, is neither normal nor a long-term condition and its emphasis has the one aim to show that the taxation system takes into consideration the element of risk in mutual business operations.

The party obliged to pay tax on profit gained is the foreign company which has gained profit by investing capital in a domestic company in order to carry on mutual business. Of the tax contributors, who bear the burden of duty to be paid, the tax payer should be differentiated who accounts and pays the tax within the term set. The foreign company is a tax contributor but the tax payer is the domestic company in which foreign means are invested. In this sence the domestic company is responsible for balancing the accounts and paying taxes on the profit gained by the foreign investor within the time set for such payment. If this is not done then the domestic company has to pay fines of 0.1% daily of the unpaid, or not paid within the time limit, tax on profits gained by the foreign investor.

The basis of tax on profits gained by the foreign investor is made by this share in the profits during one calendar year realised from mutual business operations, regardless of what shape the profit takes.

It is important to note that in confirming the profit gained by the foreign investor unstated income has to also be taken into account, which issues directly from the mutual business operations and which increases the profit gained by the foreign investor. This rule is not specially foreseen in all laws (for instance it is not foreseen in the laws of Serbia and Bosnia and Hercegovina) but it will certainly come to apply to all tax areas. We conclude this not only because of the possibilities of applied analogy but because tax on profits can be suppressed through unstated income and every tax system attempts to avoid this.

Those legal texts which foresee the above rule (for example V art. 5, point 2) do not taxatively list all the cases of unstated income but give only some individual examples. If the foreign investor provides the domestic company in which it has capital invested with primary products and semi-manufactured products or with finished products in order to carry on the mutual business operations at prices which are above the normal prices on the foreign market, the difference in price certainly represents part of the profit which the foreign investor gains through his investment. This part of the income will be added to the already stated profits gained by the foreign investor in the final account made by the domestic company, and will represent part of the taxable basis for calculating the tax on profits. The same is the case if the domestic company provides the foreign investor with products which are a result of their mutual business cooperation at prices below the normal world prices for that type of product at that time. It is also probable that the taxation authorities will take account of the nature of expenses which are deducted from the total income in calculating profits, so that one part of the profit is not shown in the shape of an expense (for example, excessive amortisation).

As far as the degree of taxation which applies to the above confirmed tax basis is concerned, there do exist differences between the tax areas. These have, as we have mentioned, come about from the need to attract the investment of foreign capital to the underdeveloped areas of Yugoslavia. The scale of taxes is as follows:

35% in Serbia, Croatia and Slovenia
20% in Bosnia & Hercegovina
15% in Montenegro
14% in Macedonia and
10% in Vojvodina.

Therefore, according to the seat of the domestic company in which foreign capital is invested, the corresponding taxation degree will apply to the profit gained by the foreign investor.

Exemption from payment of tax on profits gained also exists in two cases:

- on income from interest, which is realised by the foreign investor on the basis of the obligatory deposit with the Bank of Yugoslavia of part of the profit from the mutual business operations with the domestic company, no tax is paid,

- a specially founded international corporation for investment in Yugoslavia, in which domestic companies and international organisations which are by international agreement exempt from paying tax on profits, participate, do not pay tax on profits realised through investment in the domestic company; this exemption is the proportional share of the domestic company and the international organisation in the total capital of such a corporation.

The sense of lowering the taxation degree when taxing the profit gained by the foreign investor is clear – this is the means of stimulating reinvestment of the profits (as a whole or in part) into the same or another domestic company or its deposit in a Yugoslav bank. The amount of tax reduction depends on the annual amount of profit which the foreign investor reinvests in a domestic company as well as on the length of the cancellation term when depositing profits in a Yugoslav bank. All republican and provincial laws foresee these tax reductions but their height is not equal throughout the country. As a rule the tax reductions move within the following framework:

- if the foreign investor reinvests or deposits at least 25% of his annual profits in a domestic company or bank, the apportion of tax falling on that part of the profit will be reduced by 15%;
- if the foreign investor reinvests or deposits between 25% and 50% of his annual profits, the apportion of tax which falls on 25% of the profits will be reduced by 15% and that which falls on the profits over 25% will be reduced by 30%;
- if the foreign investor reinvests or deposits more than 50% of his profits apart from the reduction from the points above, the apportioned tax on the part over 50% will be reduced by 50%.

When depositing profits in a Yugoslav bank in order for the foreign investor to qualify for tax reduction, the following additional conditions connected with the length of the cancellation period must be fulfilled:

- if the cancellation period is less than 5 years, the foreign investor will not qualify for any tax reductions,
- if the cancellation period is between 5 and 10 years the foreign investor qualifies for half of the above mentioned reductions,
- if the cancellation period is more than 10 years the foreign investor depositing his profits in a Yugoslav bank qualifies for all the above mentioned reductions in tax.

The fate of the tax reductions depends, also, on the fact whether the foreign investor will in a given period of time transfer the reinvested profit, which is partly exempt from tax, to the same or another domestic company, with compensation. If the foreign investor does this within a period of 5 years he loses his right to the above mentioned tax reductions. However, if he does this in a period of 5 to 10 years he loses only half of the mentioned tax reduction. In both these cases the corresponding part of tax on profits will be subsequently apportioned. The tax payer in this case, too, is the domestic company in which is reinvested part of the profits while the foreign investor is the party liable for the taxation.

As the domestic company is the tax payer on the profits of the foreign investor it is as well to consider the procedure of paying taxes more closely.

The domestic company in which foreign capital is invested must show separately the income realised fron. its business operations with the foreign investor. This means that at the end of the year in its final balance of accounts it must show separately this income as well as determining the profit which falls to the foreign investor on the basis of the principles of dividing the income as confirmed in the contract on investment. The final balance of accounts together with all other necessary details for confirming the profit of the foreign investor are presented to the Public Accounting Service, which controls the correctness of the account and the payment of tax on profits. This control must be carried out within a period of 3 months from the date on which the final account is received from the domestic company. If the Public Accounting Service confirms that the tax basis has been incorrectly stated or if the tax has been incorrectly accounted, it will bring a decision by which it will prescribe to the domestic company payment of the miscalculated and unpaid tax. This decision is also sent to the foreign investor who has the right to take legal steps against this decision within a period of 60 days.

Otherwise, the domestic company during the course of a calendar year makes monthly payments on account of the tax on profits, so that the final amount of tax on profits is calculated in the final account.

The domestic company only guarantees the unpaid portion of tax on profits gained from the investment of foreign capital.

Rights on the account and apportioning as well as rights on the payment of tax on profits expire after a period of 5 years from the end of the year in which this should have been accomplished. Every action which the official body makes towards accounting and paying the tax breaks the time limit with the expiration term in any case coming into force after 10 years.

The right of the party liable for taxation to claim repayment of incorrectly or overpaid amounts in the name of tax on profits expires after a period of 5 years from the end of the year in which the payment was made.

GPSR Compliance

The European Union's (EU) General Product Safety Regulation (GPSR) is a set of rules that requires consumer products to be safe and our obligations to ensure this.

If you have any concerns about our products, you can contact us on ProductSafety@springernature.com

In case Publisher is established outside the EU, the EU authorized representative is:

Springer Nature Customer Service Center GmbH
Europaplatz 3
69115 Heidelberg, Germany

Batch number: 10824476

Printed by Printforce, the Netherlands